80286 and 80386 Microprocessors

80286 and 80386 Microprocessors
New PC architectures

A. B. Fontaine and F. Barrand

Translated by A. Rawsthorne
Department of Computer Science
University of Manchester

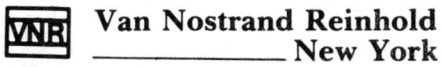

Van Nostrand Reinhold
New York

© Macmillan Education 1989
© Masson, Editeur, Paris, 1987

Library of Congress Catalog Card Number 89–9040
ISBN 0–442–30273–8

All rights reserved. No part of this work covered by the copyright hereon may be reproduced or used in any form or by any means—graphic, electronic, or mechanical, including photocopying, recording, taping, or information storage and retrieval systems—without written permission of the publisher.

Published in the United States of America by
Van Nostrand Reinhold
115 Fifth Avenue
New York, New York 10003

Printed in Great Britain by
Billing and Sons Ltd
Worcester

16 15 14 13 12 11 10 9 8 7 6 5 4 3 2 1

Library of Congress Cataloging–in–Publication Data

Fontaine, A. B. (Alain B.)
    [Microprocesseurs 80286/80386. English]
    80286 and 80386 microprocessors : new PC architectures / A. B.
Fontaine and F. Barrand : translated by A. Rawsthorne.
        p. cm.
    Translation of : Les microprocesseurs 80286/80386.
    Bibliography: p.
    Includes index.
    ISBN 0–442–30273–8
    1. Intel 80286 (Microprocessor) 2. Intel 80386 (Microprocessor)
I. Barrand. F. (Frédéric) II. Title.
QA76.8.I2927F6613 1989
004.165—dc20   89–9040
                                                    CIP

Contents

1 **Introduction**   1
   1.1   8086 and 80286 Family Standard Architectures 3
   1.2   Operating Systems 4
   1.3   Windowing Environments 5
   1.4   Networking 6

2 **Hardware Structure of the 80286**   8
   2.1   General Characteristics 8
   2.2   Principal Family Components 9
       2.2.1   82288 Bus Controller 10
       2.2.2   82289 Multibus Arbiter Circuit 11
       2.2.3   82284 Clock Generator 11
       2.2.4   80287 Numeric Coprocessor 13
       2.2.5   Other Circuits 13
   2.3   System Architectures 13
   2.4   80286 Processor Internal Structure 19
   2.5   Bus Interface 22
       2.5.1   Physical Memory Organisation 22
       2.5.2   Bus Cycle Operation 24
       2.5.3   Interrupt Structure 26
       2.5.4   Use of the 80287 Numeric Coprocessor 28
   2.6   Memory Architecture of the 80286 31
       2.6.1   Segmentation 31
       2.6.2   80286 Data Types 35
       2.6.3   CPU Registers 36
       2.6.4   Addressing Modes 39
       2.6.5   Introduction to Protection 41

3 The 80286 in Protected Mode   43
3.1 Memory Management 43
    3.1.1   Protected Virtual Addressing 44
    3.1.2   Descriptors and Descriptor Tables 46
    3.1.3   Memory Management Registers 52
3.2 Protection Mechanisms 54
    3.2.1   Types of Protection 54
    3.2.2   Implementation of Protection 55
    3.2.3   Protection and Memory Management 56
    3.2.4   Protection and Privilege Levels 56
    3.2.5   Conformant Segments 59
    3.2.6   Gates 59
3.3 Management of Tasks 63
    3.3.1   Task State Segment 63
    3.3.2   TSS Descriptor 65
    3.3.3   Changing the Context of a Task 66
    3.3.4   Using a Task Gate 67
    3.3.5   System Access Control 67
3.4 Interrupts 68
    3.4.1   Interrupts in Real Mode 68
    3.4.2   Interrupts in Protected Virtual Mode 73
3.5 Virtual Memory 80
    3.5.1   Strategy for Managing Segments 81
    3.5.2   Input/Output Management 83

4 Programming the 80286   85
4.1 80286 Programs 85
    4.1.1   Applications Code 85
    4.1.2   System Code 85
4.2 Assembly Language 86
    4.2.1   SEGMENT Directive - Defining a Segment 88
    4.2.2   Definition of Data Items 89
    4.2.3   Initialising Segment Registers 90
    4.2.4   END Directive 91
    4.2.5   Structure of Procedures 91
    4.2.6   Structures, Records and Macro Instructions 91
4.3 Modular Programming in Assembly Language 92
    4.3.1   Segment Sharing 93

		4.3.2	PUBLIC Data and Procedures	94
	4.4	4.3.3	Invoking the Assembler	95
		Development Tools		96
		4.4.1	Builder	96
		4.4.2	Binder	100
		4.4.3	Mapper	101
		4.4.4	LIB286 Librarian	101
		4.4.5	OVL286 Overlay Manager	101
	4.5	PLM/286		102
		4.5.1	PLM/286: A High Level System Language	102
		4.5.2	Variables and Constants	103
		4.5.3	Program Structure	104
		4.5.4	Arithmetic and Logical Operators	104
		4.5.5	Control Constructs	106
		4.5.6	Subprograms	107
		4.5.7	BASED Variables	109
		4.5.8	Modular Programming	110
		4.5.9	System Programming	111
		4.5.10	System Management	112
		4.5.11	Compilation Modes	113
		4.5.12	Invoking the Compiler	113
5	**Operating Systems**			**115**
	5.1	Real-time Operating Systems		115
		5.1.1	Memory Management	115
		5.1.2	Object Management	116
		5.1.3	Descriptor Management	116
		5.1.4	Exceptions	116
		5.1.5	Extensions to Operating System Primitives	116
	5.2	XENIX/286: A Development Environment		117
	5.3	Operating System Design		117
		5.3.1	Tasks	119
		5.3.2	Levels of Privilege	120
		5.3.3	Structures of Programs	122
		5.3.4	Configuring Software Systems	122
	5.4	ETR_286: A Real-Time Toolbox		123
		5.4.1	Specification	124
		5.4.2	Task Scheduling	125

	5.4.3	Task Descriptor	126
	5.4.4	Timer Manager	127
	5.4.5	Message Queue	129
	5.4.6	Semaphores	129
	5.4.7	Events	130
	5.4.8	Memory Allocation	130
	5.4.9	Input/Output Management	131
	5.4.10	Extensions	133
	5.4.11	Exceptions	133
	5.4.12	Utilities	134
	5.4.13	Creating an Absolute File	134

6 Input/Output and Networking 135

6.1	Physical Management of Input/output	135
	6.1.1 Hardware Aspects	135
	6.1.2 Software Aspects	136
	6.1.3 Local Area Networks	136
6.2	High Level Protocols	139
6.3	Open Net	139
	6.3.1 Open Net Under iRMX286	140
	6.3.2 Usage Under XENIX/286	142
	6.3.3 PC/NETWORK	142

7 The 80386 Microprocessor 143

7.1	General Characteristics of the 80386	143
	7.1.1 Software Aspects	143
	7.1.2 Hardware aspects	144
7.2	80386 Structure - the Applications View	145
	7.2.1 General Registers and Flags	145
	7.2.2 Numeric Coprocessors	148
	7.2.3 Memory and Addresses	148
7.3	System Aspects of the 80386 Structure	154
	7.3.1 System and Task Registers	154
	7.3.2 Memory Management	158
	7.3.3 Virtual Memory and Protection	161
	7.3.4 Changes of Sequence	162
7.4	Cache Memory	162
	7.4.1 Definition of a Cache	163
	7.4.2 Cache Design Criteria	163
	7.4.3 Cache Structures	164
7.5	Using an 80386	167

Appendix A	**80286 Instruction Set**	**168**
Appendix B	**80386 Instruction Set**	**191**
B.1	Double-word Instructions	191
B.2	Additional Instructions	192
Appendix C	**ETR_286 Real-time Monitor**	**195**
C.1	etr.h	196
C.2	etrstr.h	199
C.3	etrprc.h	203
C.4	etrt0.pl6	205
C.5	etrt1.pl6	206
C.6	etrtf.pl6	207
C.7	etrsched.s86	208
C.8	etrto.pl6	210
C.9	etrford.pl6	213
C.10	etrevms.pl6	217
C.11	etrfifo.pl6	221
C.12	etrmemx.pl6	223
C.13	etrmemu.pl6	224
C.14	etrbud.pl6	225
C.15	etrcnf.pl6	229
C.16	etrdrv.pl6	230
C.17	etrexp.pl6	235
C.18	etrut.pl6	238
C.19	etrmain.pl6	242
C.20	etrinit.pl6	246
C.21	etres.pl6	249
C.22	etr286.bld	252
Bibliography		**256**
Index		**258**

List of Figures

2.1.1	The 80286	8
2.2.1	82288 Bus controller	10
2.2.2	82289 Bus arbiter	11
2.2.3	82284 Clock Generator	12
2.2.4	80287 Pinout	12
2.3.1	Multiprocessor system	14
2.3.2	Local and system buses	15
2.3.3	Multibus wiring	17
2.3.4	Using the 80287 numeric coprocessor	18
2.3.5	A complex system architecture	19
2.4.1	80286 Internal structure	20
2.4.2	Pipelining	21
2.5.1	Memory organisation	23
2.5.2	Transferring a misaligned word	24
2.5.3	80286 Bus read cycle	25
2.5.4	Table of interrupt descriptors	26
2.5.5	Processing simultaneous interrupts	27
2.5.6	Using the 8259A interrupt controller	27
2.5.7	Internal structure of the 80287	29
2.5.8	Numeric coprocessor register set	30
2.6.1	Segmented memory	31
2.6.2	Displacements or offsets	32
2.6.3	Address calculation in real mode	33
2.6.4	Reserved memory in real address mode	34
2.6.5	Format of a segment selector	35
2.6.6	Physical implementation of data	36
2.6.7	General purpose registers	37
2.6.8	Addressing in protected virtual mode	39

List of Figures xi

2.6.9 Status and control words 40
2.6.10 Addressing modes 41
2.6.11 Segment descriptor format 42

3.1.1 Access to segmented data 43
3.1.2 Segment selector format 45
3.1.3 Descriptor table selection by the TI bit 46
3.1.4 Address spaces and isolation between tasks 47
3.1.5 Segment descriptor 48
3.1.6 System descriptor 48
3.1.7 Segment types 49
3.1.8 Virtual addressing mechanism 50
3.1.9 Translating virtual into physical addresses 51
3.1.10 Non global shared data 52
3.1.11 Segment registers 53
3.2.1 Gate descriptor format 59
3.2.2 Changing privilege levels using a Call Gate 61
3.2.3 Examples of calls by Call Gate 62
3.3.1 Task State Segment 64
3.3.2 Segment structures for two tasks 65
3.3.3 TSS descriptor 66
3.3.4 Task Gate 67
3.3.5 Task switch using a Task Gate 68
3.4.1 8259A Interrupt controller causing INTR 69
3.4.2 Interrupt acknowledge cycle 70
3.4.3 Sources of interrupts 71
3.4.4 Stack following an interrupt 72
3.4.5 Interrupt Descriptor Table 74
3.4.6 IDTR and other CPU Task Registers 75
3.4.7 Accessing the interrupt descriptor 75
3.4.8 Interrupt and Trap Gate descriptor format 77
3.4.9 Stack following an error exception 78
3.4.10 Relationship between two tasks 80
3.5.1 Virtual memory 82

4.2.1 A simple program 88
4.3.1 Small model 93
4.3.2 Large model 93

4.4.1 Using Builder 97
4.4.2 Using Binder 100
4.5.1 Block structure in a PLM/286 program 105
4.5.2 General layout of a subprogram 108
4.5.3 BASED variables 110
4.5.4 Accessing variables and procedures from other modules . . 111

5.1.1 Adding iRMX286 primitives 117
5.2.1 Xenix/286 organisation 118
5.3.1 Separation of data between tasks 120
5.3.2 Sharing information between tasks 121
5.3.3 System with four privilege levels 122
5.3.4 Constructing a static system 123
5.3.5 Constructing a dynamic system 124
5.4.1 Principal ETR_286 data structures 127
5.4.2 Data structures for timeouts 129
5.4.3 Message queue 130
5.4.4 ETR_286 Input/Output structures 133

6.1.1 Network subsystem using 82588 137
6.1.2 Data structures used by the 82588 138
6.2.1 OSI and CCITT protocols 140
6.3.1 iNA960 under iRMX286 141
6.3.2 Open Net file systems 142

7.2.1 General registers 146
7.2.2 80386 flags register 147
7.2.3 Translating logical addresses 150
7.2.4 Segment registers 151
7.2.5 Address mode summary 152
7.3.1 Descriptor fields 154
7.3.2 System segment descriptors 155
7.3.3 System segment descriptor registers 156
7.3.4 Principal TSS fields 157
7.3.5 Control registers 158
7.3.6 Address translation with paging 159
7.3.7 Paging mechanism 160
7.4.1 Direct-mapped 64 kilobyte cache 164
7.4.2 Direct-mapped cache hardware 165
7.4.3 Two-way set-associative cache 166

Acknowledgements

The translator wishes to thank Mr K Gallup, of Rapid Silicon, for making available facilities to compile the example programs in appendix C.

PC is a trademark of IBM, Unix is a trademark of AT&T, MS/DOS, Xenix, and Windows/386 are trademarks of Microsoft; Macintosh is a trademark of Apple Computer,Inc., Lotus 1-2-3 is a trademark of Lotus Development Corp., and Atari is a trademark of Atari Corp.

1 Introduction

The importance of sixteen-bit microprocessors has grown very significantly in the ten years since their introduction, and today only a small niche remains for the eight-bit processors. Apart from the Zilog Z80, which seems to go on and on, and excepting special-purpose sequencers and microcontrollers, the microcomputer market is dominated by 16- and 32-bit architectures. For a number of years now, the systems architect has had a number of suppliers at his disposal, and has been able to choose between numerous architectures; most current systems have, however, been based on one of two microcomputer families.

The two most significant families of microprocessor components in common usage today are the Intel 8086 and the Motorola 68000 architectures, although a number of less popular alternatives exist. The competition between these families is intense, and is based on the related bus and system architectures as well as on the capabilities of the semiconductor components themselves. Intel have developed the Multibus I and II architectures, while Motorola promote the VME bus, although it is possible to mix processors and bus architectures. Two significant influences on the adoption of these two families were the use of the Intel processor in the IBM PC and the appearance of the Motorola chip in the Apple Macintosh.

The financial rewards from a successful architecture are vast, since the investment in software for one architecture must be preserved, so semiconductor manufacturers need to hold on to their customers. One source inside Intel estimates that to date U.S. $6 billion have been spent on writing 8086 software!

In this book, we have chosen to describe in detail the iAPX 286, a successor to the 8086, with significant enhancements to help its users exploit its power. We also describe the significant enhancements brought to the Intel family by the introduction of the 32-bit iAPX 386.

The speed of progress in this area can be judged from a few figures: the 8086 processor, conceived in 1976 and introduced in 1978, has a raw performance of about 0.2 MIPS (million instructions per second) at 8 MHz. It can address 1 megabyte of memory. At the time of its introduction, this processor offered significant advantages over then-current 8-bit devices. Today, however, it has been largely superseded, for a number of reasons.

The first reason is the size of computer programs. Software sometimes seems like an ideal gas filling all available memory. For example, the IBM PC, with a maximum of 640 kilobytes, is too small for a number of applications. This restriction has encouraged Intel and Lotus (of 1-2-3 spreadsheet fame) to develop a standard means of extending the 8086 address space to 8 megabytes, at the cost of some complexity in programs that need to manage this space explicitly.

The second reason is that of speed. Simple computer applications need only a limited computer power. Evolving applications tend to be much more sophisticated, with an optimised man-machine interface, with intensive use of graphics, in multiple windows, and extensive use of network communications. It is just not possible to provide these facilities on a less powerful machine. (The reader may test this assertion by comparing the usability of the MS-Windows system on a PC/XT and on a PC/AT.)

The third reason concerns the needs of protection. In order to use a multitasking or multi-user operating system, it is necessary to provide protection between processes. Protection facilities were introduced to the Intel family in the 80286 processor.

These considerations all played their part in Intel's development of the 80286, which also, of course, represents their attempt to keep a dominant position in the microprocessor market place.

The 80286 can be seen simply as an enhancement of the 8086. In real mode, or compatibility mode, it behaves as an 8086, but 4 or 5 times faster. It approaches a performance of 1 MIP, about the raw performance of a DEC VAX 11/780, for about $50. Used in this way, it offers a significant performance with no software modifications.

The two other problems mentioned above are addressed when the chip is used in protected mode, and need operating system modifications to exploit them. In this mode, the processor offers the same raw performance, but the real addressing capacity is increased to 16 megabytes, and an individual process can address a virtual space of 1 gigabyte. In this mode, the processor supports protection, which permits applications to run without corrupting others and, by catching erroneous accesses, eases debugging during program development. So far as compatibility is concerned, investment in existing 8086 software is preserved in that while applications needing to exploit new features will need rewriting, most current applications need very few, if any, changes to run on the 286. Even assembly-language programs can be ported to the 286 with minimal changes. Only an operating system that wishes to use the protected mode will need significant changes when ported from the 8086 to the 80286.

The story continues from here, since the 80286 now has a successor, the 80386, which retains the protected mode of the 80286, but extends its power: it can address 4 gigabytes of real memory, and has a raw performance of between 3 and 4 MIPS. A number of microcomputer manufacturers (including IBM) have introduced products based upon this processor: one of the first to be introduced was a portable computer by Compaq, offering a performance of about 3 MIPS, and supporting 140 megabytes of disk, a streaming tape drive, and up to 6 megabytes of main memory. This machine showed a speed of about 3 times an IBM PC/AT, and was first offered in 1986 at a price of about U.S. $8000.

Software for the 80386 is also available now: the multitasking OS/2 is available, as are versions of Xenix and Unix System V. Some suppliers are offering concurrent UNIX and MS/DOS facilities, and one can predict the availability of "hypervisors" in the style of the VM/370 system for IBM mainframes.

1.1 8086 and 80286 Family Standard Architectures

The single most significant difference between the 8086 and the Motorola 68000 families is Intel's segmented memory addressing scheme. In order to address larger memory spaces, an address of 20 or more bits is necessary. If used everywhere, these addresses would lengthen the instructions in a program and slow its execution speed. Both architectures, therefore, allow the use of base registers, which can be loaded once with a full address, and thereafter permit data to be accessed using a short 8- or 16-bit displacement. The 68000 provides both of these and an absolute address form.

Intel, however, do not encourage the use of absolute addresses, and require the programmer to specify a Base Register and a displacement for every memory access. They call the base register a "segment register", and describe all memory accessible from that base as a "segment".

Segment sizes are limited, to 64 kilobytes in the case of the 8086 and the 80286 and to 4 megabytes in the 80386. This can be a significant constraint for an assembly-language programmer, but should be handled automatically by a high-level language compiler.

Segmentation can have advantages for the construction of large software applications, in that individual segments can be characterised by their access requirements: the 80286, for instance, monitors each access to a segment. If it is marked "read-only", no software can write to it: if it is not marked "executable" it is impossible to execute code from it. Forbidden accesses are trapped by the processor, enhancing the security of the software that is running.

A related topic to segmentation is providing virtual memory by "paging". This scheme allows an operating system to use memory and processor time efficiently by allocating memory in fixed-size "pages", which are usually between 1 and 4 kilobytes in size. Address translation hardware is needed to permit programs and their data to be loaded into non-contiguous real memory. Segments, however, are of variable size and may be much larger than an optimum page size. The choice of providing either segmentation or paging in an architecture is resolved in the 80386 by providing both.

1.2 Operating Systems

In order to exploit the characteristics of an architecture such as that of the 80286, it is necessary to use a more or less sophisticated operating system. If the architecture is aimed at general-purpose computing, it is impossible to discuss the merits of the chip itself without considering the operating system. Since its introduction, the 80286 has been closely linked with MS/DOS, with UNIX or XENIX being chosen by a minority of users. The Motorola 68000 family devices have been much more closely linked with UNIX.

In the case of the 80286, this strong link with MS/DOS is being relaxed with the introduction by IBM of their multitasking OS/2 system, and with the promotion of XENIX by Microsoft (who are the developers of both MS/DOS and OS/2!). A complete port of UNIX System V Release 3, the current version from AT&T, is also now available.

This choice of operating system is a complication for the user, since most 80286 machines do not offer the ideal of concurrently running UNIX and MS/DOS applications on the same machine. The architecture of the 80386 (especially the protected 8086 mode) makes this ideal much easier for the operating system designer to provide, and at least one commercial system now offers this concurrency.

How would a user choose between MS/DOS and, say, UNIX?

The essential difference is that UNIX is a multi-user system, sharing the available CPU power between a number of users, by the process of "time-sharing". An 80286-based microprocessor system might be powerful enough to support perhaps 10 users, depending on its memory and disk configuration.

On the other hand, MS/DOS is a single-user system, permitting only a single user access to a single application at one time. Traditionally, the provision of this much computer power to a single user, very often for a simple application, is seen as either a luxury or a waste!

Half-way between these extremes is the provision of multitasking facilities, which permit a user to interact with a number of applications running concurrently. This facility has been available for some time under "Concurrent DOS", from Digital Research, but it will be much more widely used with the advent of OS/2.

Apart from this fundamental difference, the two systems have a number of others. MS/DOS is simple and straightforward, being well suited to many of the office and management systems which are used on PCs. Unix, on the other hand, is more widespread on different architectures, and offers the software developer the prospect of portability for his application. Here again, however, the arguments are changing, as the support for "C" (the standard language of UNIX) is improved under MS/DOS, making the operating-system interface the most difficult part of porting a program. Nowadays, with a certain amount of forethought (such as defining a restricted system-call interface), it is relatively easy to guarantee the portability of software from one system to another.

UNIX and MS/DOS share a number of concepts in common, perhaps the most important being that both provide a hierarchical filestore, enabling them to offer a superficial external appearance, albeit with substantially different internal implementations.

When is each system best used? This is not a straightforward question to answer, and before investing time and effort in software development in one or other environment, it is important to consider the arguments carefully. In most cases, the decision will rest on a small number of criteria:

- The development facilities available;
- The availability of a suitable implementation language;
- Any requirement for direct access to the hardware.

It has always been difficult to make predictions about the evolution of operating systems: it is not possible at the moment to guess whether UNIX will expand in use at the rate predicted by its promoters. The current trend is for applications to hide details of the underlying operating system, in order to simplify the user interface as much as possible. One outstanding example of this direction is the "Window, Icon, Mouse" user interface provided by the Apple Macintosh.

The authors tend to the view that future operating systems will offer more diverse facilities, allowing the concurrent use of applications designed to run in different applications. One example of this is OS/2, which allows the user to run one MS/DOS application: perhaps in the future, concurrent MS/DOS, OS/2 and UNIX interfaces will be provided.

1.3 Windowing Environments

The majority of the profits from microcomputers come from their sale to professional and semi-professional employees. Apple, for example, has transformed itself from a company specialising in personal computers into one supplying professional products capable of challenging the MS/DOS world. Office products are supplied to users in the professions and to large and small organisations, industrial, service, utility and military.

The users in these markets do not need access to the direct operating system commands, whose complexity and unfamiliarity may inhibit the ready acceptance of the system. This is true of even a simple system like MS/DOS, and doubly true of UNIX. The desire to present the user with a simpler, more attractive interface gives rise to a number of software products such as TOP VIEW, MS WINDOWS, and GEM.

These products require a certain level of hardware support, typically a graphics display and controller, often supporting colour, a reasonable amount of memory (perhaps 512 kilobytes), and a mouse for positional input. Further, these window systems may support an embryo multitasking system, giving the illusion of running a number of concurrent applications.

An example of a windowing system is Microsoft's MS WINDOWS. This software is a layer above the DOS, replacing the command interpreter, and thus becoming the user interface. MS WINDOWS consists of three components: the user interface, the Graphics Device Interface (GDI), and the kernel. It is the kernel which allows DOS to be hidden, and yet provides a standard interface to the system. The same idea is used by the GDI, which translates high-level requests from the user into a series of simpler screen update operations for the hardware to carry out. For example, one hardware interface might need a series of "dot" operations to draw a simple picture, while a more complex interface might be able to draw lines and arcs: the GDI would hide this difference from the application software.

The multitasking interface is limited in that it can only support functions which can run non-preemptably. This restriction arises because DOS calls cannot be reentrant, so processes must run non-preemptably.

It is quickly apparent to a user that this type of environment is not adequately supported by the 8086 processor, and needs at least the power of an 80286.

Graphics interfaces are becoming an increasingly important area for manufacturers. Producing a low-cost machine with a high-resolution (1000 x 1000 pixels) display and a reasonable performance has been a target for a number of years, and is only now (1988) being achieved. The Atari 1040ST, for example, has been a great success since 1986. It is not only CPU components that help a designer to address these targets: the Intel 82786 graphics controller chip, for example, permits the design of very impressive systems.

1.4 Networking

The last factor to consider in the development of technologies and in the application of computers is the development of networking, both wide area, and particularly in local areas. The aim of local area networking is to provide low-cost access to computing power, to permit sharing of data between a group of users, the sharing of expensive peripheral devices, and access to databases.

It is quickly appreciated that a standard IBM PC, with a power of about 0.07 MIPS, was adequate for many simple applications, even if a PC AT, with up to 1 MIPS, depending on the model, could support more peripherals, and provide a more comfortable environment for the user. In either case, the cost of buying the equipment is very much less than buying, say, a 10 MIPS IBM mainframe, shared between 100 users, each with his own (expensive) 3270 screen.

The principal advantage of the mainframe configuration is that it is capable of supporting very large databases. Perhaps an ideal intermediate configuration would be a confederation of PC machines, each linked to a central departmental-level computer system, with further access to large mainframes to interrogate large databases. Access to the central facilities might be provided by a local network, either directly or via a gateway to a public network to the remote machine.

Such a configuration demands that each personal computer needs to be sufficiently powerful to perform network-related tasks without slowing down unacceptably.

Two principal classes of network can be identified, wide area networks and local area networks.

Almost all current wide area networks in Europe use X.25 as their interface standard. When interfaced to these networks, the 80286 processor is used in conjunction with other components specifically designed to interface to these networks. Western Digital, for example, manufacture a chip which implements levels 1 and 2 of the ISO Open Systems Interconnection (OSI) architecture, leaving levels 3 and above to be implemented in software. A new development is X.32, which CCITT standardised in 1986 to specify the interface between computers, such as PCs, and packet-switched networks via the telephone network.

Local area networks can be further subdivided into different classes. Ethernet was initially developed for use in office communications systems, and uses a contention protocol on a common interconnection bus. Other networks specify token passing over either ring or bus topologies: standards such as MAP (Manufacturing Automation Protocol) and TOP (Technical and Office Protocol) specify a complete suite of protocols spanning all layers of the OSI Reference Model.

From the viewpoint of the system architect, networking can be implemented in one of two different manners: some systems provide a single processor to do everything – handle the keyboard, paint the screen, service peripherals, implement the network protocols, while others are based upon a largely decentralised architecture, with a number of special-purpose processors, each performing one task.

Networking is one of the more actively developing areas, and we can expect to see significant developments here in the near future. The most significant influence on the future development of networking is the ISO 7 layer reference model for Open System Interconnection. It will soon be common to purchase communications software which implements all 7 layers of the reference model: this will enable all systems so equipped to interchange files (using FTAM), electronic mail (using X.400) and to support remote terminal sessions using VTP.

Having briefly examined the current context of the Intel 16- and 32-bit processor chips, the following chapters examine their architecture in detail.

2 Hardware Structure of the 80286

2.1 General Characteristics

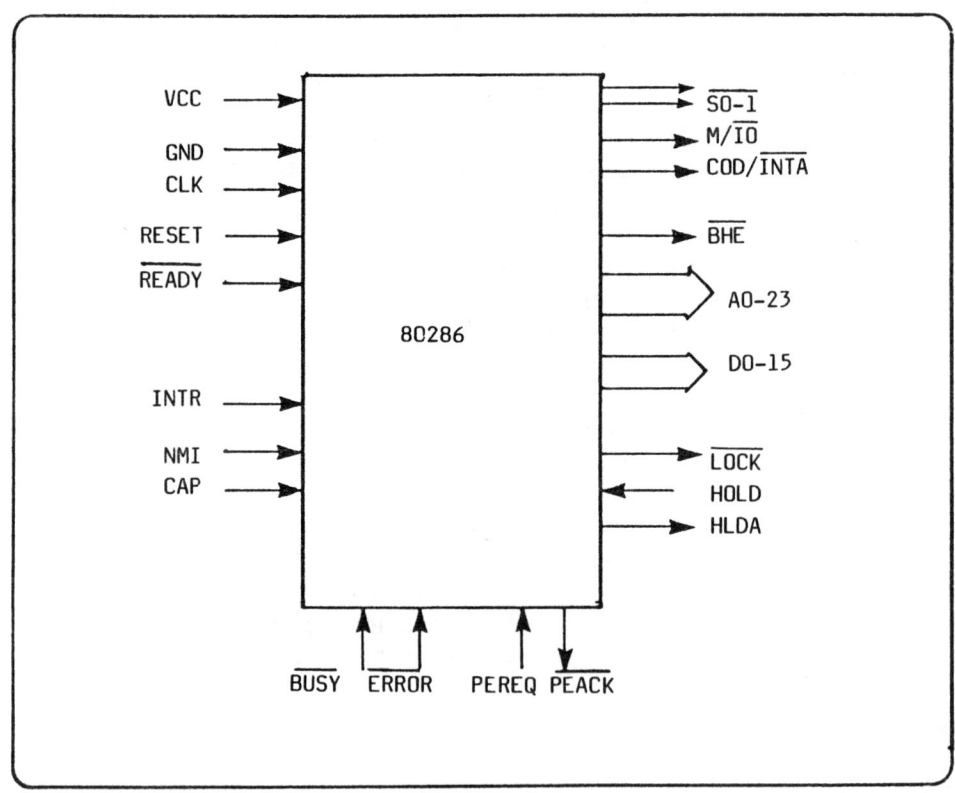

Figure 2.1.1 The 80286

The 80286 CPU operates at 8 or 10 MHz, and offers a performance of about 6 times faster than a 5 MHz 8086; its input/output bus can transfer data at 8 or 10 megabytes per second.

A range of circuits for use with the 80286 processor has been developed: a clock generator chip, the 82284, a bus arbiter, the 82289, for use in multiprocessor architectures, a numeric coprocessor, the 80287, a DMA controller, a dynamic RAM controller circuit, and circuits for implementing error-detection and error-correction codes in memory.

The memory address space of the 80286 is larger than in the 8086: using 24 address lines gives the CPU the ability to address 16 megabytes of real memory. The address lines are driven by a mechanism which supports protection, and which implements virtual memory supporting over 8000 tasks, each of which can address 1 gigabyte of virtual memory.

Address translation is based upon an indirect addressing scheme which is implemented very efficiently: each memory segment is addressed via a descriptor which indicates a type, a privilege level, and a maximum size. Data access is made as fast as possible by integrating the address-translation and protection circuits onto the CPU chip.

The 80286 CPU can function in two different modes, real mode and protected mode.

Real mode uses the same addressing scheme as is implemented on the 8086, implementing the same instruction set with a few additions.

Protected mode provides facilities for:

o Supporting multitasking and context switching,

o Protecting data using a multi-level privilege scheme, and

o Restricting program accesses to pre-allocated memory areas.

These characteristics allow the 80286 to be used in significantly different hardware configurations from the 8086. It can be used with very large main memories and, with a suitable operating system such as Xenix/286, can run a number of simultaneous applications for different purposes.

All of the advanced facilities are described in this book. It is worth noting that the 80286 is used in the IBM PC/AT and some of the PS/2 computers; MS/DOS, however, does not take advantage of the more advanced features of the CPU.

This chapter describes each member of the 80286 family of components, and explains how they may be interconnected to form convenient system architectures. It concludes by describing the internal operation of the CPU chip itself and the operation of its input/output bus.

2.2 Principal Family Components

Since the 80286 processor is a direct descendant, it is not surprising that its family of related components is similar to that of the 8086. The aim of the design of this family is to give the hardware designer flexibility to fashion many different computer systems around the same CPU chip.

The raw power of any CPU chip will be determined by its maximum clock rate, by the instruction set, the number of general-purpose registers, the addressing modes available, the usable memory space, and so on. As soon as a chip is used in a system, the overall system performance will depend on the environment of the CPU chip: the speed of input and output, the bus performance, the performance of special-purpose coprocessors, and so on.

It is for this reason that a range of components has been designed specifically for use with the 80286 processor: a similar range of circuits available with the 8086 contributed to its widespread success.

2.2.1 82288 Bus Controller

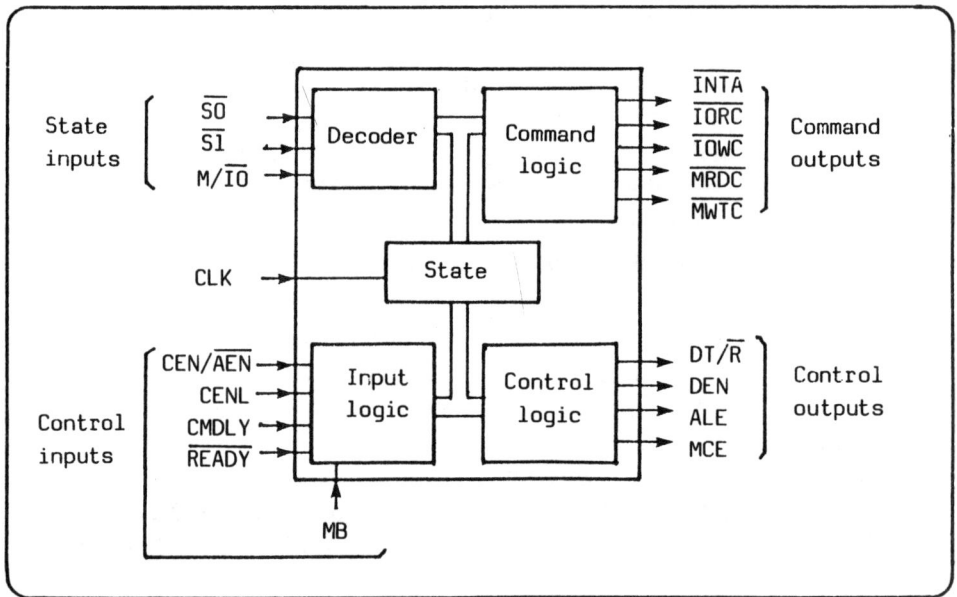

Figure 2.2.1 82288 Bus controller

The first circuit considered is the 82288 Bus Controller. This chip decodes the status signals from the 80286 and generates bus control signals (read, write, memory, IO, timing signals and interrupt acknowledgements). Memory and IO read and write signals are each decoded separately in order to simplify hardware design.

As in the 8086, it is possible to segregate different buses, and, for example, to have separate IO and memory buses. This bus controller chip is designed to interface with the next chip, in applications using Multibus, to produce multiprocessor systems.

2.2.2 82289 Multibus Arbiter Circuit

The Multibus, now standardised as IEEE 796, was originally designed for use with the 8086 processor. Fortunately, the standardisation process was sufficiently far-sighted to provide facilities for the 80286 processor.

Multibus is intended to facilitate the design of systems with a multiprocessor architecture in which all resources can be shared between all the processors.

Interfacing the 80286 processor to a Multibus is handled by the 82289 chip, which performs the same functions as the 8289 which preceded it. This chip resolves priority clashes that arise from simultaneous accesses to the Multibus from different processors, and provides a bus-locking mechanism during critical memory updates. A number of different algorithms can be used to determine how priorities are resolved: the 82289 can implement serial priority, parallel priority, or rotating priority schemes, depending upon exactly how it is wired.

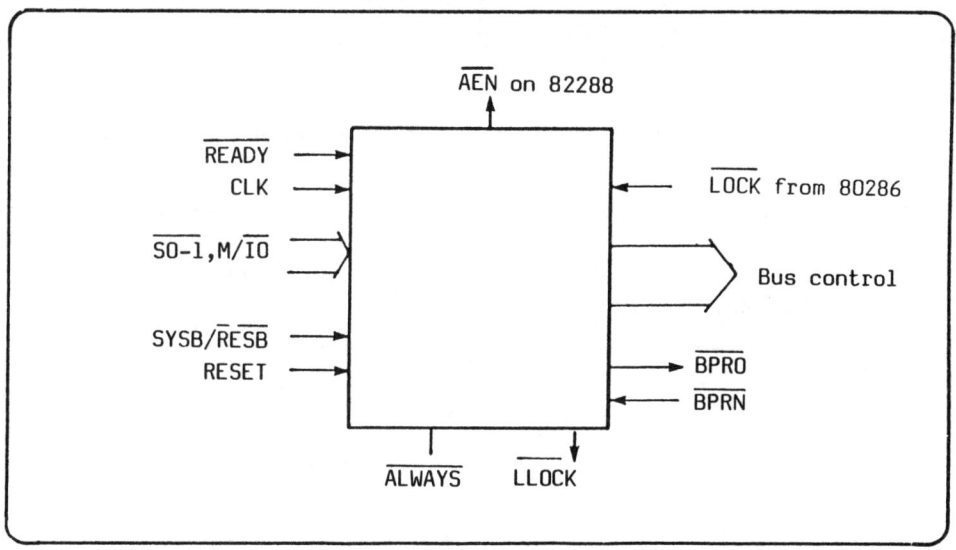

Figure 2.2.2 82289 Bus arbiter

2.2.3 82284 Clock Generator

The timing signals necessary for an 80286 system are provided by the 82284 chip, which performs two additional functions in addition to generating the master clock frequency: it provides a synchronised RESET signal, and it synchronises the READY signal which is used to delay bus cycles for slow memory or IO devices.

Figure 2.2.3 shows that the clock may be derived from one of two sources; either a normal quartz crystal or an external clock signal. The external clock

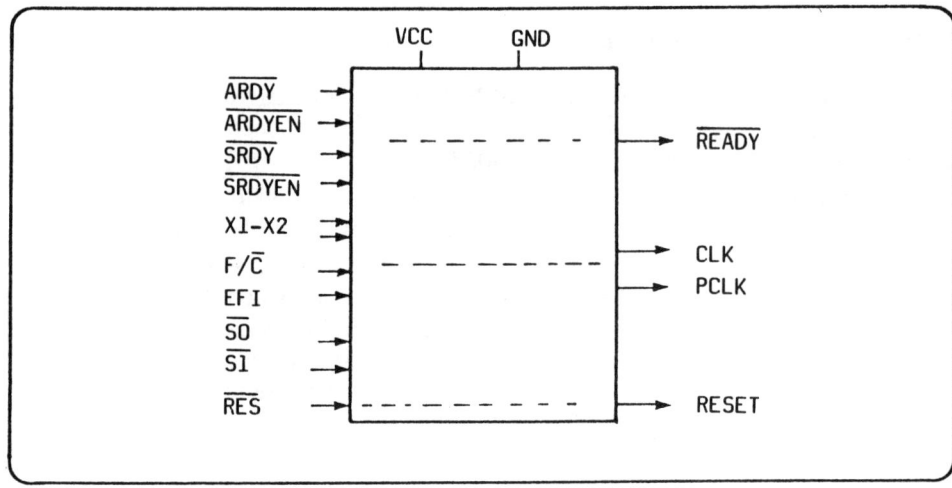

Figure 2.2.3 82284 Clock Generator

signal may be used in multiprocessor systems to ensure that all processors operate synchronously.

As in the case of the 8086 family clock generator, the 8284A, the READY signal may be derived from synchronous or asynchronous input signals. This flexibility is important to permit the simple interfacing of different peripheral circuits and to optimise the speed of access to memory.

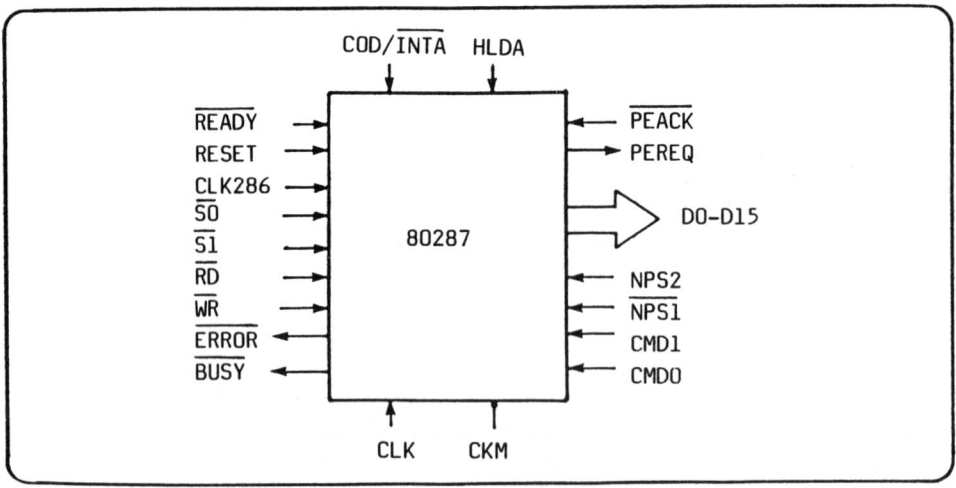

Figure 2.2.4 80287 Pinout

2.2.4 80287 Numeric Coprocessor

The most impressive members of the Intel CPU families are the numeric coprocessors. The coprocessor designed for use with the 80286 is the 80287 (see figure 2.2.4). This chip provides hardware to implement arithmetic operations on reals and extended integers, and can speed up applications by a factor of 100 or more. An interesting feature of this chip is its interface to the 80286 chip: the two buses are connected in parallel and synchronised, permitting the 80287 to recognise and implement its own special-purpose instruction set, while relying on the main processor to interpret the 80286 addressing modes. The use of the numeric coprocessor is yet further simplified for the programmer by two alternative mechanisms for dealing with hardware which does not provide it: either the same program may be recompiled with a switch that tells the compiler to use a different library, or the floating-point instructions may be left to cause traps to the operating system, which then emulates the effect of the instructions themselves.

2.2.5 Other Circuits

Some other circuits that can be used in the design of 80286-based systems are:
- The 8207 dynamic RAM controller
- The 8286 and 8287 bidirectional buffers
- The 8282 and 8283 latches
- The 8259A Interrupt controller.

Compatibility of design of the IO bus means that the majority of the circuits designed for use with the 8086 can also be used with the 80286.

Having introduced the various components, let us proceed to an examination of some examples of 80286 system architectures, considering various different options.

2.3 System Architectures

Different system architectures may have different bus architectures. A multiprocessor system using an 80286 may have two different types of bus:

A local bus, consisting of the signals directly produced by the processor itself, and

A system bus, which connects the processor to global memory and IO devices. The system bus permits global resources to be accessed by different processors, each of which has its own local bus and private resources such as memory or IO devices.

The 80286 provides control and synchronisation signals which can be used to share buses in two ways; the local bus is shared between the processor and coprocessor, and the system bus may be shared between a number of processor modules. Figure 2.3.1 shows the different elements which appear in a typical architecture.

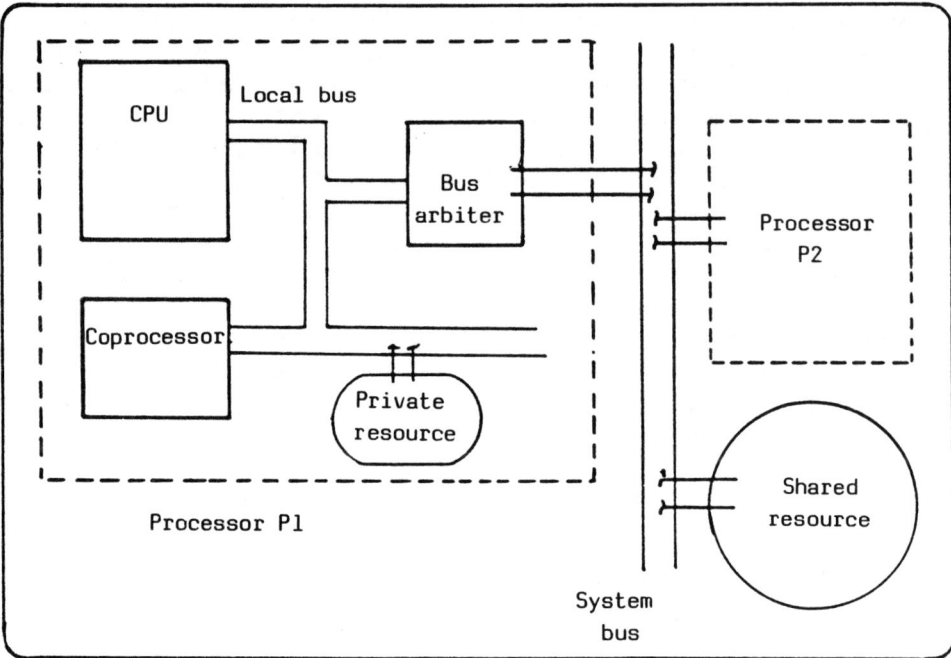

Figure 2.3.1 Multiprocessor system

Figure 2.3.2 shows one module of a multiprocessor architecture in more detail. In this example, the 80286 is interfaced to both the local and system buses, both of which are "buffered". The buffering isolates the two buses, permitting them to operate independently, and also increases the signal drive capability of the 80286 chip. This enables a large number of memory and IO modules to be connected to the system.

This diagram shows two distinct 82288 bus controllers, individually selected by an address decoder which classifies accesses from the 80286 as "local" or "system".

The purpose of having two different buses may not be immediately apparent: in most cases, it is a performance optimisation. Private memory connected to the local bus will have a fast access time, and the 80286 will be able to use its "pipelined" structure to the full. A number of these modules would be able to run concurrently provided that they all access only their local memory. Global memory, accessed via the system bus, will be slower, but will permit communication between all processors in the system (subject, in the case of the 80286 family, to all of the normal protection mechanisms).

Hardware Structure of the 80286

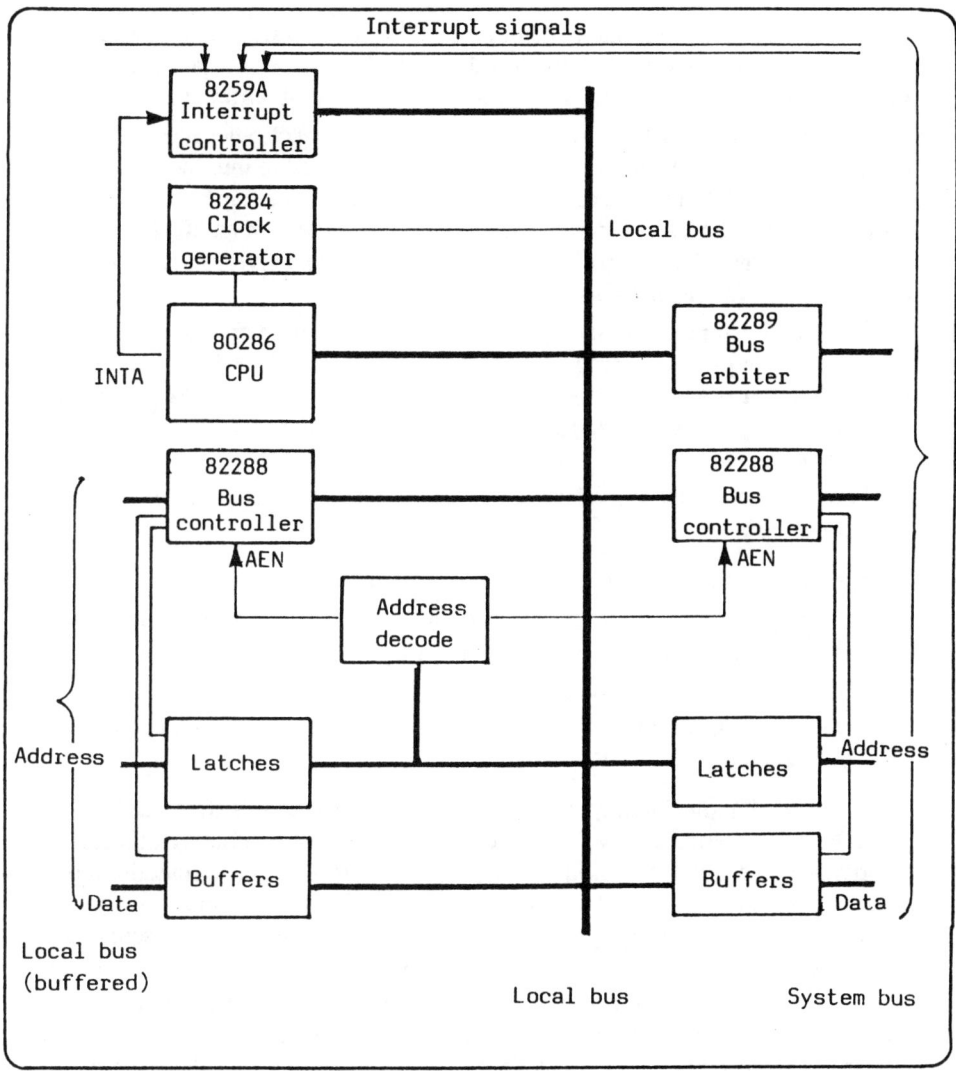

Figure 2.3.2 Local and system buses

Multiprocessor architectures need a method of resolving the conflicts that arise when multiple requests for a common resource arise simultaneously. In the context of a Multibus architecture using 80286 processors, this arbitration is performed by the 82289 which appears on each Multibus master module, so there is only one 82289 bus arbiter, since only the system bus (not the local bus) is subject to requests from a number of different processors.

Peripherals and input/output devices are connected in the same way as memory: they may be connected locally, for the exclusive use of one processor, or they may be connected to the system bus, for the shared use of all processors.

Multibus 1, in its IEEE 796 standard form, can connect other types of processors: in particular, special-purpose processors can be used to interface I/O devices with very high data rates. For example, one could connect an 80186 processor, with two DMA channels, serving high-speed peripherals, and an 80286 processor on the same bus. The 80286 could usefully devolve the activities associated with driving a disk, for example, to the 80186.

This architecture encourages the partition of the required processing into tasks that run on one particular processor. Subdividing applications into tasks is not a new idea, but it is an increasingly valuable way of building complex applications as processors get more powerful and as their addressing mechanisms get more sophisticated.

Some of the advantages of using a multiprocessor architecture built around a system bus are:

- Particular tasks can be assigned to specific processors;
- The system throughput can be increased by exploiting parallel processing;
- The system reliability can be enhanced by isolating the different functions of the overall application; and
- The overall design can benefit from using a hierarchical, modular design and implementation methodology.

The key to implementing this local/system bus structure is the 82289 bus arbiter. It is this component which solves the problems of conflicting accesses, of priority, and of mutual exclusion. In the past, these problems have sometimes been addressed in software, increasing the complexity of programs, and slowing them down, or in hardware, leading to the use of considerable amounts of discrete logic on circuit boards.

The flexibility of the bus arbiter comes from the ability to control the arbitration and locking functions by software: for example, the LOCK prefix to an instruction causes the corresponding locking signal to be active during the whole instruction execution time.

For example, the instruction LOCK XCHG Reg, Semaphore would permit the implementation of a semaphore in memory to control access and provide mutual exclusion to a shared resource.

Intel have now introduced Multibus 2, a natural progression from Multibus 1. Its principal characteristics are:

- Parallel, non-multiplexed address and data buses, each 32 bits wide
- A serial CSMA bus
- A local bus for use within modules

Hardware Structure of the 80286

- A programmable configuration system that avoids the use of jumpers or switches on circuit boards
- A hardware-based message-passing system, presenting a simple applications interface, independent of which bus (local, system or serial) is used.

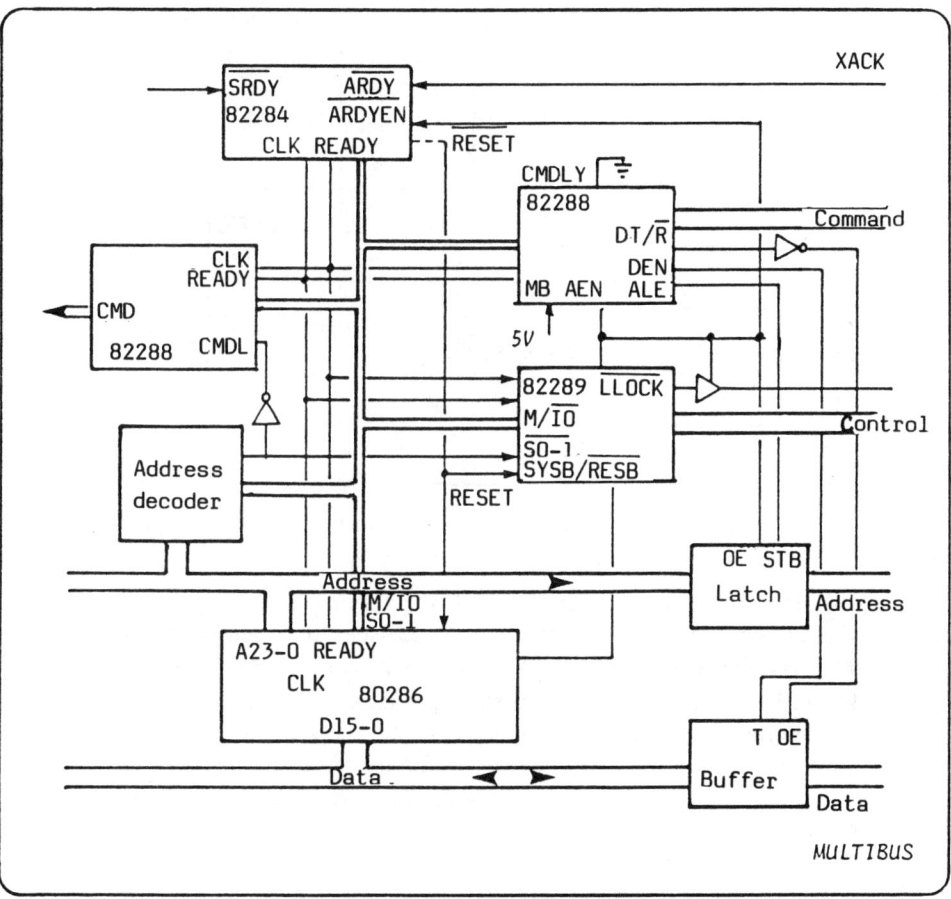

Figure 2.3.3 Multibus wiring

Figure 2.3.3 gives a more detailed diagram of the connections between an 80286 and a local and a system bus.

The capabilities of the 80287 numeric coprocessor have already been outlined above; figure 2.3.4 shows the principal connections between the coprocessor and CPU.

There are, of course, limits to the size of complex systems built from individual modules: figure 2.3.5, for example, shows a complex system with a number of

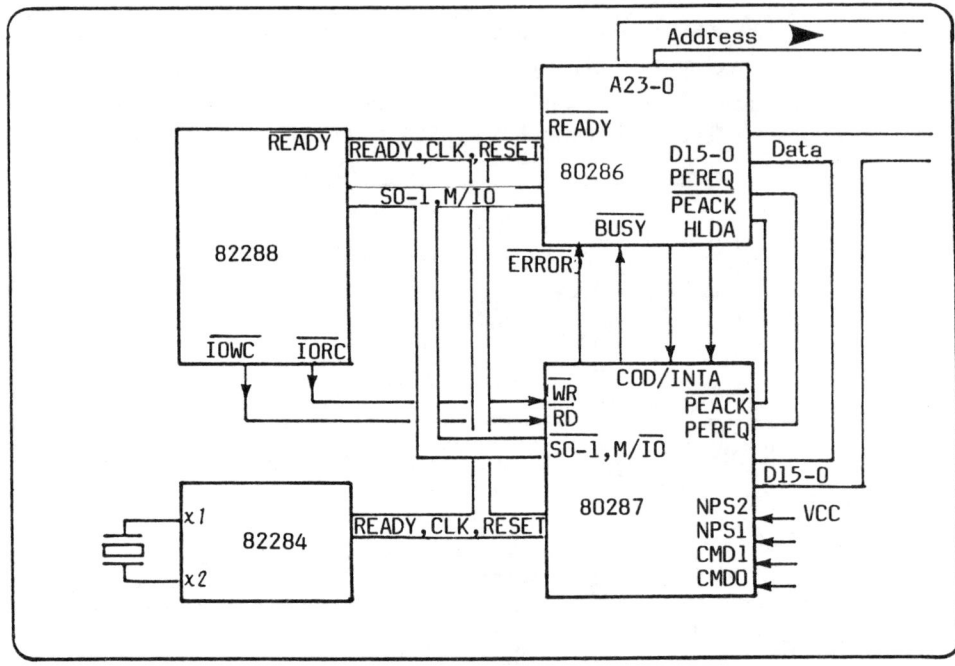

Figure 2.3.4 Using the 80287 numeric coprocessor

special-purpose subsystems. Depending on the operation of the system, it is possible that in this architecture, contention for the use of the main system bus might occupy a significant fraction of time, thereby degrading the overall performance.

The initial planning of a system structure must take this consideration into account; in order not to saturate the bus and prevent any useful work, the designer must consider the bus loading imposed by each software module. The overall design is limited by hardware constraints and by the techniques that will be adopted by the software specialists.

The APEX System

The APEX system (Advanced Processor EXtension) is a hardware architecture which enhances the performance of 80286 systems. This architecture, proposed by Intel, integrates up to four 80286-based processors. Operating under Xenix, this multiprocessor architecture gives the user a machine whose performance can approach 4.8 MIPS, by partitioning tasks between the processors in a manner transparent to the user. In order to achieve this increase in performance, each processor needs a private memory, attached directly.

This system extends the notion of multiprocessor systems, providing a "pool" of general-purpose processors, with dynamic assignment of tasks to processors.

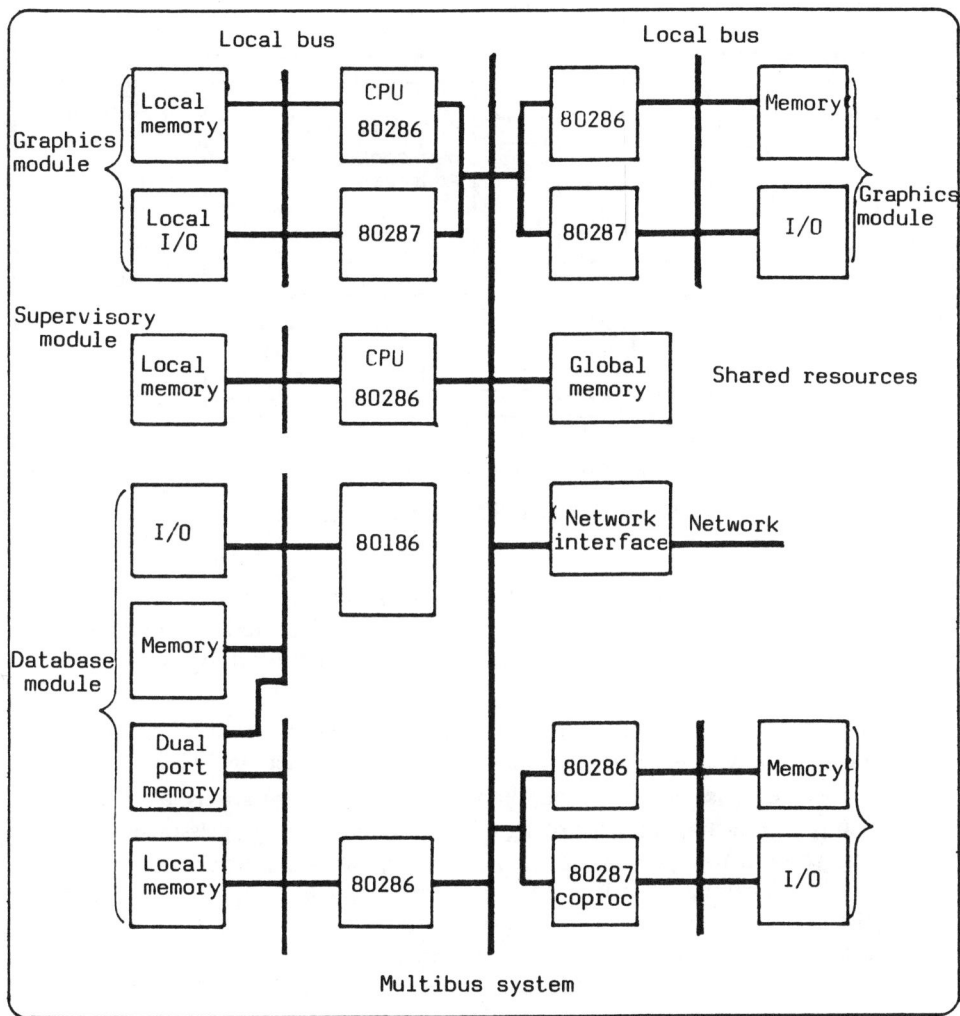

Figure 2.3.5 A complex system architecture

2.4 80286 Processor Internal Structure

Derived from the original 8086 CPU, the 80286 was conceived as a 16-bit multiprocessor for use in a multitasking, multi-user environment. The multitasking, multi-user criterion was to be met, not as with previous microprocessors which needed significant MSI circuitry and layers of supervisory software, but by directly implementing on-chip the necessary mechanisms to support a suitable operating system.

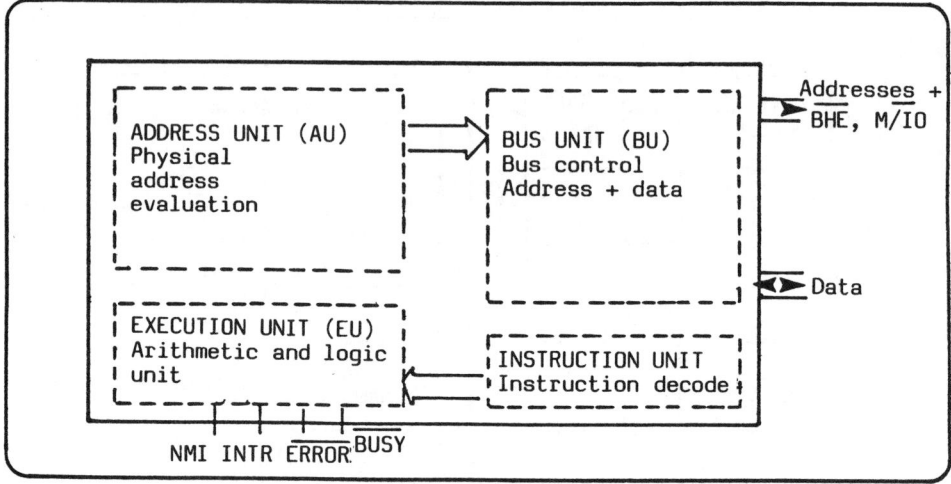

Figure 2.4.1 80286 internal structure

The principal built-in features are memory sharing, protection using a ring-structured privilege system, prevention of accesses outside a task's boundary, and task and context switching. Pipelining, already a feature of the design of the 8086, is used extensively in the 80286 CPU.

The hardware implementation of this functionality gives rise to a very complex chip design, which is divided into four relatively independent modules.

The Bus Unit implements input/output and memory operations, address calculation, data transfer, and control signal generation for the processor bus. This unit also controls the synchronisation between coprocessors, which need to share access to the local bus. The Bus Unit uses a pipelining technique, by reading instructions before they are needed, and storing them in the Instruction Unit. This unit can store up to 6 bytes of instruction, which are stored independently of the alignment within words. The read-ahead operations occur when the bus is inactive, with neither read nor write operations in progress, and allow a significant performance enhancement.

The Instruction Unit gets instructions from the queue of 6 bytes fetched by the Bus Unit, decodes these instructions, and stores the decoded form in a queue containing up to three fully decoded instructions.

The Execution Unit fetches decoded instructions and executes them. In the process of execution, it may need to call upon the Bus Unit to gain access to the bus in order to read or write data.

The fourth processing unit is the Address Unit. This unit is of central importance in that it implements all the operations necessary to generate real addresses to pass to the Bus Unit to present to external circuitry. The translations that this unit implements use 24-bit arithmetic, addressing 16 megabytes of real memory.

Hardware Structure of the 80286

The protection mechanisms provided in "protected virtual" mode, and described in chapter 3 are also implemented in the Address Unit; their chief purpose is to simplify the implementation of multitasking systems with different privileges, for example separate "user" and "supervisor" modes.

Figure 2.4.2 gives an example of the pipelining that occurs among these four units, and shows how this mechanism speeds up the overall execution rate. Not shown is the disruption to the pipeline that occurs when a straightforward instruction sequence is broken, by a jump, a procedure call or an interrupt.

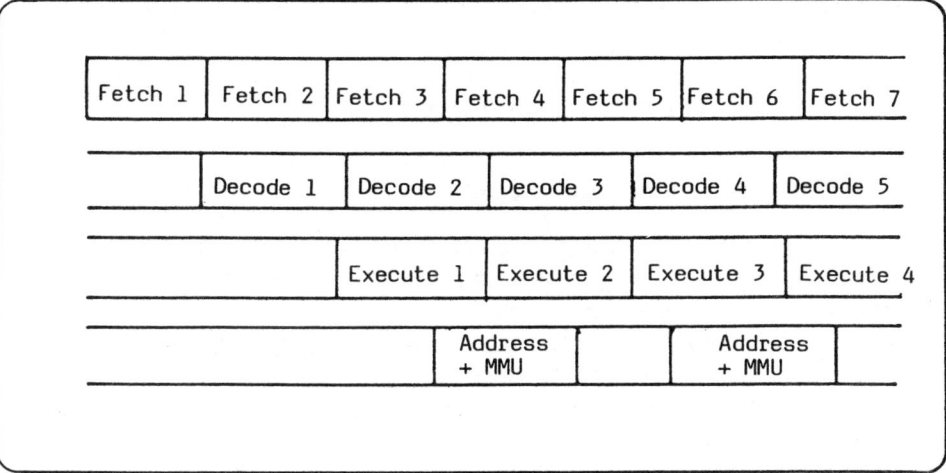

Figure 2.4.2 Pipelining

The internal processor structure permits operation in two different modes.

In "real address" mode, the 80286 accesses a maximum of 1 megabyte of memory using 20-bit addresses, which are formed in the same way as in the 8086, that is by adding a 16-bit segment number (multiplied by 16) to a 16-bit offset (see figure 2.6.3). In this mode, the 80286 appears to be an improved 8086, in that software designed for the 8086 will run unchanged. This mode was widely used for initial applications of the 80286 in PCs: they could run an unmodified version of MS/DOS.

A second mode is called "protected virtual" mode, which allows access to the full 16 megabytes of memory. In this mode, an internal cache in the Address Unit speeds up the translation of addresses and permission checking. The term "virtual memory" is used because the address space in this mode is much larger than the maximum physical memory; it is possible to relegate certain regions of memory to a disk, and to have the operating system retrieve them only when an access to the particular area is made.

2.5 Bus Interface

The 80286 is connected to memory devices by a parallel bus, consisting of 24 address signals, 16 data lines, and a number of control signals.

The operation carried out on this bus is decoded from the states of the processor signals COD/INTA:L, M/IO:L, S0:L and S1:L by the 82288 bus controller chip, which outputs the more conventional signals for bus control and synchronisation.

A number of related signals, such as HOLD and HLDA are used for such purposes as sharing the local bus between CPU and a DMA device. In a workstation, for example, an 82586 network processor could share the CPU bus in this manner.

Lastly, there are a few miscellaneous signals; ERROR:L signals an error indication to the CPU; INTR requests an interrupt; BUSY:L causes the CPU to wait for a coprocessor, and RESET:L initialises the CPU.

2.5.1 Physical Memory Organisation

The size of addressable memory depends upon the operating mode of the processor, but the physical organisation of memory is the same in both. One view of memory is of a succession of 8-bit bytes. The data bus of the 286 is 16 bits wide, but the programmer is able to access 16-bit words at any byte location. This organisation, carried over from the 8086, has both advantages and disadvantages, the chief of which is the difference in access times for words with different alignments. An aligned word (at an even address) can be accessed in one bus cycle, while a non-aligned word (with an odd address) needs two cycles for its access.

Figure 2.5.1 shows how the logical address space can appear as a succession of bytes, or as two parallel areas, juxtaposed to provide 16-bit words. Depending on the processor mode, up to 512 K words or 8 M words can be accessed.

Figure 2.5.1 also shows that memory devices are connected to the high or low-order bits of the data bus, depending upon the least significant address bit. Aligned words have their low-order bytes at an even address, and successive words are accessed using successive even addresses.

When the CPU needs to access the high-order byte within memory, the BHE:L (Byte High Enable) signal is activated. The use of this signal, and the use of the least-significant address bit, A0, is coordinated in order to cause different patterns of memory accesses, depending on the type of memory access (word/byte, aligned/non-aligned) requested by a program. Figure 2.5.2 shows how the two signals are used as "chip selects" for the two bytes of memory to perform non-aligned word accesses.

Figure 2.5.2 also illustrates the major disadvantage of this type of memory structure, as it shows how accesses to non-aligned data cause two bus cycles to fetch a single word: the first cycle is carried out with A0 high and BHE:L low, to fetch the low-order byte from the odd address, the second with A0 low and BHE:L

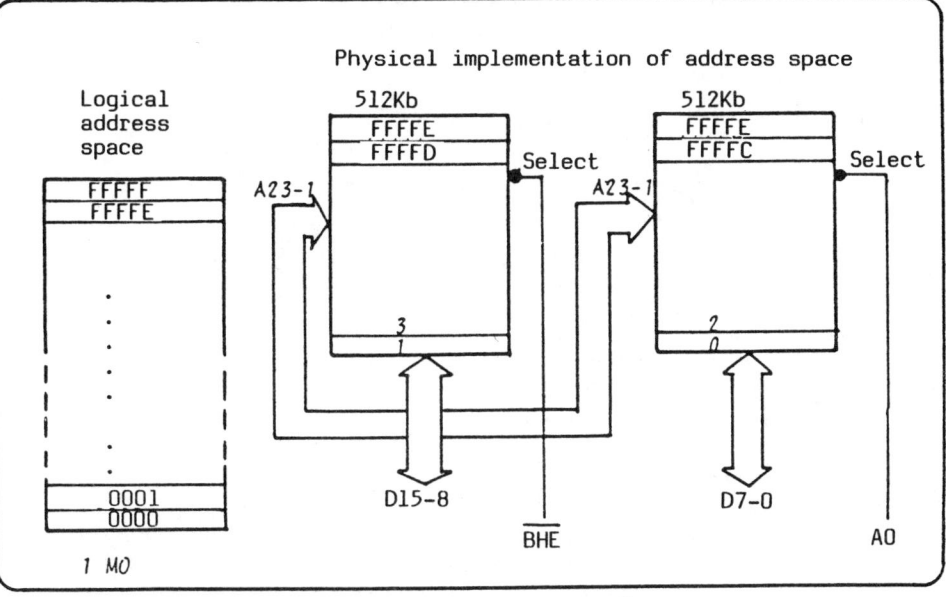

Figure 2.5.1 Memory organisation

high, to fetch the even address. Two cycles are necessary because the CPU cannot supply the necessary different addresses to both banks of memory during the same cycle.

The alignment problem is worse during write operations than during reads: during the execution of a "mov al,variable" instruction, the 286 will sample the relevant halves of the bus in each cycle if two cycles are necessary. In a write operation, however, the signals BHE:L and A0 must be used to inhibit writing to the "unused" half of each word in each of the two successive bus cycles.

Since the structure of memory is preserved from the 8086 CPU, many of the same solutions can be used with the 80286. One advantage for the modern hardware designer is the appearance of 16-bit wide EPROM devices, which are ideal for bootstrap or BIOS code, and which are usable with the 80286 since they do not need to respond to write operations.

Access to input/output locations is provided using the IN and OUT instructions, and is subject to exactly the same constraints. The programmer can regard the I/O space as 64K byte locations or 32K word locations. Eight-bit wide peripheral devices may be connected to the low-order or high-order bits of the data bus, but 16-bit devices must be situated at even addresses, so that a 16-bit IN or OUT operation can be carried out in one bus cycle.

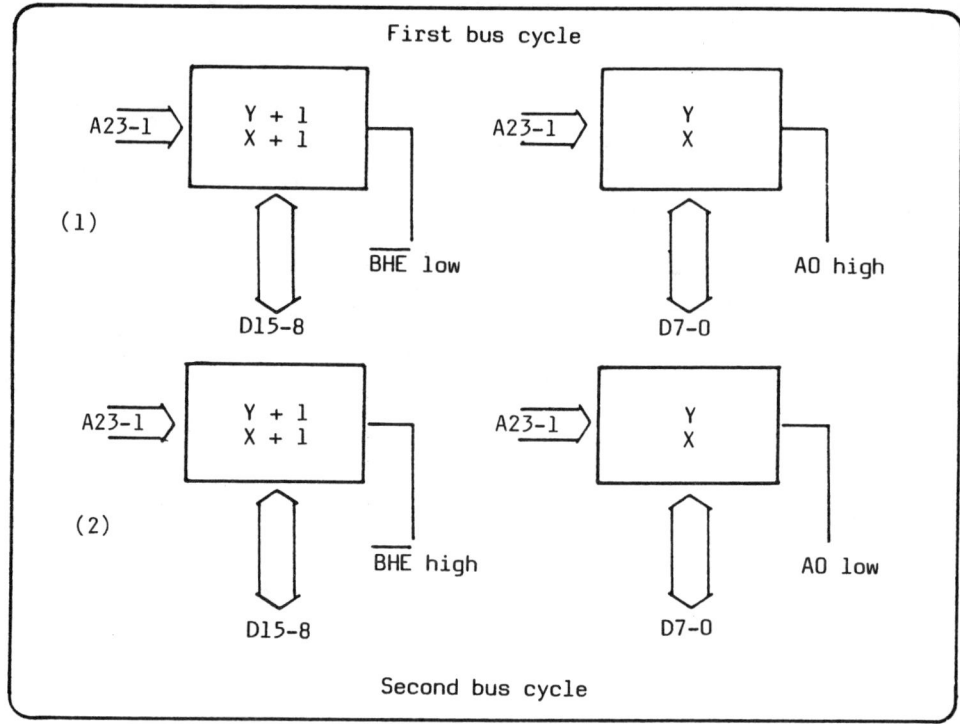

Figure 2.5.2 Transferring a misaligned word

2.5.2 Bus Cycle Operation

The basic clock frequency supplied by the 82284 generator chip, at 8 or 10 MHz, is divided by two within the processor to form an internal clock at 4 or 5 MHz. A bus cycle consists of a minimum of two internal clock cycles (500 or 400 ns), but may be extended by activating the READY:L signal to interface with slow memory devices.

The bus cycle timing is optimised using a pipelined addressing scheme, so that a second bus cycle starts (its address becoming available) before the data from the preceding cycle is sampled. (Pipelining is illustrated in figure 2.4.2.) This mode of operation is possible in the 80286 because the data and address buses are distinct, rather than multiplexed as in the 8086, and because of the relative independence of the Address Unit and the Bus Unit in the processor. The use of this mode, however, imposes a hardware restriction: a set of latches is necessary on the address lines in order to preserve the current address for the full duration of a cycle.

Figure 2.5.3 shows a timing diagram of a bus cycle, showing details of the timing of auxiliary signals (ALE, DEN, DT/R:L), which are provided to facilitate interfacing the 80286 CPU to common peripheral circuits.

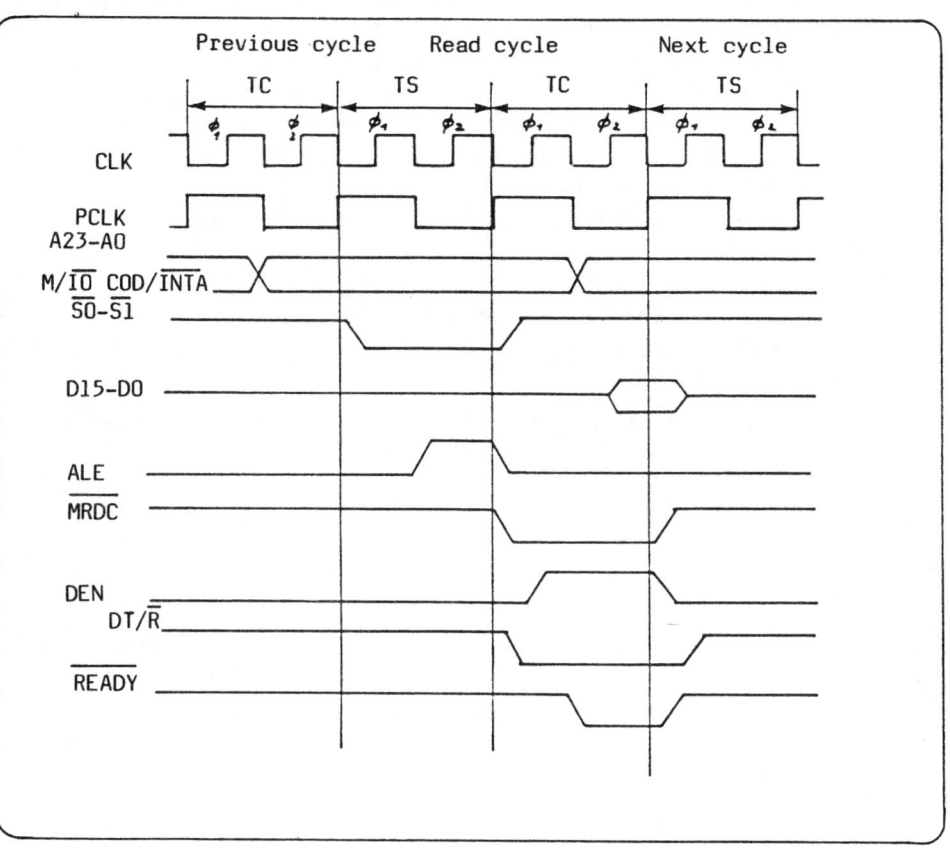

Figure 2.5.3 80286 Bus read cycle

Major reasons for the high speed of the 80286 processor are prefetching up to 6 bytes of instructions, and pipelining the bus accesses. Pipelining enables the rate of bus input/output from the processor to reach the relatively high rate of 8 megabytes per second at 8 MHz, for aligned accesses. This limit is reached during the execution of "string" instructions, which are simple instructions with a prefix to cause repetition (see the description of the REP prefix and the CMPS instruction in appendix A).

2.5.3 Interrupt Structure

The 80286 accepts interrupts from two distinct sources, in the same way as the 8086. Hardware interrupts are caused by the activation of the INTR or NMI signals, while software interrupts are caused by the execution of INT k instructions or the occurrence of some exception condition in the program.

Interrupts caused by the NMI (Non Maskable Interrupt) signal are always accepted, while the INTR signal can be masked by software. The sequence invoked by an interrupt signal depends upon the processor mode, real or protected; the different data structures are summarised in figure 2.5.4, and interrupts in protected mode are described further in section 3.4.2.

The INTR signal is slightly anomalous in its operation: in real mode, when an INTR is accepted, further response to the INTR signal is inhibited until either the software signals its readiness, or until the interrupt service routine is completed. In protected mode, however, the inhibition of the INTR signal within a service routine is explicitly specified in a descriptor describing the interrupt action, attached to the particular interrupt vector.

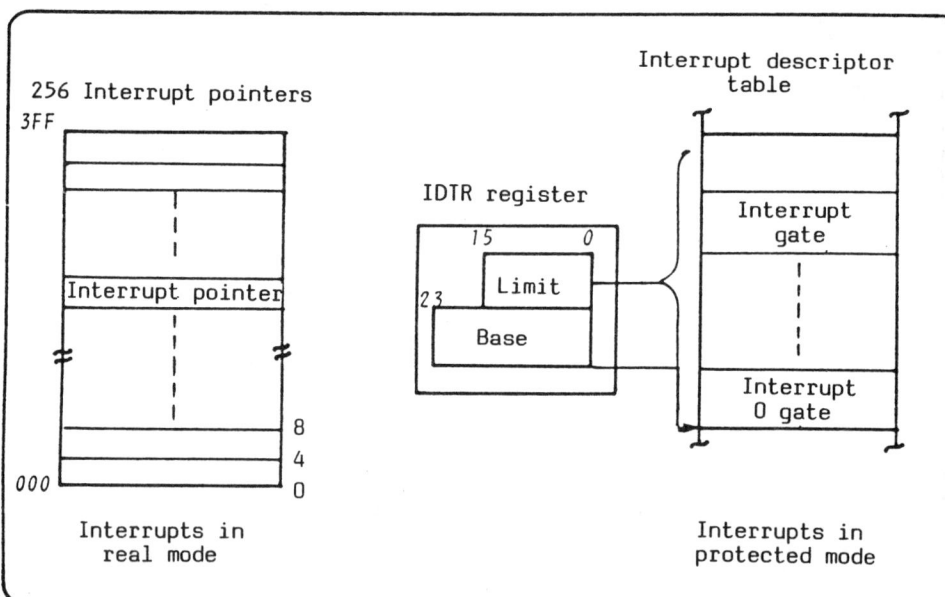

Figure 2.5.4 Table of interrupt descriptors

As in most other systems, systems implementors must be aware that the interrupt signals are sampled between instruction execution, and the maximum latency before an interrupt is recognised is the maximum instruction time.

The different causes of interrupts have a priority order: this is shown in figure 2.5.5, although some entries in the table are mutually exclusive events.

Processing order	Interrupt source
1	Instruction exception
2	Single step
3	Non-maskable interrupt (NMI)
4	Coprocessor segment overrun
5	INTR (hardware interrupt request)
6	INT n instruction

Figure 2.5.5 Processing simultaneous interrupts

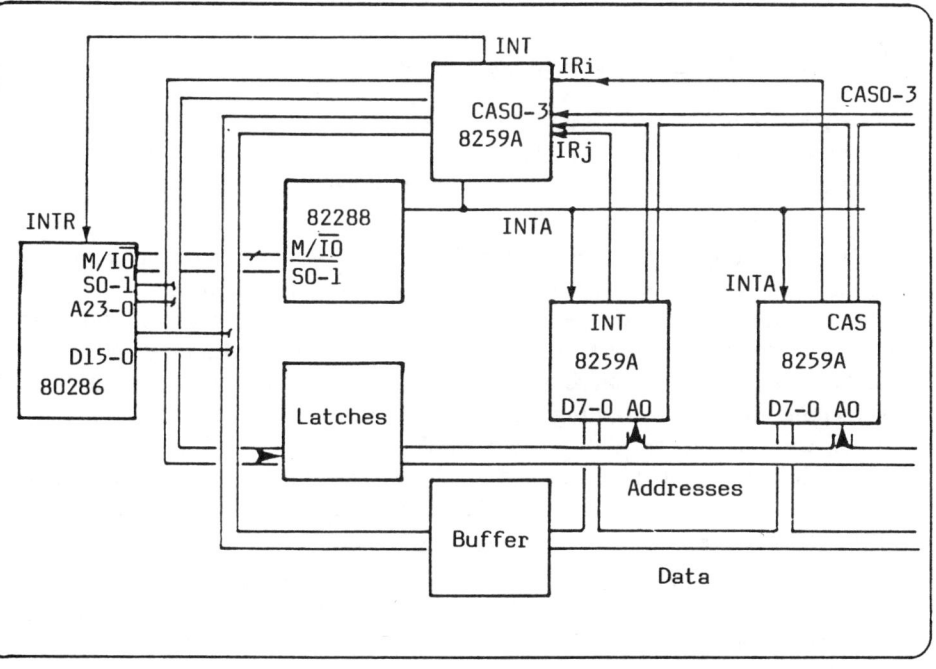

Figure 2.5.6 Using the 8259A interrupt controller

The 80286 is capable of responding to 256 different interrupt vectors, but the vector numbers do not themselves convey any sense of priority. Any externally generated interrupt is accepted immediately, unless it is on the INTR pin while that pin is inhibited. This implies that any hardware priority required in an application must be implemented externally to the CPU, before the relevant pin is asserted. This gives the designer the freedom to design a priority system exactly suited to the purpose of the hardware—correct priorities are essential for a real-time system, for example. Figure 2.5.6 shows that the general hardware for implementing interrupt priority is the same for the 80286 as for the 8086. The INTA:L signal is similar in both systems, permitting the 8259A Programmable Interrupt Controller to be used effectively in single or cascaded mode. This structure can be extended to cope with between 8 and 64 different interrupt sources.

A diagram of the interrupt acknowledge cycle of the 80286 is shown in figure 3.4.2. The LOCK signal is asserted throughout the cycle, to permit an 82289 chip to lock the Multibus during an interrupt acknowledge in a large multiprocessor system. Note also that in a large configuration, using cascaded interrupt controllers, an adequate settling time for the interrupt signals is necessary—this may require the interrupt acknowledge cycle to be extended using the READY signal. Interrupt hardware follows the practices adopted in the 8086 family.

2.5.4 Use of the 80287 Numeric Coprocessor

The 80287 numeric coprocessor adds about fifty instructions to the instruction set of the 80286, implementing addition, subtraction, multiplication, division, exponentiation, and other operations including simple arithmetic operations, logarithms, and trigonometric functions.

The close coupling between the coprocessor and the CPU permits them to operate as a single entity, rather than as two separate processors. The 80287 behaves as an extension to the 80286, being directly connected to its status lines and to its local bus. The CPU executes a program in the usual way, with the coprocessor watching the data bus, identifying those instructions prefixed with an ESC op-code, intercepting them and executing them. The 80286 can access the 80287 directly through the fixed input-output locations 0F8H, 0FAH, and 0FCH. This means that these addresses must not be allocated to any peripheral device, and demands that if the local data bus of the 80286 is buffered, the bidirectional buffers are disabled when the CPU reads these dedicated addresses.

Figure 2.3.4 shows a block diagram of the principal interconnections between the coprocessor and the CPU. This diagram shows that different clock frequencies can be used for the coprocessor from the CPU, giving a higher overall speed of operation in some situations.

The two processors are necessarily synchronised on their local buses; they share the status signals S0, S1, COD/INTA:L, READY, RESET, HOLDA. The 80287 monitors the state of these signals in order to recognise its own instructions, to find out when to carry out its calculations.

Connecting the BUSY:L signal to the equivalent pin of the 80286 implements the synchronisation of the two processors, using the WAIT instruction which samples the state of the TEST pin. When the WAIT instruction is used, processing is suspended until the TEST pin becomes active: this has the disadvantage of

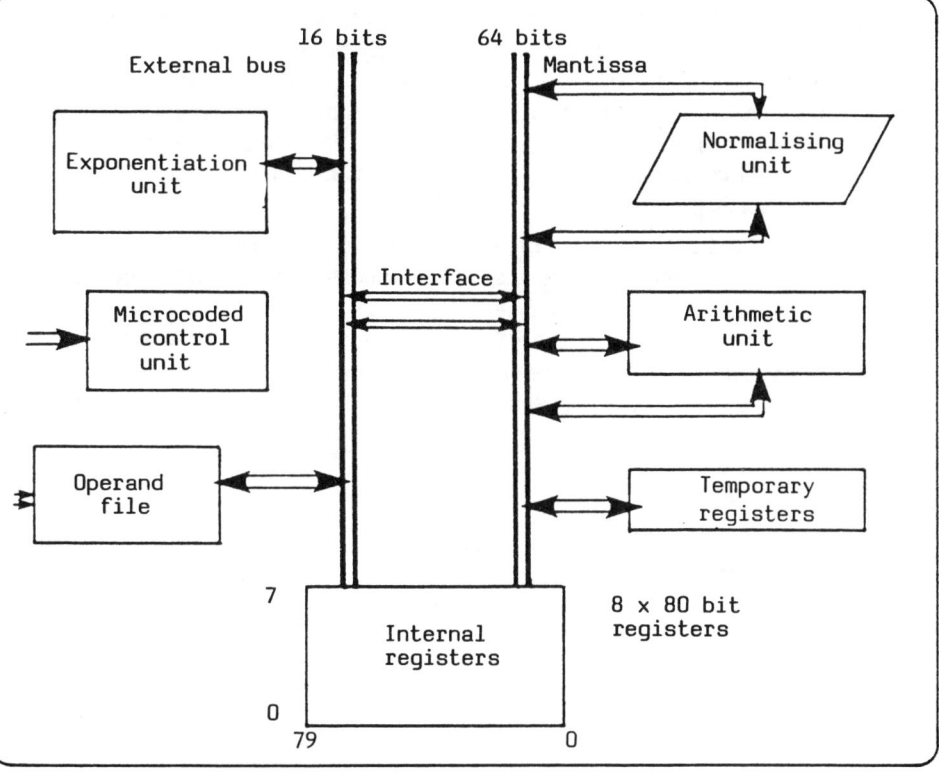

Figure 2.5.7 Internal structure of the 80287

slowing overall processing speed, and an interrupt-based scheme might be used to permit a different task to proceed while a numeric computation is completed.

Apart from the automatic input-output operations generated by the 80286, the coprocessor control signals NPS1:L, NPS2, CMD0, and CMD1 need to be generated. Address decoding circuits to achieve this need to be added to figure 2.3.4.

The 80287 needs to access data in order to carry out its operations. These data accesses are carried out over the local bus shared by the two coprocessors. Bus access and transfer requests are synchronised between the two processors using the signals PEREQ and PEACK:L, which are 80286 inputs and outputs respectively. Memory accesses by the 80287 are like DMA accesses, but take place under the control and supervision of the 80286. This arrangement allows the 80286 to perform address calculations using its native addressing modes, and causes these accesses to be subject to the normal privilege checks and address field checks (in protected virtual mode) within the processor. This cooperation shows how closely integrated the 80287 coprocessor is into the 80286 family.

When the 80286 processor encounters an ESC instruction in a program, it needs to know whether a coprocessor is physically present to execute the instruction. If an ESC instruction is executed by a processor with no coprocessor present, an exception is generated which can be used to enter a software emulation routine. This information is present in the Machine Status Word (MSW) and must be initialised before the coprocessor is used, using a standard routine to detect whether the coprocessor is present.

The 80287 has a structure similar to that of the 8087, the numeric coprocessor in the 8086 family. Calculations are carried out on data stored in an 8 word register file 80 bits wide. All intermediate results can be stored in this extended, temporary real format. The object code of the 80287 is, of course, compatible with that of the 8087, ensuring compatibility between iAPX86/20 and iAPX286/20 systems. (Intel use a /20 suffix to indicate the presence of a numeric coprocessor in a system.)

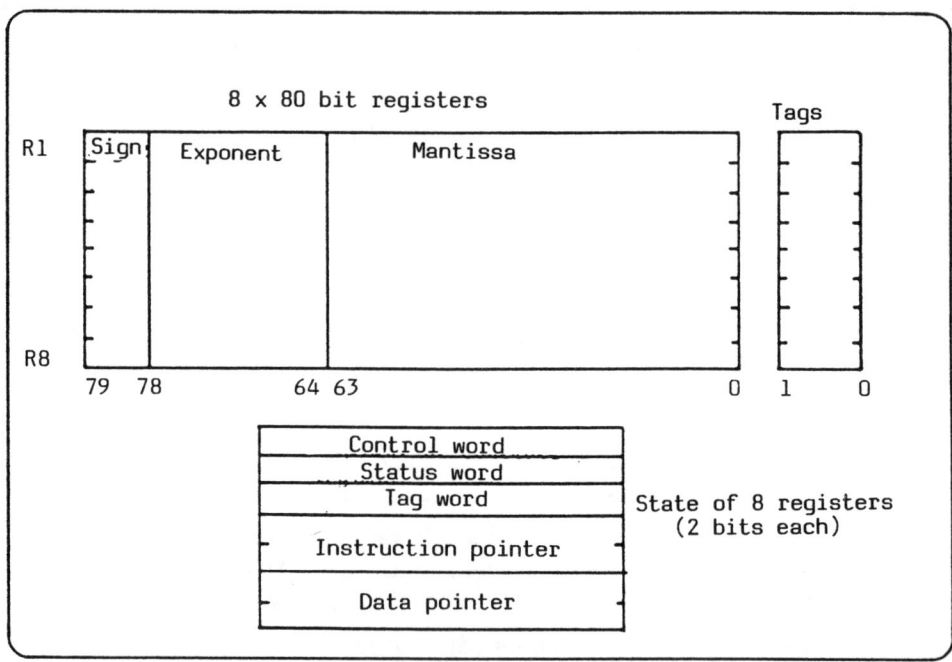

Figure 2.5.8 Numeric coprocessor register set

Figures 2.5.7 and 2.5.8 show the internal structure of the 80287 and its internal register set; these registers can store integers of 16, 32 and 64 bits and reals of 32, 64 and 80 bits in the format defined in IEEE 754.

To illustrate the speed of the coprocessor, a 5 MHz 80287 can carry out an exponentiation in 100 microseconds, a square root in 36 microseconds, and a tangent calculation in 90 microseconds.

Most software for scientific applications is written in a high-level language, rather than in assembly language, and compiled before execution. Hardware that includes a coprocessor is often fast enough that the usual arguments for writing code in assembly language, such as increased speed and smaller size, do not give sufficient advantage to warrant the extra effort. The value to the programmer of the 80287 numeric coprocessor is further enhanced by the transparency it gives to the hardware configuration: the programmer does not need to know if a coprocessor is to be present until the compiled high-level program is linked to a library, either one accessing the coprocessor directly or one emulating its operation.

2.6 Memory Architecture of the 80286

2.6.1 Segmentation

As with the earlier 8086 processor, the programmer writing code for the 80286 needs to bear the segmentation scheme in mind. We have already seen that the 80286 implements address translation and protection schemes, described in more detail in chapter 3, further to the simple scheme provided in the 8086. Nevertheless, the concept of segmentation applies whether the 80286 is used in real or virtual protected modes, and care must be taken by the programmer whenever a larger area than 64 kilobytes is used.

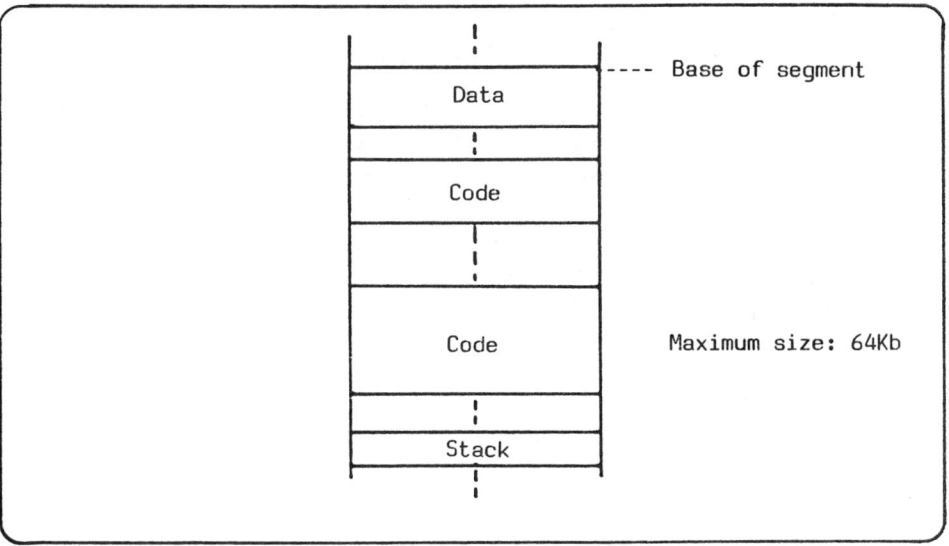

Figure 2.6.1 Segmented memory

Segmentation Principles

Segmentation is a memory management method which shows explicitly the logical structure of programs and data. For example, the data which is relevant to one portion of an application may be logically independent from the rest of the code. This data could be gathered up and allocated to a unique segment defined by the user.

This definition of segmentation is logical only, but the hardware implementation of segmentation imposes additional physical constraints on the scheme. In the 80286, as in the 8086, addressing limits the size of individual segments to 64 kilobytes. The processor is equipped with segment registers which are used to point to the beginning of a segment situated somewhere in memory, and a number of address registers are used to evaluate an offset which is a displacement from the base of the segment. (See figures 2.6.1 and 2.6.2.)

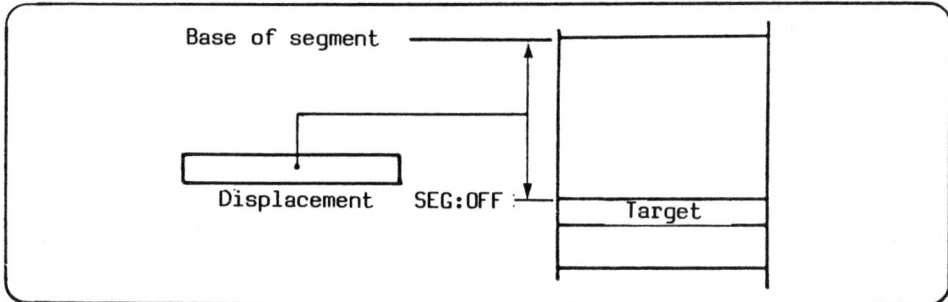

Figure 2.6.2 Displacements or offsets

Logical segmentation is therefore a structure imposed on a program by the programmer, who accesses a physical data item using a systematic addressing mode, specifying an offset and a segment.

For example:

```
Segment definition - base of data segment
    definition of data items X, Y, Z
- end of segment

- base of code segment
    initialisations..
    ..
    ..
    initialise segment register to point to data segment
    ..
    access variable X using the segment register
    ..
- end of code segment
```

Segmentation in real mode

In real mode, only 20 address bits are generated by the processor, giving access to a physical memory space of 1 megabyte, the same size as the 8086. In this mode, address bits A20 to A23 are not used.

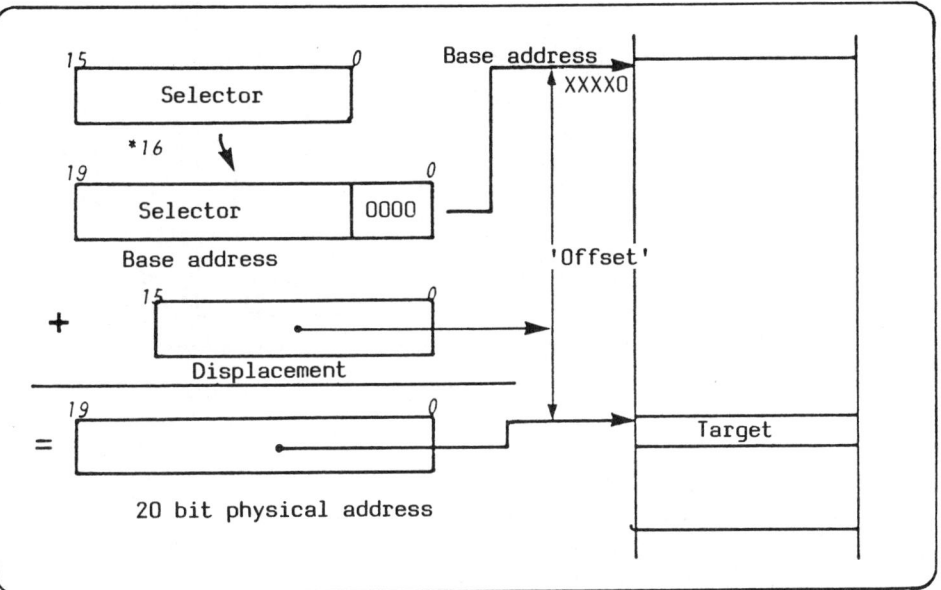

Figure 2.6.3 Address calculation in real mode

Segmentation is implemented in exactly the same way as in the 8086, and address evaluation is carried out as shown in figure 2.6.3.

In this mode, the 16-bit value in the "selector" (segment register) is multiplied by 16 and added to the displacement or effective address, giving a 20-bit real address.

Segmentation in virtual protected mode

In protected mode, the 80286 address calculation has three additional features:

1. The notion of virtual memory, permitting each task to address a maximum of 1 gigabyte of memory, some of which may reside on secondary storage devices.
2. A modification of the mechanism for forming a real address using indirection via a system table. This is essential once a virtual addressing scheme is introduced.

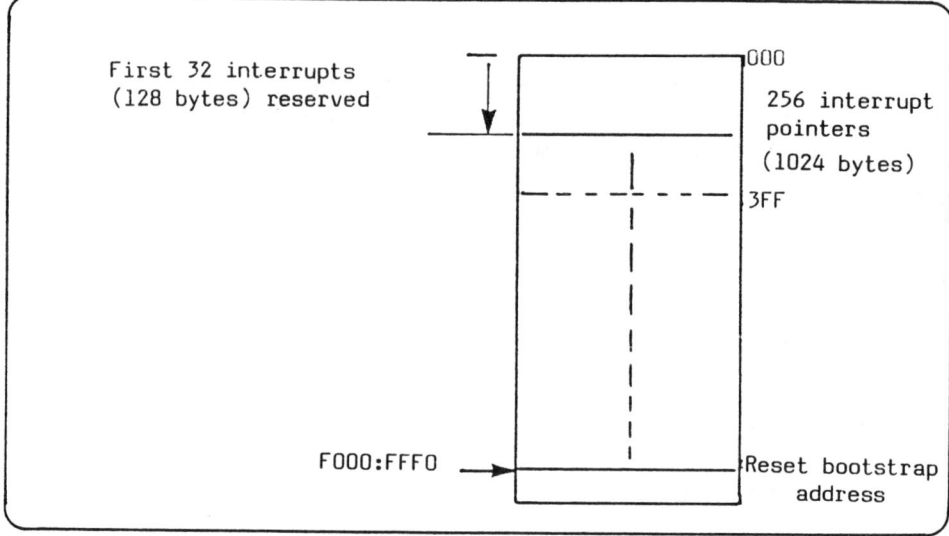

Figure 2.6.4 Reserved memory in real address mode

3. Protection is provided, permitting the notion of hierarchies of privilege for executing code and for the associated data. The protection principle is simple: a routine with a low privilege level is prohibited from accessing data with a high privilege. This scheme has the benefit of protecting sensitive data from access by unauthorised programs, regardless of whether a malicious attack or a faulty access caused by a bug is attempted.

In protected mode, the segment registers play a different role: they serve as indices into a segment descriptor table. A descriptor table may contain up to 8192 entries, each entry describing a physical segment varying in size up to 64 kilobytes.

Two different segment descriptor tables may be accessed by each task. This means that an individual task may access up to $2 \times 8K \times 64K$ bytes of memory, or 1 gigabyte. Thirteen bits of the segment register (bits A3 to A15) select the entry within the segment descriptor table (see figure 2.6.5).

Although in protected mode the physical segments are accessed via the descriptor table, they are defined by the programmer in the same way as logical segments are defined in real mode.

The system structures for tasks, segment descriptors, the descriptor tables, and logical segments are built up with the aid of a configuring program, BLD286. The programmer can attach a certain privilege level to each code segment and data segment, and declares the privilege level required to permit access to each procedure. Privilege levels vary from 0 to 3, 0 being the most privileged and 3 the least.

When a program modifies a segment register (a selector), the modification causes the related segment descriptor to be loaded into a memory translation cache.

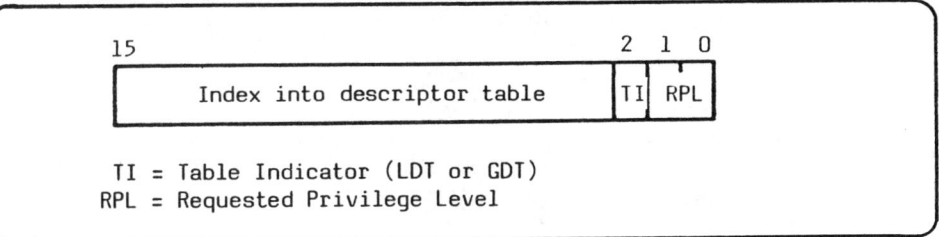

Figure 2.6.5 Format of a segment selector

2.6.2 80286 Data Types

Memory is organised as a bank of bytes. The unit of addressing implemented in the 80286 is the byte, and a number of instructions operating on byte quantities are implemented. A number of 8-bit registers are provided in the CPU for these operations. Also provided are 16-bit registers and operations, and since the data bus of the processors is 16 bits wide, the 80286 is normally described as having a 16-bit word size, with each word made up of two bytes.

These two basic quantities, the byte and the word, are used in the order code and the status bits in the machine to implement operations on data in a number of different formats. In particular, there are operations which can be carried out upon:

- unsigned 8- and 16-bit integer quantities
- signed 8- and 16-bit integers
- boolean values represented in a byte
- address pointers, consisting of a base (or segment) in one word and a displacement in a second word
- binary-coded-decimal (BCD) items, coded one digit per byte, and compact BCD with two digits per byte.

Operations on floating-point numbers are not directly implemented by the 80286, but need the intervention of the 80287 numeric coprocessor, or implementation using an emulation library.

Unlike some other processors, any data item can reside at any alignment in main memory: any data item consisting of more than one byte has its least significant byte at the lowest memory address.

Figure 2.6.6 shows some examples of the appearance of bytes, words and pointers in main memory.

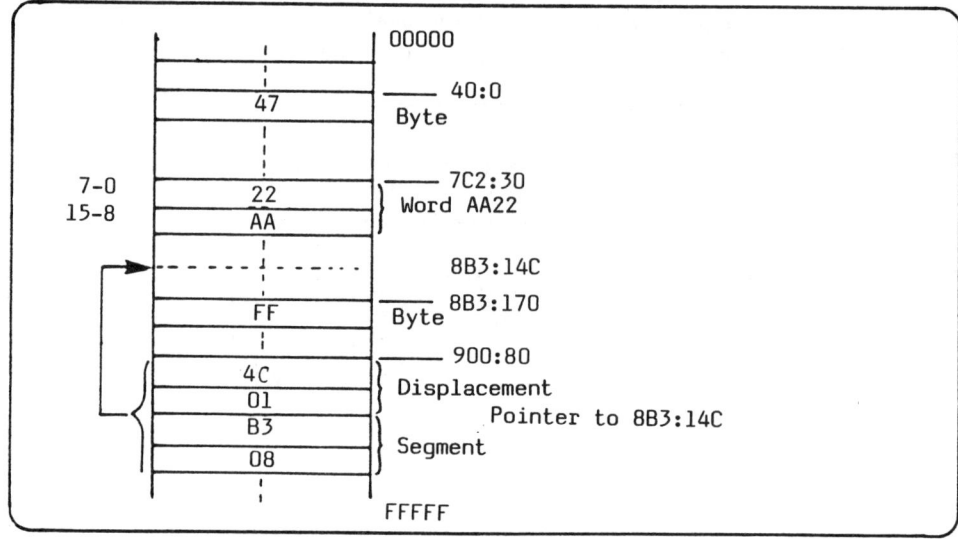

Figure 2.6.6 Physical implementation of data

Notice that a pointer to a data item is represented as two 16-bit words. When the pointer is used, the appropriate address translation mechanism is used, ensuring that the pointer is converted to a 20-bit or 24-bit real address, depending on the processor mode.

2.6.3 CPU Registers

Figure 2.6.7 shows the similarity between the registers of the 80286 and those of its predecessor, the 8086. The registers can be divided into three groups: general-purpose registers, segment registers, and status and control registers.

The 80286 CPU implements an additional set of registers not present in the 8086, used to implement the address indirection needed by the protected virtual memory mode.

General-purpose registers

There are 8 general-purpose registers, each 16 bits wide, called AX, BX, CX, DX, SI, DI, SP and BP, used in exactly the same way as in the 8086 CPU. No dedicated accumulator register is provided, as most of the general-purpose registers can serve as source or destination of arithmetic and logical operations.

Some of these registers are closely linked with certain operations: the most significant of these are that

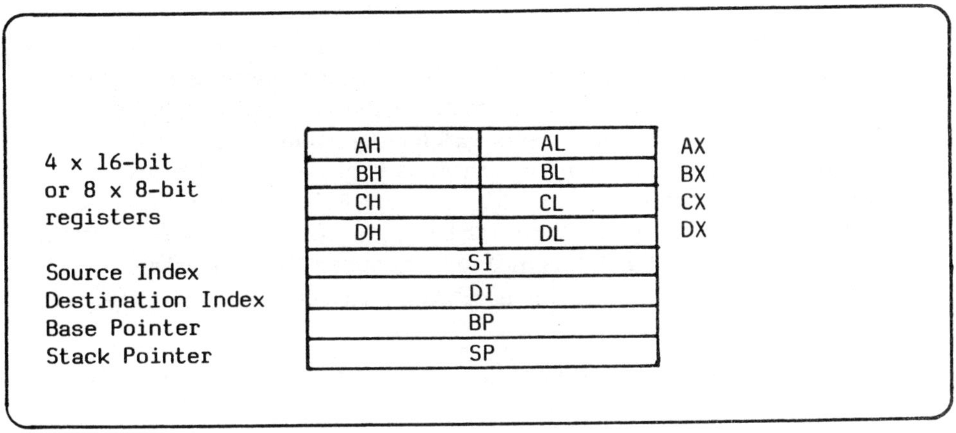

Hardware Structure of the 80286

```
                        AH      |   AL      AX
4 x 16-bit              BH      |   BL      BX
or 8 x 8-bit            CH      |   CL      CX
registers               DH      |   DL      DX

Source Index                  SI
Destination Index             DI
Base Pointer                  BP
Stack Pointer                 SP
```

Figure 2.6.7 General purpose registers

- AL and AX are always used as one operand of multiply and divide instructions, and are the most convenient source and destination for output and input instructions.
- CX is used as a dedicated count register for the LOOP instruction and during instructions operating on strings.
- DX contains the address used by some input/output instructions, and is used for the most significant half of 32-bit operands and results of divisions and multiplications.
- SP is the stack pointer.
- BX and BP are frequently used in indirect addressing modes, and are thus frequently called base registers. BP is provided for accesses within the current stack segment, and is used to access the parameters passed by a calling procedure and local variables declared within the current procedure.
- SI and DI serve both as additional base registers for indirect addressing, and as indices for indexed indirect addressing, and are thus called index registers. They are used for string instructions to hold the memory addresses of the operands.

Segment registers

The advantage of segmentation, apart from the readability and the convenience it introduces during software development, comes from the optimisation of code which it enables. For example, if memory references are implicitly associated with a particular segment, data items grouped together can be accessed using short operand addresses of 8 or 16 bits since it is only necessary to specify the displacement from the beginning of the segment, rather than needing the full 20 or 24 bits needed to identify a full absolute real address.

The 80286 is equipped with four 16-bit segment registers, CS, SS, DS and ES, permitting immediate access to four different current segments. The purpose of these registers is to identify the segment to aid in the formation of the physical address of each main memory access. Each register points to the base of a physical segment. The offset from this segment base is given by another 16-bit value, derived usually from one of the registers IP, SP, BP, BX, SI or DI. In most cases, the programmer need only specify the offset, because a set of implicit rules determines which of the segment registers is used to perform the address translation.

The four segment registers are each associated with accesses of a particular type:

- CS, the Code Segment register, points to the segment containing the currently executing code.
- SS, the Stack Segment register, contains the base of the segment within which the current stack is active, being accessed by the Stack Pointer and Base Pointer registers SP and BP.
- DS, the Data Segment register, indicates the segment containing the current data to be accessed.
- ES, the Extra Segment register, serves as an extra Data Segment register, and permits access to a second segment of data, albeit at the cost of an extra byte in each instruction that needs to use it. ES is also used implicitly in string instructions.

The full address of a data item, then, is given by a pair of sixteen bit quantities:

`SEGMENT:OFFSET ; offset is displacement from segment base`

The address of the current instruction, for example, is represented by the pair of 16-bit registers CS and IP (the Instruction Pointer).

The manner of forming a physical address depends upon the mode of operation of the CPU. In protected virtual mode, in particular, the value in the segment register is used not as a physical segment base address, as in real mode, but as an index into a segment descriptor table. The most significant 13 bits form the index, into one of two tables, giving a maximum table size of 8192 descriptor entries. Since each descriptor classifies a segment which may vary in size up to 64 kilobytes, this limits the virtual addressing of a particular task to 1 gigabyte. Figure 2.6.8 summarises the formation of real addresses in protected virtual mode.

State and control registers

The Flags register (see figure 2.6.9) contains indications about the results of recent CPU operations, and has the same bit configuration as in the 8086. Two extra fields meaningful only in protected mode appear: the NT (Nested Task) bit indicates the relationship of linked 80286 tasks, and IOPL is a 2-bit field which limits the programmer's use of certain input/output instructions to tasks with a certain privilege.

Hardware Structure of the 80286

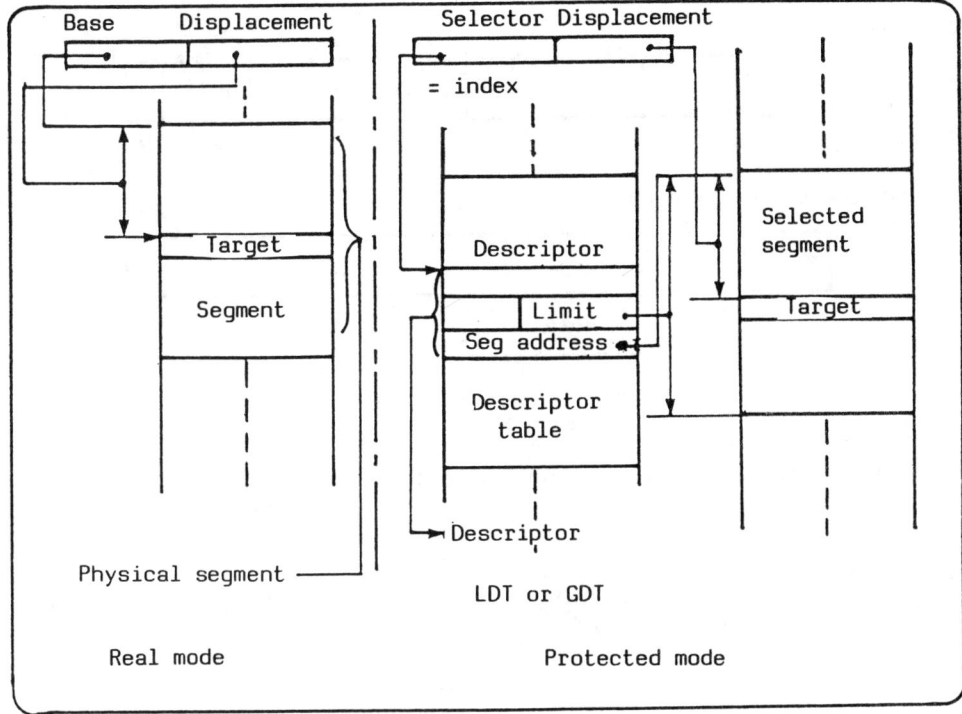

Figure 2.6.8 Addressing in protected virtual mode

The control register MSW indicates the protection mode of the processor and the presence and status of the numeric coprocessor. It is set to zero (real mode) by the reset signal, while software setting it to "1" causes entry to protected virtual mode.

2.6.4 Addressing Modes

Different addressing modes provided by the 80286 CPU allow the programmer to access data items in memory and carry out operations on them. The CPU provides facilities for accessing immediate operands (whose value is specified in the instruction) and operands in registers, but also implements a number of different modes for accessing memory, both simple and more complex. The addressing modes of the 80286 are the same as in the 8086, and are described briefly in this section for completeness.

Direct addressing has the offset of the data contained in the instruction.

```
MOV AX,COUNT
```

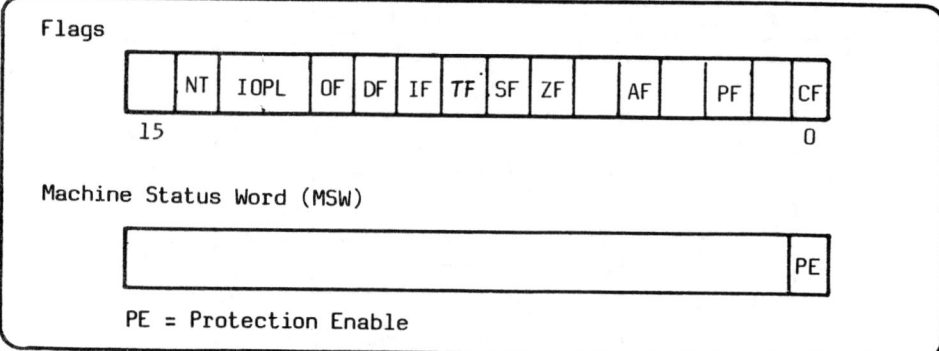

Figure 2.6.9 Status and control words

Register Indirect addressing has the offset of the operand in one of the registers SI, DI, BP or BX.

```
MOV AX, [BX]
```

In Based Addressing, the offset of the operand is obtained by adding a displacement to the contents of BX or BP.

```
MOV AL, [BX+2]
MOV AX, [BP+12]
```

Indexed Addressing is almost equivalent to register indirect addressing. Using one of the SI or DI registers, it is used in the processing of tables, and in the instructions which process strings of bytes.

```
MOV BYTE PTR ES:[SI], 35H
```

Based Indexed Addressing involves the calculation of an effective address by adding one of the base registers BX or BP to one of the index registers SI or DI.

```
XOR DS:[BP][SI], AL
```

Based Indexed Addressing with Displacement is used, for example, in the processing of tables of structures, and calculates the offset by adding a base register (BX or BP) to an index register (SI or DI) and a displacement specified in the instruction itself. In the example, the word "field" refers to an element in a data structure defined by the programmer.

```
example STRUC
field0 DW ?
field1 DB ?  ; at address 2 in the structure
example ENDS
```

```
MOV AL,ES:[BX][DI].field1
```

Figure 2.6.10 is a schematic representation of the addressing modes showing indirection and indexing.

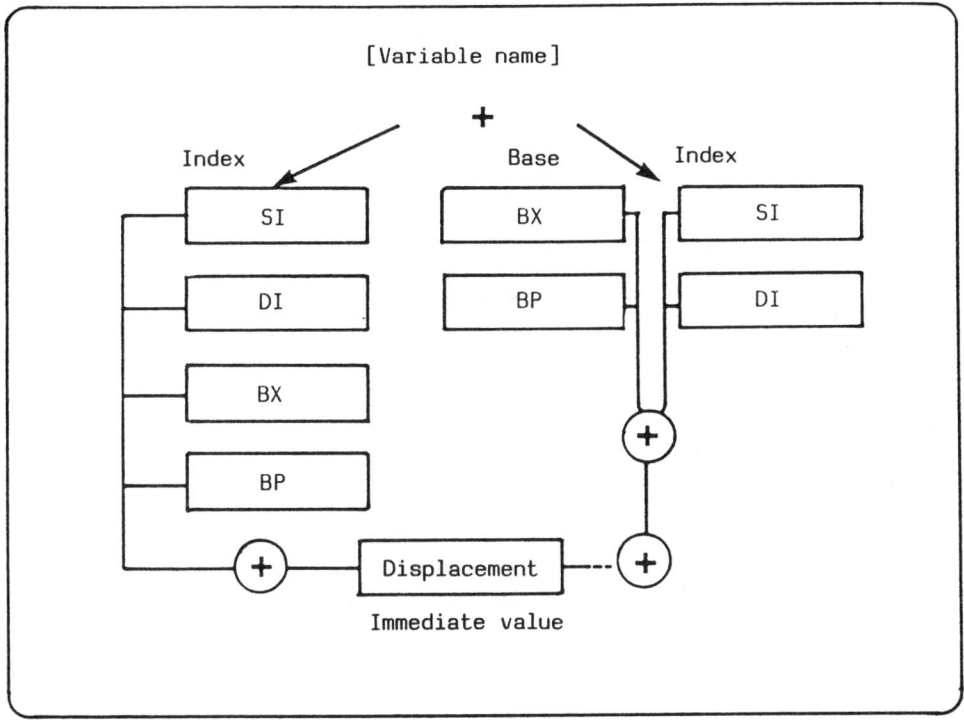

Figure 2.6.10 Addressing modes

2.6.5 Introduction to Protection

We have seen that in protected mode, symbolic addressing relies upon an extra level of memory indirection provided by the segment descriptor tables. Each descriptor describes the physical address and the size of its associated segment. Figure 2.6.11 gives the general layout of individual descriptors. Full details of the use of the fields within a descriptor are given in chapter 3, but it will be instantly apparent that the descriptor contains certain information which is necessary to implement a protected system.

These fields are:

P: indicates whether the segment is present in or absent from main memory

DPL: is the privilege level associated with this segment

S: identifies the descriptor as a Segment Descriptor

A: is a bit set by the hardware when the segment is accessed

TYPE: is a field which indicates the modes of access permitted within this segment: read only, read/write, modifiable privilege, etc.

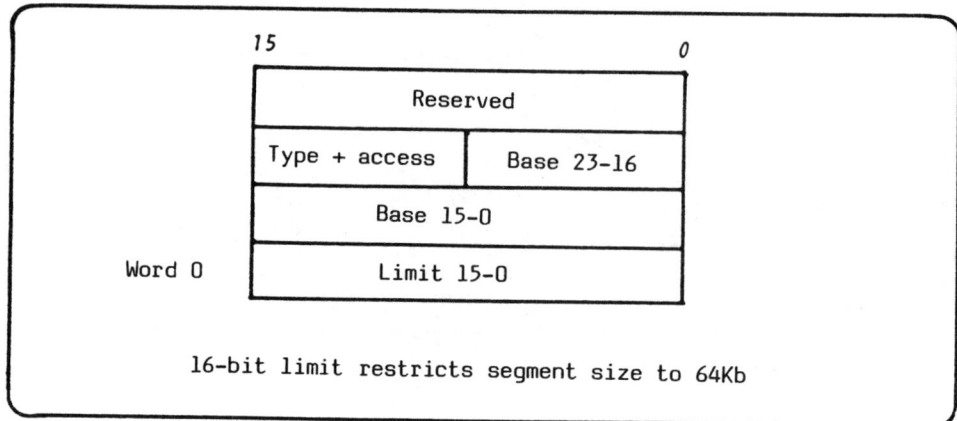

Figure 2.6.11 Segment descriptor format

It is apparent from the appearance of these bits within the segment descriptor that the CPU will need to refer to them constantly during instruction execution. The requirement for fast processing means that copies of the current descriptors are kept within the CPU.

The detailed mechanisms of protected virtual mode are examined in more detail in chapter 3, "the 80286 in protected mode".

3 The 80286 in Protected Mode

3.1 Memory Management

In the preceding chapter, the three fundamental aspects of protected virtual mode were introduced: virtual memory, translation into physical memory addresses, and protection.

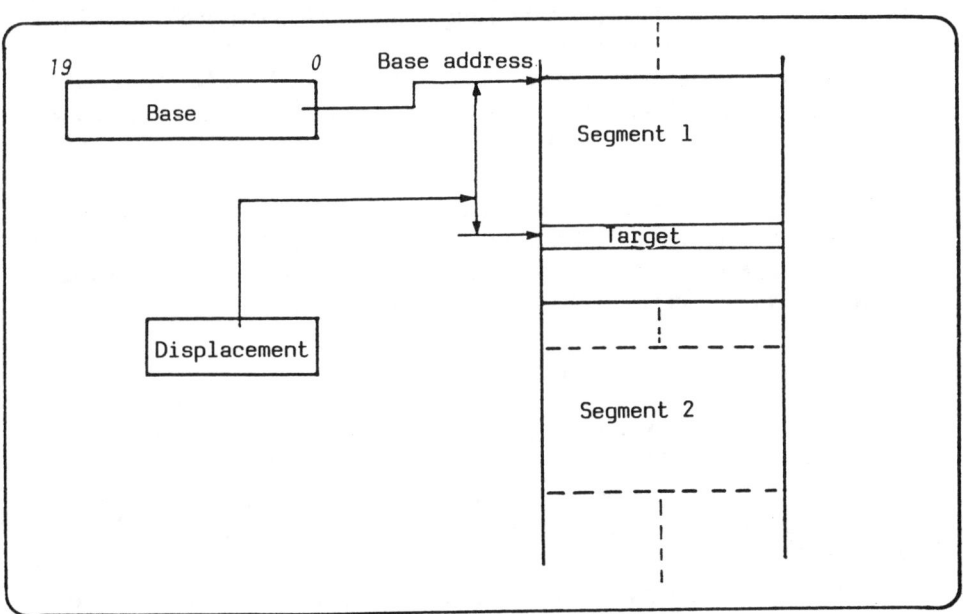

Figure 3.1.1 Access to segmented data

These facilities are starting to appear in today's microprocessors because of their benefit in the structured development of software and the structuring of data. This is of value in writing large, complicated applications.

This structuring gives rise to the need for individual data areas to be accessed by the relevant instructions, but to be protected from access by a different, possibly bug-ridden program running in the same machine. The increase in the volume of data that can be processed by a modern microprocessor means that it is an advantage to be able to address data using virtual addresses rather than real addresses. The first step in this direction was the ability to reference data using a symbolic name, without worrying about its exact address in memory. The second step, taken in the 8086, was to introduce the concept of logical segments, into which symbolic objects can be grouped, each segment being accessed via a segment register.

At this stage, it becomes apparent that the microprocessor will need to contain circuits whose task is to translate the address of each data reference, using the value in the relevant segment register and the symbolic address.

This scheme includes some principle of a "virtual address", because it is only when the program is actually running that the exact relationship between the symbolic addresses used in the program and the exact location of data in main memory is made. The advantage of this scheme is that it removes certain physical constraints related to the machine in use, from the programmer. The constraints are satisfied at the last moment, using link editors and loader programs.

The concept of virtual memory can be further enhanced: the programmer might be permitted to manipulate data items using their logical address when these items are present in main memory, but might also be permitted to access data items which are not currently in memory. This technique can be implemented only if the CPU knows how to detect that a particular data item is missing from main memory, and how to cause it to be fetched into main memory from a secondary storage device such as a magnetic disk.

When discussing virtual memory and memory protection, it is convenient to introduce the concept of a "task". For the moment, it is sufficient to define a task as a "context" active in the machine, carrying out a specific processing purpose, and accessing a specific set of data related to this application.

3.1.1 Protected Virtual Addressing

In the 80286 protected mode, programs use only virtual addresses, without any access to the real addresses generated by the translation unit within the CPU.

The virtual address is always composed of two parts, the displacement and the segment selector. The displacement is a 16-bit value, and is sometimes called an offset (within a segment) or an effective address.

The segment selector specifies exactly which segment contains the data to be accessed. The selector is also a 16-bit item made up of three distinct fields which are described later.

The (displacement, selector) pair together makes a 32-bit pointer, which represents the full virtual address of the object to be accessed.

These 32-bit pointers can be manipulated as a whole by the programmer when coding: if pointers are always treated as these 32-bit quantities, an 8086 program will also run on a 80286 in both real and protected virtual modes. In this last case, protection information needs to be added to each segment; this may be introduced after compilation in a final phase of module construction using a specific software tool (Builder, described in section 4.4.2) for the purpose.

We have seen in chapter 2 that this scheme has the advantage of reducing the code size necessary to access a particular data item. Experience shows that in many cases, 64 kilobytes is sufficient to contain the data to be accessed by a particular module of a program performing a clearly defined task. This allows us to use a 16-bit address within the program module, relying on the address translation hardware to generate a physical address of 24 bits.

The segment selector contains different information, depending upon the mode of processing: its use in real mode is shown in figure 2.6.3.

In protected mode, the selector is made up of three fields, shown in figure 3.1.2.

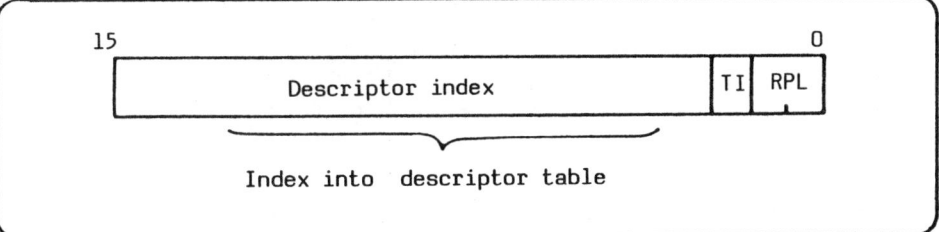

Figure 3.1.2 Segment selector format

In this format, only the 14 most significant bits are used in the address calculation. We can thus access 2^{14}, or 16384 different segments, which since each segment can have a maximum size of 2^{16} bytes gives us a virtual memory space of 2^{30} bytes, or 1 gigabyte. The least significant of these 14 bits is the Table Indicator (TI) bit, which selects between two segment descriptor tables (see figure 3.1.3). Each table may have up to 2^{13} entries, describing up to 8192 segments.

One of these tables, the Global Descriptor Table (GDT), is shared between all of the programs running in the machine.

The second, the Local Descriptor Table (LDT), is local to the currently executing task or context, so that the virtual address space of 1 gigabyte is a per-task limit. Since each task may have its own LDT, it may have a "private" address space of up to $\frac{1}{2}$ gigabyte and a "global" address space, shared with all other tasks currently executing, of another $\frac{1}{2}$ gigabyte.

The global space is commonly used for the operating system, for shared library routines and data, and for access to global resources of the system.

Providing one local segment descriptor table per task enables the separation of data belonging to different tasks, giving an increase in the reliability of the system, and reducing the consequences of programming errors.

Figure 3.1.4 shows a configuration of three tasks, demonstrating how each task's data is private, while certain data is shared between all three.

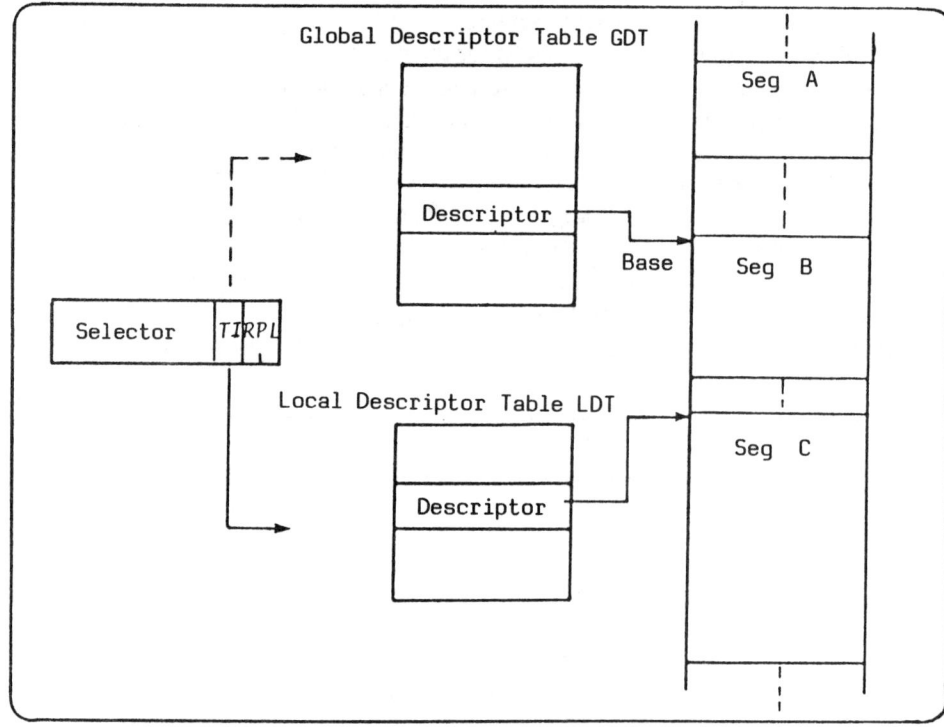

Figure 3.1.3 Descriptor table selection by the TI bit

3.1.2 Descriptors and Descriptor Tables

A table of descriptors, indexed by the segment selector, must be resident in main memory during the task's execution. The table is used as an indirection table for the management of protection and for the generation of physical addresses for every memory access. It serves as the means of translating a 32-bit virtual pointer into a 24-bit physical address.

In its execution, each task may reference the GDT and the LDT. Nevertheless, it is possible to envisage an application which only uses the GDT. This might simplify understanding the addressing mechanisms that are in use, but it would also destroy the principle of separating the data between tasks, and thus diminish the protection between programs. In this type of system, it would be impossible to limit or forbid task A from accessing the data which logically belongs to an independent task B.

In the 80286 system, maximum flexibility is provided by delaying the construction of the descriptor tables until after all the stages of compilation, and using a tool (Builder) which allows the tables to be fully configured by the user.

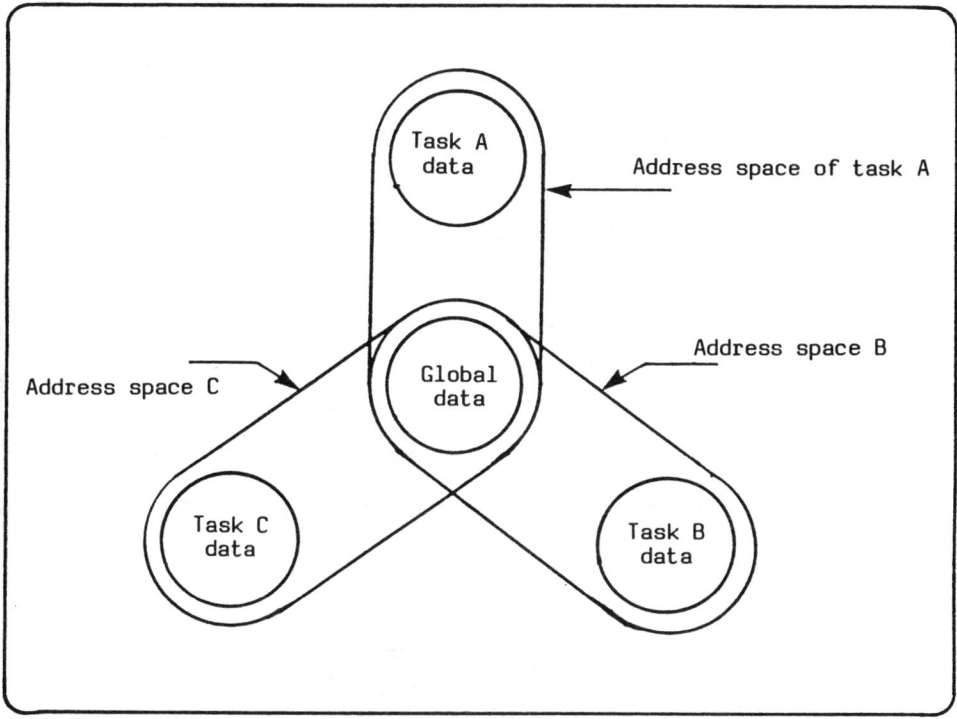

Figure 3.1.4 Address spaces and isolation between tasks

A segment descriptor table consists of a vector of 8-byte quantities, called descriptors. A table may have up to 8192 entries, so a full-sized table exactly fills one segment.

The 80286 system provides two different types of descriptors, segment descriptors, and system descriptors, used for different control operations, such as task switching, interrupt entries, or for describing special types of data segments.

System descriptors will be described in greater detail in sections 3.2, 3.3 and 3.4, where tasks and their support are discussed. Figures 3.1.5 and 3.1.6 show the format of descriptors of each type.

The largest field of a descriptor is the 24-bit base address, which is the real address of the start of the segment in main memory. A second field gives the real physical size of the segment, which must be less than or equal to 64 kilobytes.

The remaining byte contains a number of interesting fields, used in the management of memory and in its protection. This byte concerns the access rights of the segment.

The three "type" bits are described (for segment descriptors) in figure 3.1.7.

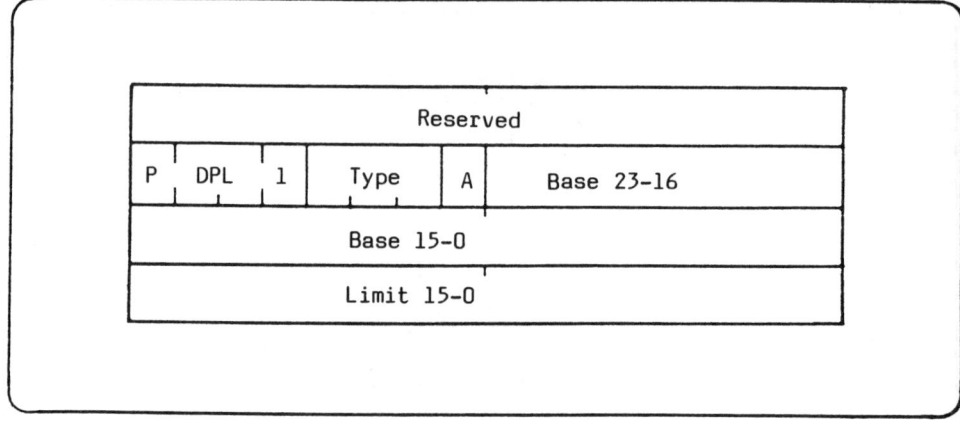

Figure 3.1.5 Segment descriptor

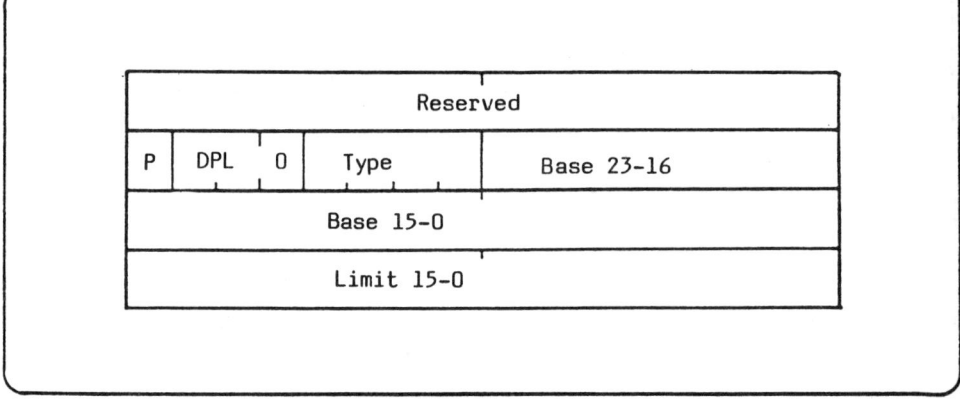

Figure 3.1.6 System descriptor

The "P" bit defines the presence (1) or absence (0) of the segment from main memory. This bit is used by the operating system process that migrates segments between main memory and secondary storage.

The "DPL" bits define the rank or protection level attached to the segment, and is initialised by the Builder program during the final stage of program construction.

The "A" bit is set by the hardware whenever an access is made to the segment.

The full protection mechanisms of the 80286 are described in section 3.2, but it will be apparent from the above description of segment descriptors that at least two independent protection checks may be implemented, preventing accesses to unallocated parts of segments, and preventing accesses to code and data at the wrong privilege levels.

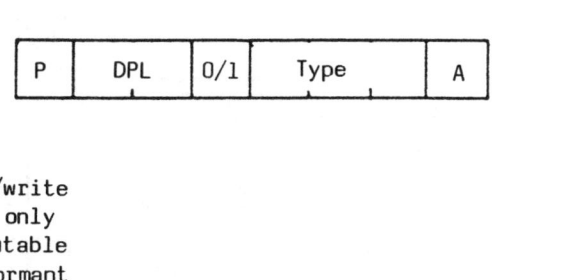

Segment type:
- read/write
- read only
- executable
- conformant
- 'expand down' (stack)

P indicates presence in main memory
A indicates segment has been accessed

Figure 3.1.7 Segment types

In order to be accessed, every segment defined by the programmer must be described by a segment descriptor appearing in one of the LDT or GDT descriptor tables. The LDT itself is a segment in its own right, and its descriptor must reside within the GDT.

The system can only have one GDT. The segment containing the GDT is defined by the contents of a dedicated CPU register, the Global Descriptor Table Register (GDTR).

Figure 3.1.8 summarises the full address translation mechanism for virtual addressing. The figure shows the Local Descriptor Table Register (LDTR) in the CPU, which points to the descriptor in the GDT describing the LDT for the currently executing task.

Once these mechanisms are understood, it is straightforward to explain the steps involved in translating a virtual address into a physical address.

1. The TI bit of the pointer selects either the GDT or LDT descriptor table (figure 3.1.3).
2. The address of the table is obtained from the CPU register GDTR or (indirectly via the GDT) LDTR.
3. The index (13 most significant bits of the selector), multiplied by 8, gives the displacement within the table of the descriptor for the segment which is to be accessed.
4. Reading this descriptor gives the address of the base of this segment (if it is present in memory), to which is added the displacement from the pointer, to obtain the full 24-bit real address (see figure 3.1.9).

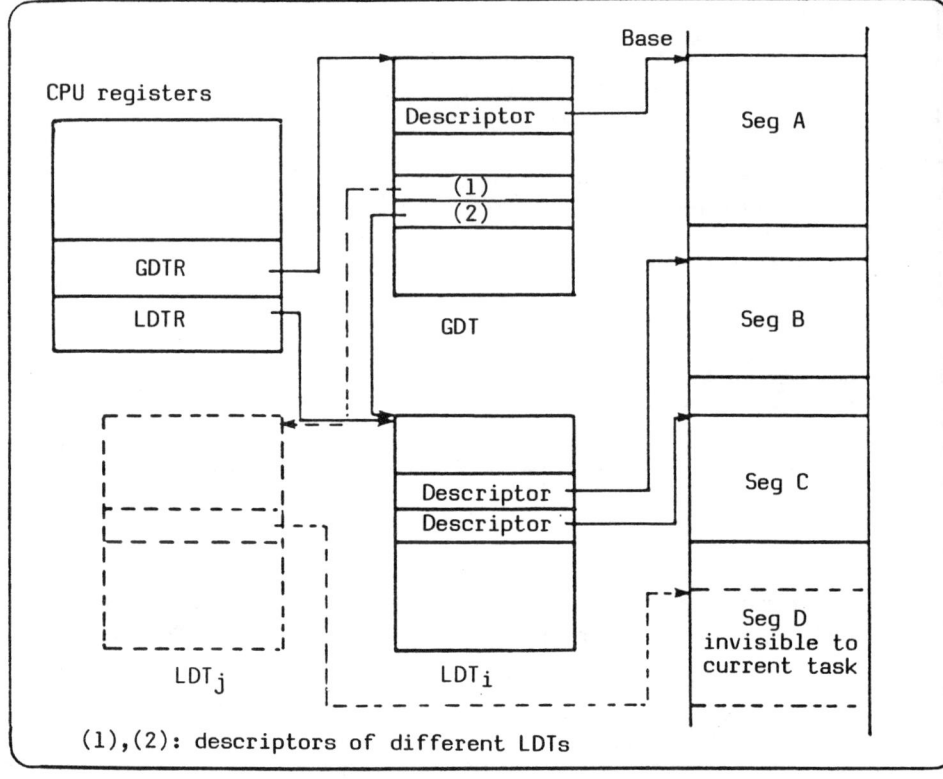

Figure 3.1.8 Virtual addressing mechanism

The checking of access permissions and limit checking take place during this address translation process.

Having met the address translation scheme of the 80286, we may reflect on some of the advantages of this method.

As in the 8086 family, the management of memory resources is based on the concept of segments. Unlike in the 8086, however, the 80286 does not fix the size of a segment, but permits it to be exactly the right size for the data it contains. This flexibility encourages programmers to adopt structured analysis and modular programming techniques, which tend to give rise to applications made up from a number of functional modules, each closely associated with some relevant data. These programming guidelines have been developed in response to the need for efficiency and the requirement for reliable, bug-free software.

Looking at figure 3.1.8, it is apparent that there are different options available for managing the visibility of segments: each segment must be described by a descriptor, present in at least one table (GDT or LDT), but a descriptor might be present in several different LDTs.

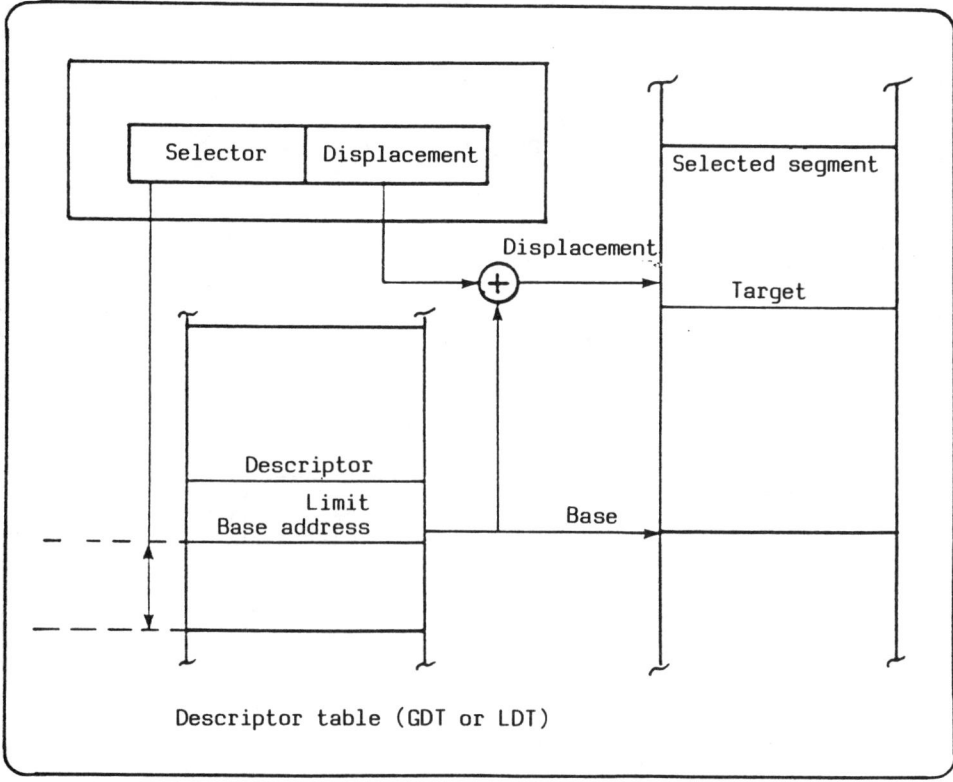

Figure 3.1.9 Translating virtual into physical addresses

This gives rise to the possibility of sharing data segments between different tasks, without making them global. Figure 3.1.4 may be modified to produce figure 3.1.10, which shows tasks 1 and 2 sharing the data area 1–2, but if the descriptor is missing from the LDT of task 3, this task will not be able to access that area.

Aliasing

An individual descriptor contains a size, protection information, and a physical address. If it is required to change the value of one of these fields, it could be done in situ, or by making a copy of the descriptor with most fields identical, modifying only those that are required to be different. This technique creates an "alias", that is a second virtual address which may be used to access the same underlying data. This technique is often used in operating systems to manage the segments which belong to them. For example, consider the case of a system creating a process table.

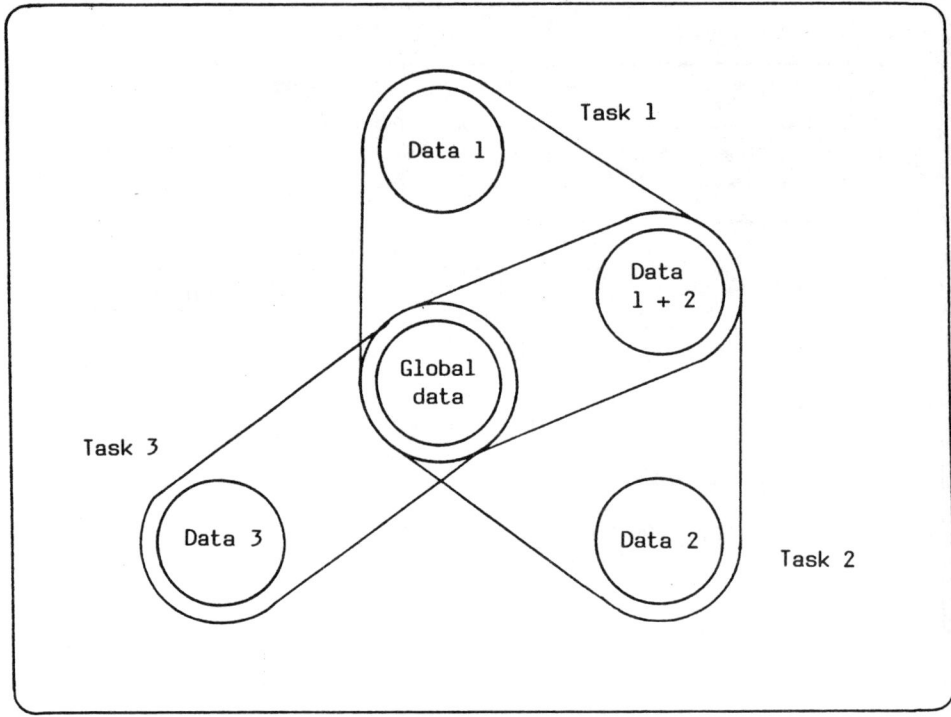

Figure 3.1.10 Non-global shared data

The process table must be protected from writing by any other code within the system, and must therefore be read-only. Since the operating system needs to modify the table (to change state bits, for example), it creates an alias, with read/write permission, which can only be used by the operating system.

Another example might be to group a number of segments with different characteristics together as a single system segment, so that it can be treated as a complete entity. In this case, the size and the protection properties of the alias will be different from those of the underlying segments.

3.1.3 Memory Management Registers

The segment selector is manipulated by the programmer using one of the segment registers DS, ES, CS or SS.

Figure 3.1.11 shows the four registers and the two Descriptor Table registers GDTR and LDTR, which make up the address translation cache of the CPU. In this figure, the "selector" part of each line is visible by the programmer, but each line also contains a 48-bit field which is not programmer-accessible. It is this hidden area which is the cache memory of the machine.

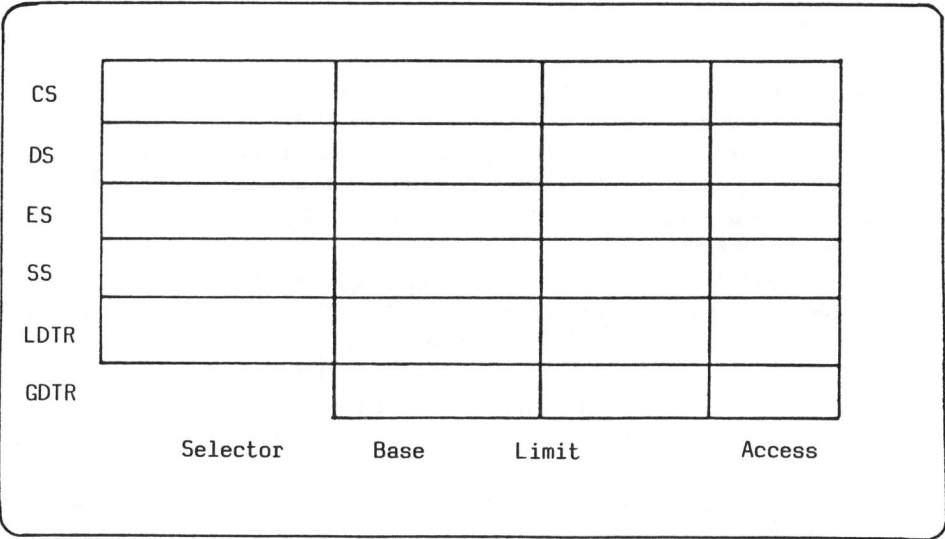

Figure 3.1.11 Segment registers

Some instructions which change segment registers are LDS, LES, MOV, POP, CALL, and JMP.

When one of these instructions changes a segment register, the visible portion of the line is loaded with the INDEX, DPL, and TI information. In addition, the processor uses the information from this selector to read the designated segment descriptor from the appropriate descriptor table, selected by the TI bit, and to write the 6 least significant bytes of the descriptor into the relevant translation cache line. (The first two bytes are present in the segment descriptor for upwards compatibility with the 80386 and successor products and are ignored.) This mechanism ensures that when future accesses are made using the same selector, all the relevant information, the base, the limit, and the access rights of the segment are already present in the cache memory of the processor.

The descriptor table registers LDTR and GDTR also appear in this memory cache. These registers are accessed by privileged instructions. They also appear in the same format as a descriptor. The instructions LGDT, SGDT, LLDT and SLDT are provided to load or store the contents of these registers. It will be normal to load the GDTR register once, just before protected mode is entered, but the LDTR will be changed on other occasions, especially when the current task is suspended and a different one resumed in a task-switch. The index portion of LDTR is a selector in the normal format, since we have already observed that the LDT is a segment in its own right, whose descriptor must lie within the GDT (see figure 3.1.8).

3.2 Protection Mechanisms

The protection of programs plays an important part in the overall quality, reliability and performance of a computer system. Memory protection has two different advantages, in that it helps in the development and testing of software, speeding development time and reducing development costs, and also limiting the effects of a faulty program in a production environment, preventing it from interfering with other, correct programs.

Testing and debugging is an essential step in the development cycle of software: during this phase, one significant difficulty can be to isolate the underlying cause of faulty program behaviour. This difficulty arises because an initial bug may just cause the modification of an internal state, while the observable bug is caused by an otherwise correct operation which relies upon this state. This process is particularly common in a real-time multitasking system, for example. A protected system can, in most cases, speed the debugging process by eliminating the delay before a bug causes an observable effect, by trapping on the initial, faulty access to the state variable.

The principle of the protection mechanism is straightforward: it is to halt an inappropriate access by the current task immediately, and give enough information to the programmer for him to interpret the cause of the faulty access. This principle is easily explained, but the implementation is sometimes tricky; the checking needs to take place in real time at the same time as program execution is occurring. This means that specific circuitry on the CPU chip is needed to carry out this checking, validate the result, and to warn the user when a fault occurs.

The protected mode of the 80286 implements these protection and fault detection circuits, introducing hardware and software facilities to enable the designers of systems to implement more or less complicated protection regimes and error reporting mechanisms.

3.2.1 Types of Protection

The 80286 includes three distinct mechanisms of protection:

- separation of system tasks and applications,
- isolation between different user programs, and
- controlling access to different types of objects, such as data, procedures, and stack objects.

The first type of protection is based upon a hierarchical structure which uses four distinct levels of privilege, numbered 0 to 3. The privilege level is an indication of the reliability of a routine, since the lower the number, the higher the privilege, and the more important it is that the program is bug-free. The software with the highest privilege (0) is protected against all software running with a lower privilege.

A good analogy of these different levels of privilege is given by the classification of documents in industrial or military institutions; each document is given a security classification, and each person receives his or her own security clearance. Reliable people might receive the highest clearance, and with this may view all documents classified at their level or below.

Historically, software running at privilege level 0 would be called supervisor mode software, which can access all of the different resources of the machine. In order to guarantee the correct operation of the system overall, it might be necessary to restrict access to this software, so that only some of the routines in this level 0 code can be called by less privileged software. The most privileged software generally consists of the "kernel" of the operating system, and is made up of modules whose behaviour and operation is tested and demonstrably correct. The programs associated with the less privileged levels are application programs, in production or in course of development. This applications software must not be permitted direct access to the physical resources of the machine, only to the resources that have been granted by the operating system.

This multilevel privilege structure is adopted to good effect in the design of multitasking operating systems, where a structured design gives rise to a series of modules with limited functions, each processing a limited area of data.

The second aspect of protection, protection between tasks, limits each task to accessing its own data. The task that is currently executing cannot change the data of a task that is currently waiting, since it has no means of generating a virtual address that translates to a real address within a different task.

The third aspect of protection is a mechanism which gives additional protection even within a single task. Its purpose is to restrict the accesses to individual data items to those accesses which are necessary on that particular type of data. For example, if a program tries to write into a code segment or a read-only data segment, or to jump into a stack segment with only read/write permission, the access is interrupted and an error condition is signalled. This protection again localises the effect of any bug, so that an error is notified as soon as possible after its original cause.

3.2.2 *Implementation of Protection*

The protection mechanisms implemented in the 80286 apply these different constraints in an attempt to limit every access to code, data or input/output ports to actions that are specifically permitted, depending on the current context.

In one check, the protection mechanism monitors every access against the types of access permitted by the type field of the relevant segment descriptor, and prevents any access that is at variance with those permitted accesses.

In a second check, each access is monitored for the appropriate protection level, since each code and data segment has a privilege level stored in its descriptor.

The procedure call mechanism serves to implement a barrier between "system" and "application" software, in order to maximise the reliability of the system. In order for an application module to call a system module, recourse is made to a descriptor, called a "Gate Descriptor". In overall terms, applications programs are protected from one another by the addressing mechanism, and the priority control system protects the operating system from applications software. (With four levels available, the priority control system protects trusted software from untrusted programs or from software in course of development.)

The combination of the two mechanisms offers the maximum flexibility for the system designer to build different configurations with different rules for accessing code, data and input/output ports. Input/output protection is discussed later, and the notion of allowing even non-privileged tasks access to input/output ports is introduced.

3.2.3 Protection and Memory Management

Protection attributes are applied to an individual segment, and appear in the segment's associated descriptor. This descriptor is normally defined and created after all the compilation phases by Builder, the appropriate software tool.

The information defined by the segment descriptor's protection information is threefold:

- the type of the segment (code, data, read-only, etc.)
- the level of privilege (0 to 3), and
- the size or limit of the segment.

Section 3.1.3 above describes how the information in a descriptor is present in the CPU chip at the time of the access, since it is loaded into the address translation cache memory when the segment register is loaded. Loading these segment registers is also an operation to which protection checks are applied: it is not possible, for example, to load the Stack Segment (SS) register to point to a segment that is marked read-only, since to operate as a stack, the processor needs both read and write access.

All of the size, type and privilege checks are carried out before the start of the bus cycle which would access the data. The time that this operation takes is hidden by the pipelined operation of the address generation unit and the bus interface.

3.2.4 Protection and Privilege Levels

As described above, additional protection measures are necessary to prevent an application program from incorrectly accessing operating system kernel routines or kernel data.

When any access to a segment is made via its descriptor, the 80286 carries out the following protection checks:

Privilege: the access is validated by comparing the privilege level of the current program (in CPL; see below) with the privilege level of the descriptor that is being accessed (DPL).

Type: the type of a segment is specified in the access control byte of its descriptor; this check prohibits writing to a read-only segment, for example.

Limit: on every access to a data item, regardless of the addressing mode, the CPU checks the effective address against the segment size, contained in the "limit" field of the descriptor. A stack segment, which grows downwards, is marked with the "expand down" bit, and the hardware checks that the access lies in the allocated upper part of the segment, rather than the unallocated lower part.

Levels of privilege

Each descriptor contains a two-bit field which specifies the privilege level of the associated segment, numbered from 0 to 3 (0 being the most privileged). Each segment, therefore, has its own privilege. The comparison of privilege levels in this hierarchy of protection serves to check the validity of every access by a program.

For example, the operating system code and its data, at privilege level 0 cannot be accessed by programs running at levels 1, 2 or 3. Conversely, programs at level 0 can access data which has any of the different privilege levels. In general, code running at a particular privilege level can only access data in segments with an equal or larger privilege number.

The partitioning of a complex system into levels is completely configurable by the designer of the system, who uses the relevant configuration tools to achieve the desired structure. This structure may be the classic two mode (supervisor and user) operating system structure, or may be a more modern multi-level ring structure.

Configuring the protection structure of a system using these and related facilities means that the 80286 presents choices to the system designer that were not available or necessary with earlier processors. The ability to build structured, protected systems will appeal to developers in many different fields. The benefits, and the problems, of writing parts of an application to run at the most privileged of levels will be readily understood.

It is not essential to use all four privilege levels in a system; it is possible to use just one level, omitting the level-based protection checks, or to use two, to implement "supervisor" and "user" modes. Nevertheless, the possibility of using all four levels can give increased flexibility to large systems, with, for example, a number of input-output processes.

The idea of privilege is applied directly to tasks and to three types of descriptors:

1. Memory segment descriptors,
2. GATE descriptors, and
3. Segments which hold task state information.

The privilege of a running task varies from moment to moment, and is determined by the privilege of the segment from which the task is executing instructions. The privilege level contained within a descriptor is called the DPL. The current privilege level for a running task is called the CPL. The CPU ensures that the CPL is numerically less than or equal to the DPL of every segment descriptor before that descriptor is loaded into the address translation cache.

In more detail, the privilege checking of accesses relies upon three distinct pieces of information:

CPL (Current Privilege Level), contained in bits 0 and 1 of the current CS register. This value indicates the level of privilege to be given to the current program, thereby determining what privilege of data can be accessed.

DPL (Descriptor Privilege Level), contained in the access byte of the descriptor which is being accessed. This value indicates the level of privilege assigned to the segment to which access is being made.

RPL (Requested Privilege Level), contained in bits 0 and 1 of the selector that is being used.

The purpose of RPL is to indicate the privilege level of the program on whose behalf the current access is being made. For example, a program at level 3 may call a routine at level 1, and pass it a pointer to a data item. In order to avoid violating the protection scheme, the level 1 routine must use the pointer at an effective level of 3, to ensure that data which is inaccessible from level 3 is not inadvertently accessed. An RPL of 3 is used in the selector part of the pointer which is passed to the level 1 routine, and in general, RPL is used to indicate the privilege level of the originator of a pointer.

Ultimately, the following rules are observed:

- a program at a certain CPL can only access segments if their DPLs observe the relationship
  $CPL <= DPL$
- if the selector used to access the segment descriptor was loaded by software running at a different level from the current, the access is only permitted if
  $RPL <= DPL$

These checks can be summarised by introducing the concept of an Effective Privilege Level (EPL), which takes the higher value of CPL and RPL. Accesses are permitted only if

$EPL = maximum(CPL, RPL)$, where $EPL <= DPL$

The notion of EPL ensures that both the currently running code and the code which created the segment selector are sufficiently privileged to access the segment indicated by the descriptor.

The instruction ARPL (Adjust RPL – see appendix A) is provided to load the RPL field of a segment selector with the evaluated EPL. In the example above, the ARPL instruction could be used in the level 1 routine to insert the value 3 in the selector passed by the level 3 routine.

3.2.5 Conformant Segments

Some software routines can be used at a number of different privilege levels, meaning that they need to maintain the CPL which was in use before they were called (especially if they were called at a low privilege level!). Examples of these routines might be library software, which does not explicitly manage an operating system resource, but is shared between modules running at different levels.

A "conformant" segment is indicated by setting bit 2 in the access byte of the segment descriptor. When this bit is set, the segment can be accessed by a CALL or JUMP instruction even if the CPL is numerically greater than the DPL in the descriptor. After the call, the CPL is unchanged, and the code continues in the same privilege level as the calling segment. This is the one and only case when the comparison of CPL and DPL is not carried out.

3.2.6 Gates

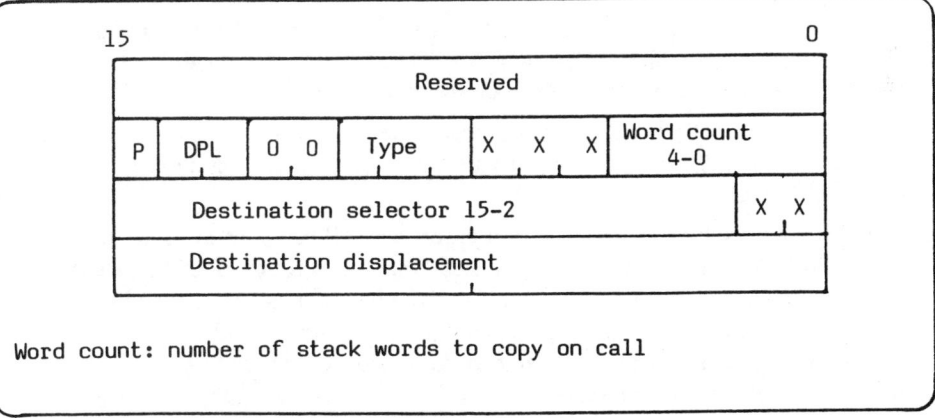

Figure 3.2.1 Gate descriptor format

An Operating System will be constructed from many different procedures, but non-privileged code may only be permitted to call a small number of these routines. For example, it would be unusual to permit applications routines to call the operating system scheduling routines directly. Every procedure call that changes privilege level must be checked to ensure it is permitted. In the case of the 80286, this check is enforced by permitting privilege changes only through specific "Gates".

A gate is a system descriptor which specifies an object which the user wishes to access. Figure 3.2.1 shows a gate descriptor, containing the following fields:

P   presence bit

DPL two bits indicating the protection level of the gate descriptor. The gate cannot be used from code with a CPL higher than DPL.

Type indicates the type of the gate, showing the type of object which it guards:
  4 Call Gate, for procedure calls
  5 Task Gate, for task switching
  6 Interrupt Gate, to be placed in the Interrupt Descriptor Table, pointing to an interrupt procedure
  7 Trap Gate, with the same function as an Interrupt Gate, but pointing to an error-handling routine

WC   a Word Count, the number of words which are copied from the callers stack to the stack reserved for the privilege level of the procedure associated with this gate (used only for Call Gates).

SDST Selector Destination, indicating the selector of the destination code; in the case of a Call Gate, this is a selector of a code segment, and the new CPL will be the DPL of this segment.

OFFSET the entry point of this routine in the destination segment.

A Gate is a data object which must be visible to a particular routine in order to access the object which it describes. It is therefore necessary that the CPL is less than or equal to the DPL of the gate itself.

Further, it is not possible to call a procedure at a less privileged level, even using a call gate. Such a call can only be carried out by calling a different task, using a task gate.

Figure 3.2.2 shows an example of a procedure call using a Call Gate installed in the GDT. Procedure P, at level 3, is accessing a procedure PROC.OS, at level 0, using a call gate at level 3. The figure shows how there is an indirection via the descriptor table (GDT or LDT), which contains the descriptor which points to the destination segment indicating the start of the PROC.OS procedure. Procedure P can only make this call to PROC.OS because the system designer has created the gate to permit this particular call.

The gate is given a protection level of 3 so that it may be accessed by an application program. Thus an ordinary CALL instruction carries out the privilege change. The example program given below shows a call in ASM/286. The reader will observe that exactly the same program would be used on the 8086 processor, in which none of this checking occurs.

Example:
```
EXTRN  PROC.OS:FAR
PUSH   PAR1         ;First parameter
PUSH   PAR2         ;...and the second
CALL   PROC.OS      ;Call via Gate
```
Only the selector of the pointer used in the CALL instruction is used, the binder program placing the selector of the call gate in the code. The new segment and the displacement of the entry point is given in the gate descriptor.

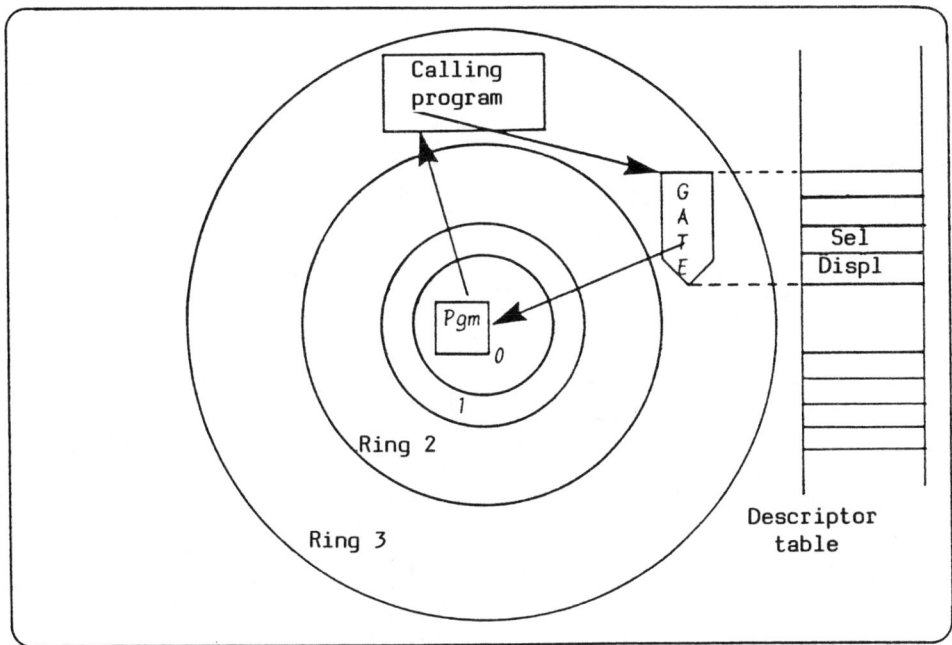

Figure 3.2.2 Changing privilege levels using a Call Gate

When a call results in a privilege change, the CPU switches from the current stack to the stack defined for the new privilege level. The called procedure can access parameters passed on the stack as the CPU copies them (the number of words is given in the WC field of the gate descriptor) to the new stack area, which must be defined with sufficient space available. The WC field in the gate descriptor is initialised by the Builder program.

Once the procedure PROC.OS has finished execution, it executes a RET 4 instruction, which has the effect of unstacking the parameters copied for the level 0 code, readjusting BP and SP for the level 3 code, and returning to the calling procedure. The gate in this example has facilitated a procedure call to a more privileged level.

A CALL instruction through a Call Gate may not result in a privilege level change, if the destination code runs at the same level as the current code; this does not cause a change of stacks. In this case, a JMP instruction could be used instead of a CALL. (JMP cannot be used to change privilege level.)

The purpose of using a Call Gate without changing the privilege level is to enable a particular procedure to be accessed using a fixed selector, rather than by an address which will change every time the program is recompiled. The calling code is therefore unmodified, even if the called code changes its address.

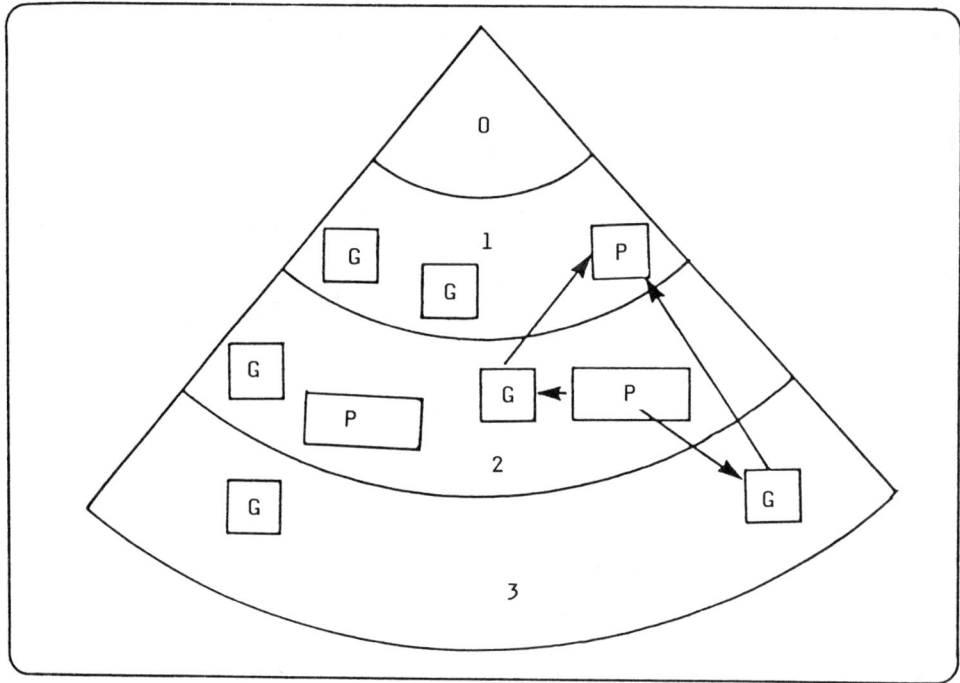

Figure 3.2.3 Examples of calls by Call Gate

Gates may be situated in the GDT (and thus visible by all running applications), or in the LDT (and usable only by the relevant task), or in an Interrupt Descriptor Table (IDT). In this last case, the gates point to entry points of interrupt procedures (Interrupt Gates), or procedures to manage exceptions (Trap Gates). A gate may also transfer control to a new task, as described in the next section.

The Gate mechanism is restrictive in the manner shown in figure 3.2.3. Three possible causes of error arise:

- if the gate is at a lower level than the caller
- if the gate transfers to a less privileged level
- if a call to a more privileged level is attempted without using a gate.

3.3 Management of Tasks

The real-time features of the 80286, particularly those concerned with task management, clearly indicate that the designers wanted to include in the architecture a set of mechanisms to facilitate the writing of real-time monitors and operating systems. A task is defined by a minimal execution context, consisting of its registers and its stacks. Four stacks are provided for each task, one for each privilege level, so that each stack can be protected from other levels.

A task is also defined by the accesses it can make to other objects in the system. Two descriptor tables, one global (GDT), the other local to a task (LDT), provide this extended or limited visibility.

One of the more interesting features of the 80286 is its ability to switch from one task context to another within a very short time (22 microseconds at 8 MHz), by saving the registers of the old context and reloading those of the new.

The 80286 distinguishes between tasks switched by software, whose context is loaded by an explicit program call, and tasks switched as a result of hardware action, usually an interrupt.

One can further distinguish between task management carried out in the microprocessor, which only needs to change the hardware context, and the more complex management of tasks in the sense of an operating system which provides a fuller context. The hardware task switching mechanism provides the base functions on which can be built a real-time executive, such as ETR_286, described in chapter 5.

3.3.1 Task State Segment

The principal table describing a task is the Task State Segment (TSS). This table is a memory segment of at least 22 words. Figure 3.3.1 shows the structure of a TSS.

The fields within this table are mostly self-explanatory; the following areas will be observed:

- The general registers AX, BX, CX, DX, SI, DI, SP and BP.
- The four segment registers holding selectors: ES, CS, SS and DS.
- The stack pointers for the three more privileged levels: SS0:SP0, SS1:SP1 and SS2:SP2.
- The program state register, containing the flags.

The remaining two fields need some additional explanation: the LDT selector is a selector (indexing into the GDT) to the local LDT belonging to this task, and the back link selector is written during a task switch so that the new TSS contains a reference to the previous TSS.

TSS segments are always defined within the GDT (rather than an LDT) so that tasks may be entered at any time.

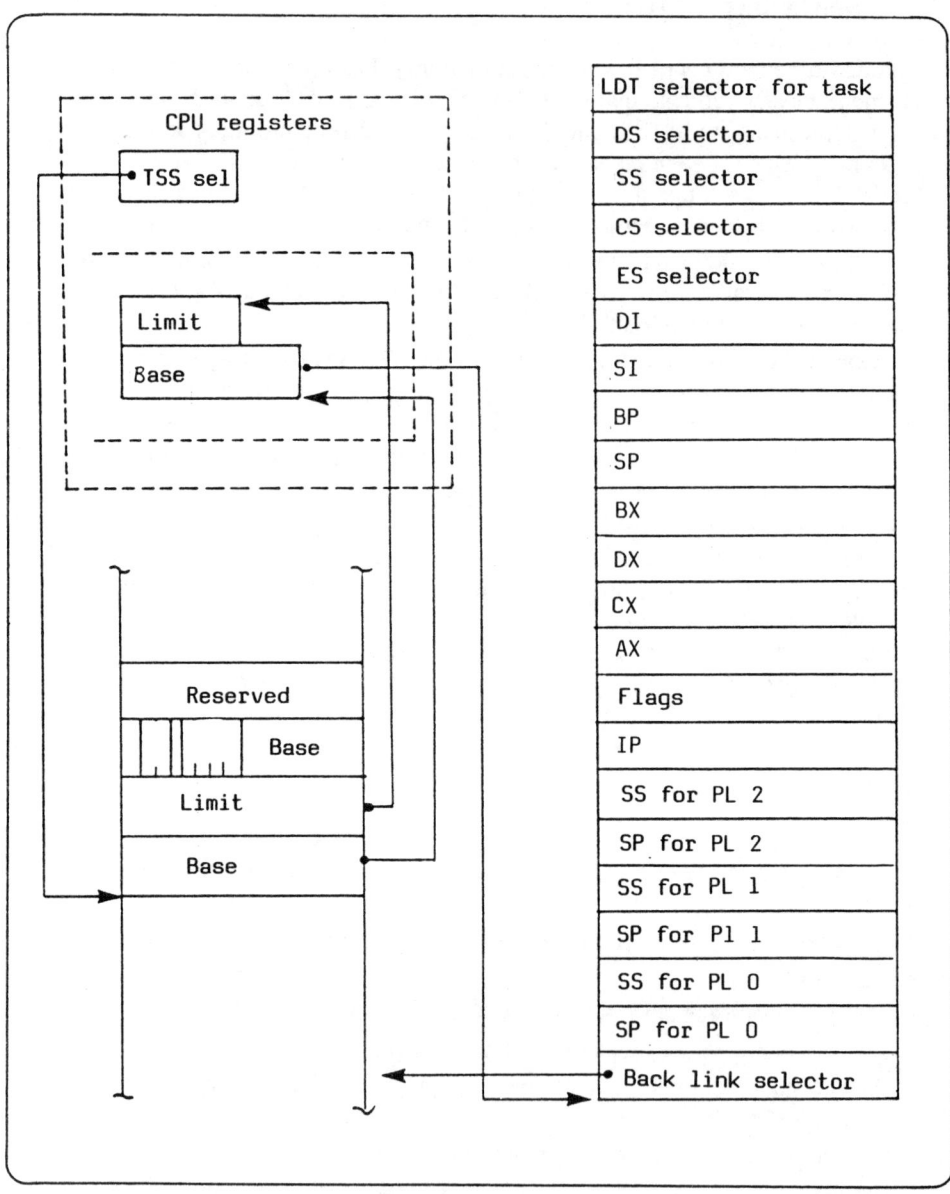

Figure 3.3.1 Task State Segment

In addition, while the processor is executing a particular task, it holds the address of the current TSS within a CPU register. This register is called the Task Register (TR), and contains the current TSS selector. When tasks are switched, TR and the base and the limit of the new TSS are loaded in an invisible manner.

Figure 3.3.2 gives an example of the entries in the GDT and LDTs for a system with two tasks.

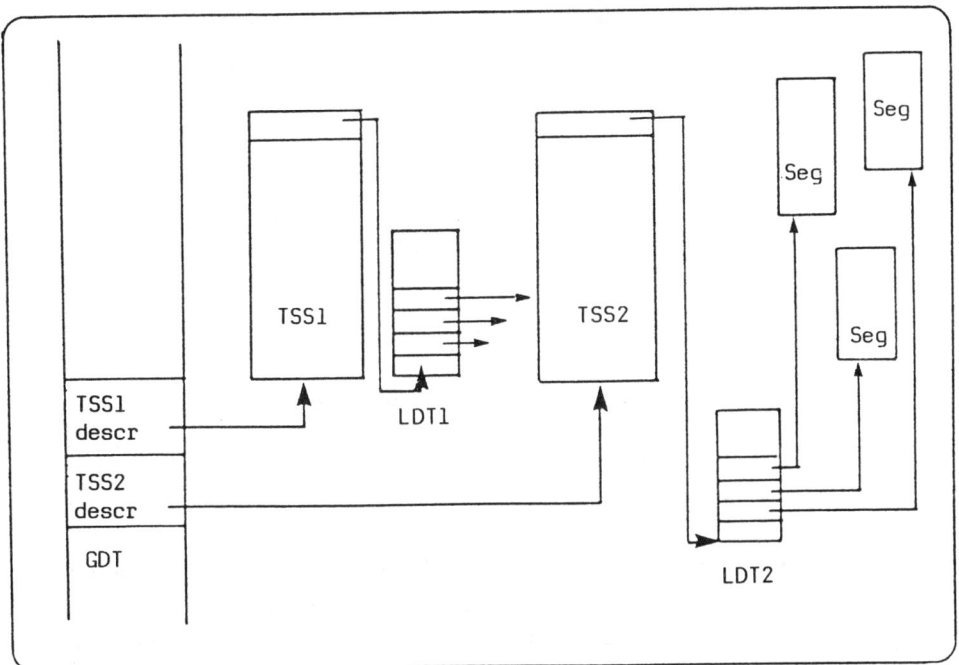

Figure 3.3.2 Segment structures for two tasks

3.3.2 TSS Descriptor

The TSS descriptor, shown in figure 3.3.3, contains the following fields:

Base: the 24-bit base address of the TSS

Limit: the 16-bit TSS size

P: Presence bit, indicating that the segment is present (1) or absent (0) from memory

DPL: Descriptor Privilege Level

B: "busy" indicates that a task is active (if 1) or not (0). This is necessary as tasks are not reentrant. If an attempt is made to enter an active task, an exception is generated.

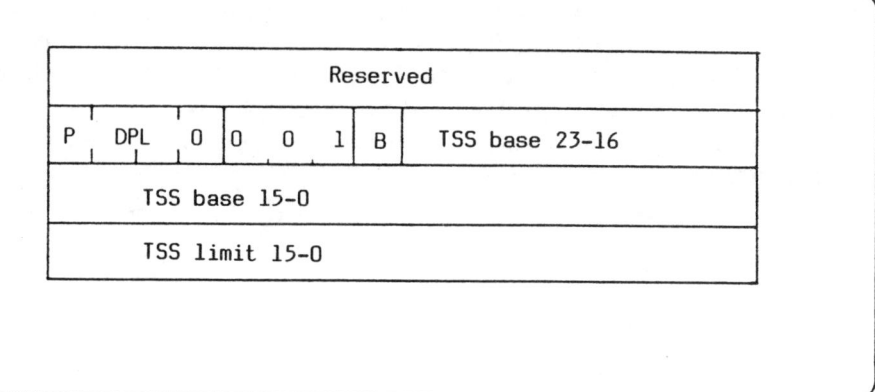

Figure 3.3.3 TSS descriptor

3.3.3 Changing the Context of a Task

When a program is running on the 80286, it is executed in the context of the current task, defined by the current TSS and LDT. The construction tools used to create an 80286 program are used to define at least one initial task. Some software systems may execute entirely within one task, and never perform a context switch.

Tasks are generally used in a modular fashion: one task is created per function to be performed, and task changing is carried out in order to change function.

The LDT defines the local address space of the task, and may be shared by a number of tasks, or may be unique to a specific task. This decision is made by the designer of the system. The GDT is, of course, global to all tasks.

Context switches may be caused by either hardware or software.

A programmed context switch is caused when a JMP or CALL instruction references a TSS. The use of a JMP instruction implies that there will be no return to the calling task, while the use of a CALL implies that a return to the calling task will be made using an IRET instruction within the new task. The use of JMP instructions for task switching will normally be limited to a real-time executive which is scheduling tasks.

Context switches may also be caused by hardware when an external or internal interrupt occurs (see also section 3.4.2). If the interrupt descriptor is an Interrupt or Trap Gate, the current task is suspended and a new task is entered. The new task is linked to the interrupted task using the "back link" field of the new TSS. When a task is preempted by a new task to service an interrupt, the Nested Task (NT) bit in the flags register of the new task is set to 1. When the interrupt service routine is finished and an IRET instruction is executed, a reverse task switch back to the interrupted task is made.

3.3.4 Using a Task Gate

The user may cause a process switch by using the selector of a TSS (which must be in the GDT) in a JMP or CALL instruction. It is also possible to perform the call using a Task Gate. This introduces an additional level of indirection. The selector of the Gate is used in the CALL or JMP instruction, and points into the GDT or LDT. The gate in the descriptor table contains the selector of the TSS for the new task, from which all the necessary information can be determined. This gives a certain stability to the code, meaning that only the selector in a gate needs to be changed to change the destination. The layout of a Task Gate Descriptor is shown in figure 3.3.4.

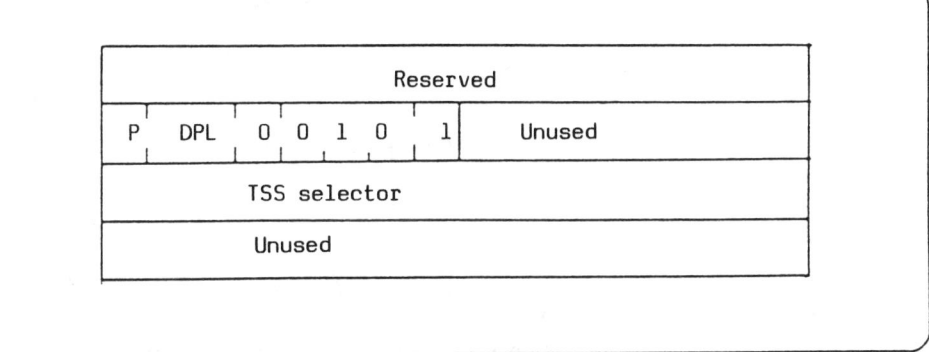

Figure 3.3.4 Task Gate

The rules of access to a task gate are the same as for a call gate. The Effective Privilege Level (EPL) of the destination selector must be (numerically) less than or equal to the DPL in the Gate. Figure 3.3.5 shows the use of a Task Gate to access a new task.

3.3.5 System Access Control

As described above, an 80286 operating system will provide entry points to applications to verify that no invalid calls are made. These entry points are seen by the application as particular virtual addresses, and are task or call gate selectors. This mechanism gives three advantages: the entry point is controlled by a gate descriptor; the entry points form a set of fixed virtual addresses, since a gate is accessed by indexing into the GDT or LDT tables; and the allocation of gates to specific privilege levels allows each system call entry point to be given its own appropriate protection.

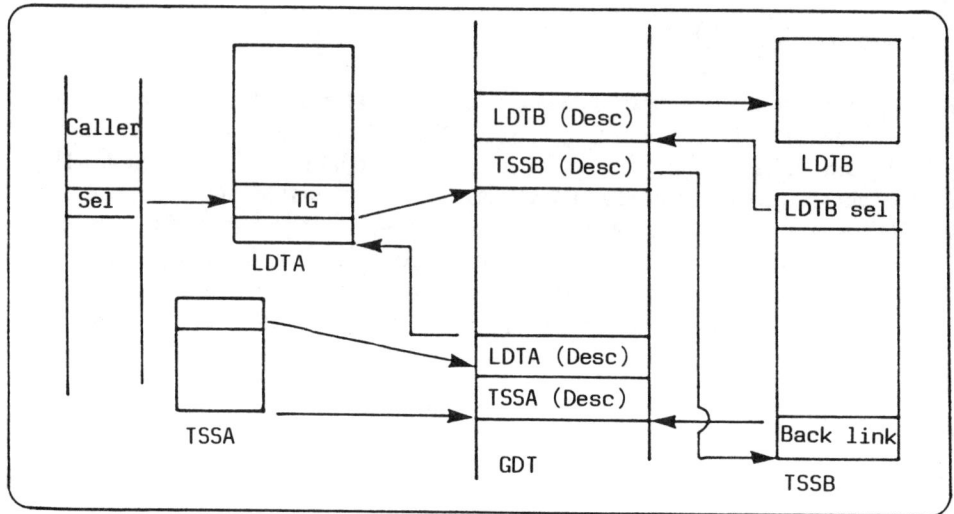

Figure 3.3.5 Task switch using a Task Gate

3.4 Interrupts

Interrupts are today a generally accepted and useful facility, provided by all commercial microprocessor architectures. As with other families, the 80286 is equipped with hardware and software facilities for coping with interrupts, described in this section. As for other facilities, it is necessary to distinguish between real mode and protected virtual mode, which use different techniques to accept interrupts and handle them.

3.4.1 Interrupts in Real Mode

In real mode, the 80286 accepts interrupts in very much the same way as its 8086 predecessor; two sources of interrupts are distinguished, internal and external.

An internal interrupt is caused by either the execution of an INT n instruction (where n is the number of the interrupt), or by the occurrence of an exception condition (such as division by zero, or execution of an invalid op-code) which automatically generates an interrupt to an exception handler.

In addition, two external pins on the 80286 allow it to respond to two asynchronous external events, interrupting the current task and making entry to the appropriate interrupt handler. The signals are INTR (Interrupt Request) and NMI (Non-Maskable Interrupt). An active transition on NMI causes an interrupt which is not maskable in any way, making it suitable for signalling some urgent fault condition, such as a parity failure or a watchdog timeout. Interrupts caused by the INTR pin may be inhibited by a bit, IF, in the flags register.

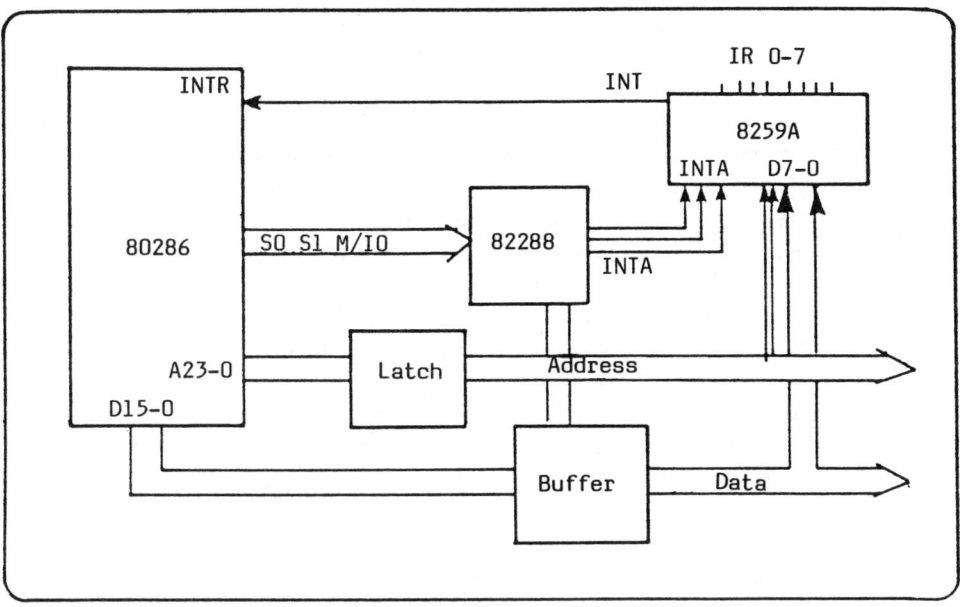

Figure 3.4.1 8259A Interrupt controller causing INTR

Figure 3.4.1 shows the 8259A Programmable Interrupt Controller, used with the 80286 as with the 8086 family. The figure shows a single 8259A, but these devices may also be used in a cascaded mode, in which one "master" component is connected to a number of "slave" interrupt controllers, in order to prioritise more than eight interrupts in a tree-like manner. This scheme allows the construction of a system of 64 levels of hardware interrupt priorities. After initialisation such a system responds automatically to the highest-priority interrupting device without further software intervention.

Regardless of the source of interrupt, internal or external, it is important for the processor to respond as quickly as possible, by suspending the current process, saving its state, and entering an appropriate handler routine. These steps are independent of the source of the interrupt, the only difference being the selection of the handler routine, which is made using a single "interrupt number", an 8-bit value which selects one of 256 interrupt handlers. The interrupt number has no implicit priority function, all priorities being defined by the internal circuitry and external interrupt controller.

In some cases, the interrupt number is defined implicitly by the cause of the interrupt: for example, the NMI signal always causes an interrupt using number 2, and a division by zero uses an interrupt number of zero.

In the case of programmed interrupts, the interrupt number is specified in the instruction, for example:

```
INT 127 ; Cause Interrupt Number 127
```

When an interrupt is caused by an active level on the INTR pin, however, an interrupt number is read from the Interrupt Controller via the external bus using an interrupt acknowledge cycle.

The interrupt acknowledge cycle is indicated by the processor asserting the INTA:L signal, which is interpreted by the Interrupt Controller chip as a read signal. This process is shown by the timing diagram in figure 3.4.2. The purpose of the first cycle is to freeze the state of the interrupt controllers and make sure that priority arbitration is complete before the interrupt vector is returned to the CPU during the second cycle.

Once the interrupt number is determined, it is used as an index into the interrupt table to select a pointer to the relevant interrupt handler routine. In real mode, the 80286 uses a full address, consisting of a 16-bit segment number and a 16-bit offset. The interrupt table is a one kilobyte table of 256 pointers starting at address 0.

The programmer is responsible for initialising all relevant entries in this table, to handle internally generated exceptions and external interrupts correctly. Typically, an operating system would initialise all table entries to cope with all 256 possible interrupt sources.

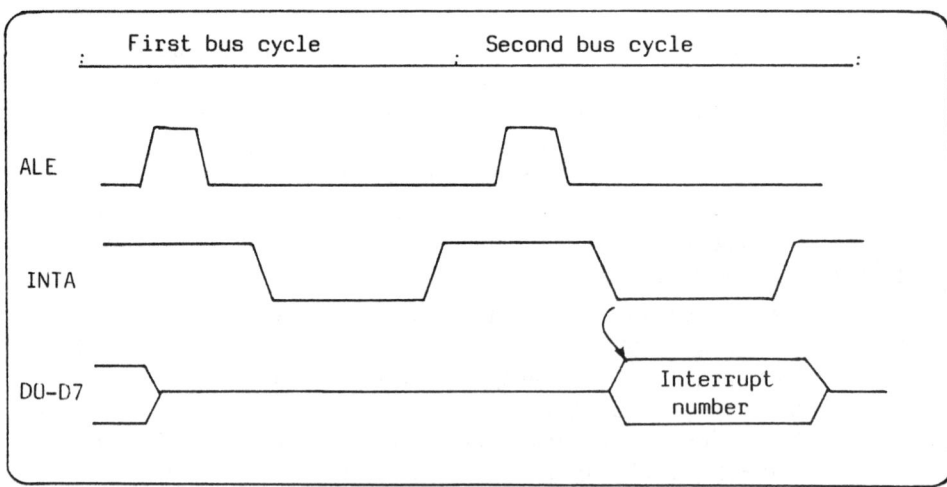

Figure 3.4.2 Interrupt acknowledge cycle

If a number of external interrupts occur simultaneously, the one with the highest priority is accepted first. If both NMI and INTR are simultaneously activated, NMI has precedence, and INTR is normally inhibited during NMI servicing: in real mode, the IF flag is cleared by the hardware when an NMI is accepted, and in protected mode, the programmer will usually direct NMI interrupts through an interrupt gate, again clearing the IF flag.

It is useful to remember that an interrupt is serviced as soon as it is accepted. Figure 3.4.3 summarises the different sources of interrupts, and shows how a programmable flag bit, IF, is used to defer recognition of the INTR signal.

Accepting an interrupt

Accepting an interrupt consists of the following operations:
- the Flags register is stacked;
- the current CS and IP are stacked;
- the single-step (TF) and interrupt (IF) flags are cleared, to prevent further interrupts being accepted;
- an interrupt number is read or generated;
- an interrupt pointer is read from the interrupt table, indexed by the interrupt number; and
- execution is resumed at this address.

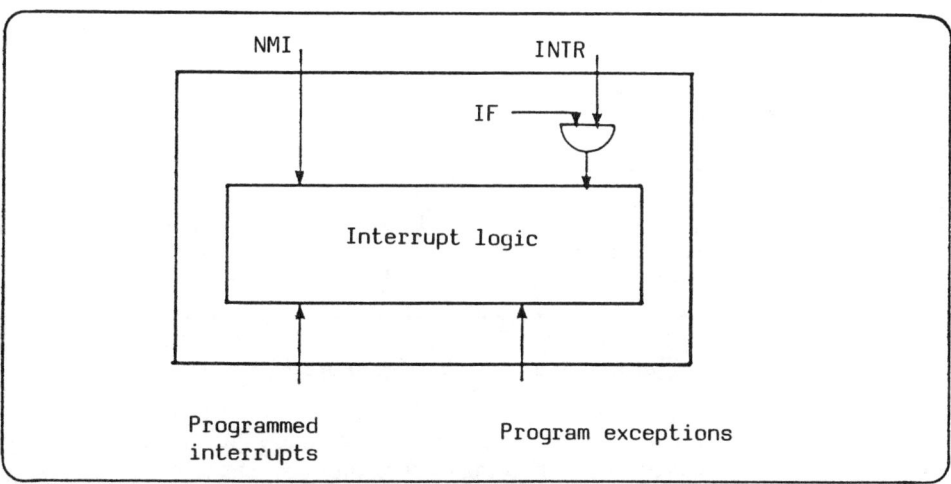

Figure 3.4.3 Sources of interrupts

Figure 3.4.4 shows that three words containing context information from the interrupted program are stacked by the hardware; any further state information must be preserved by software. At the end of the interrupt handler, the software-saved state must be restored; return can be made to the interrupted code using the IRET instruction, which restores the Flags register, CS and IP from the stack.

In particular, IRET can restore the values of TF (the single-step flag) and IF (the interrupt enable flag). IF may be manipulated using the STI (Set IF) and CLI (Clear IF) instructions, to enable and disable interrupts at any time. Needless to say, the correct operation of an interrupt-driven system will depend upon the correct use of these instructions.

The structure of an interrupt handler routine will normally look like this:

```
COD SEGMENT
IH  PROC    FAR
    PUSHA       ; save all registers
    ...         ; handle interrupt
    POPA        ; restore registers
    IRET        ; resume interrupted code
IHD ENDP
COD ENDS
```

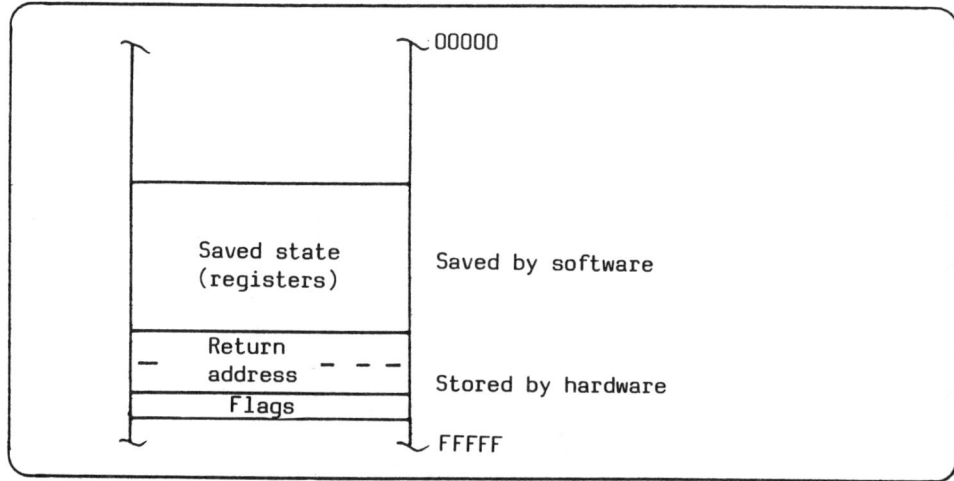

Figure 3.4.4 Stack following an interrupt

It is essential to cope with the implicitly-defined interrupt numbers for two reasons; it is necessary to avoid choosing these numbers when selecting interrupt numbers to be supplied by external interrupt controllers, and it is also prudent to initialise the interrupt pointers for these numbers to indicate a suitable procedure, even if this procedure performs a null action by consisting of a single IRET instruction.

The interrupt numbers that are implicitly defined in the 80286 are:

0: Divide by zero. This exception is generated by the CPU by a DIV or IDIV instruction when the result is too great for the destination register.

The 80286 in Protected Mode 73

1: Single step. This interrupt occurs after every instruction if the TF flag is set. This facility is widely used by debugging programs to enable the user to single-step through a program under test.
2: NMI.
3: Breakpoint. The INT 3 instruction is coded in a single byte, and can be substituted by the programmer or by a debugger for any other instruction, in order to cause a program under test to pause for intervention.
4: Overflow, caused by the INTO instruction which is used to test for overflow following arithmetic instructions.
5: Bound Check, caused by a BOUND instruction which checks that an address lies between two limits. If the limits are exceeded in either direction, the interrupt is caused. This instruction may be generated by high-level language compilers for Pascal, for example, to verify that an array access does not lie outside the space allocated.
6: This interrupt is caused when an undefined instruction is executed. This may mean that the program code has been overwritten by a previous error.
7: This interrupt indicates that the numeric coprocessor is absent when required by the program. It is possible to emulate the function of the coprocessor in software in order to permit the same application program to execute more slowly in less well-provided hardware systems.

3.4.2 Interrupts in Protected Virtual Mode

Protected mode naturally has a more sophisticated manner of dealing with interrupts. In protected mode, the manner of handling interrupts is completely integrated with the protection and multitasking facilities of the processor. As is the case in real mode, exceptions, programmed and external interrupts are dealt with identically in protected mode.

Handling an interrupt may take place in one of two different environments, depending upon the choice of the implementor: the interrupt procedure may execute in the context of the interrupted task, using the same stack, the same local descriptor table and the same TSS, or the interrupt procedure may be written as a specific task, needing a context switch to get into and out of it.

The choice of environment in which to handle a specific interrupt is entirely up to the user, and will depend upon the extent of the function to be performed by the interrupt and the degree of isolation that is desired in the system. It is possible to envisage a mixed organisation, in which some simple interrupts are handled within the current context, and others cause context switches into their own defined environments.

As in real mode, interrupts in protected mode are characterised by an interrupt number of between 0 and 255. Certain of these numbers (a superset of the real-mode set) are again implicitly associated with specific events. The interrupt

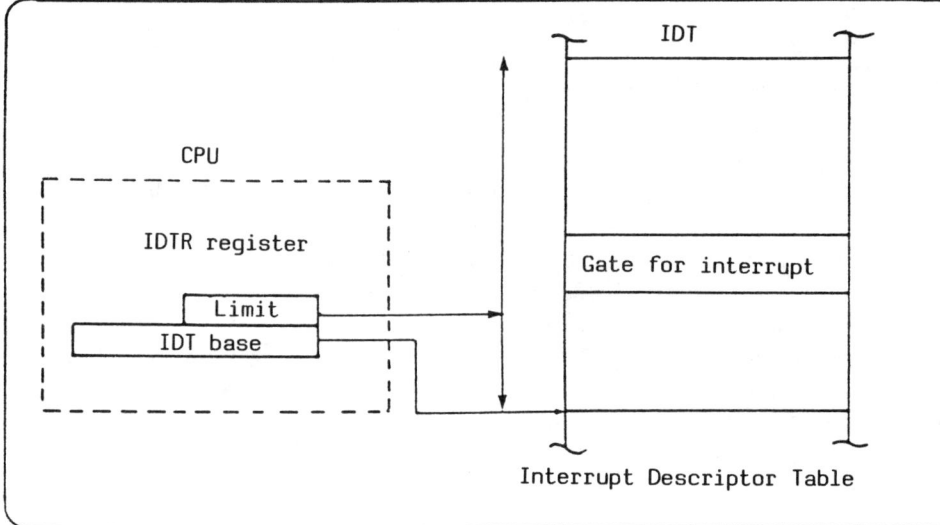

Figure 3.4.5 Interrupt Descriptor Table

number is again used as an index, but into the Interrupt Descriptor Table which, as its name suggests, contains an array of descriptors indexed by interrupt numbers. The table is a segment identified to the CPU by the contents of the IDTR register, which is initialised using the privileged LIDT instruction when protected mode is entered. Figure 3.4.6 shows the CPU descriptor table registers including the IDTR.

The Interrupt Descriptor Table may reside anywhere in memory, and its entries must all be Gate Descriptors. Since a descriptor is 8 bytes long, the table may be up to 2 kilobytes in size. The gate descriptors may be of three different types:

- Interrupt Gate (see figure 3.4.7)
- Trap Gate
- Task Gate

Context switches take place only when Task Gates are used. In the case of Interrupt or Trap Gates, the interrupt-handling code is run in the context which is active when the interrupt is accepted.

In a particular system, the user may not wish to dedicate a maximal-sized segment, and may not wish to provide handlers for all possible interrupt numbers. The CPU hardware checks on every interrupt that the descriptor accessed is valid and lies within the allocated size of the segment, generating an error exception if either of these checks fails.

We have seen that the first few interrupt exceptions are reserved to specific exceptions. In order to assure compatibility with future hardware and software

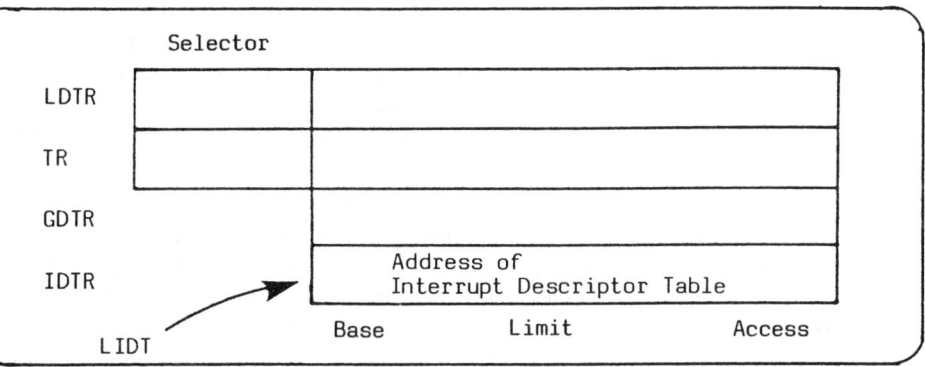

Figure 3.4.6 IDTR and other CPU Task Registers

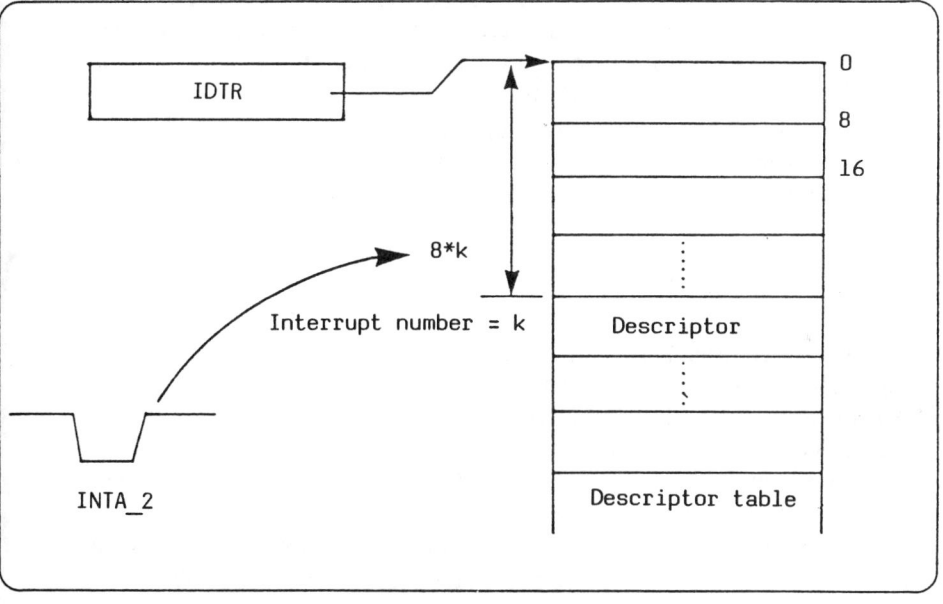

Figure 3.4.7 Accessing the interrupt descriptor

products, Intel reserve interrupt levels 0 to 31, and suggest that users restrict their numbers to the range 32 to 255.

The hardware of interrupt circuits driving the INTR or NMI pins remains the same in protected mode as in real mode. The one minor difference is the treatment of the interrupt flag IF.

External interrupts on the INTR pin are disabled if this flag is set to zero (by the CLI instruction, for example). This bit has no effect on external interrupts caused by NMI or on program-generated interrupts or exceptions. The IF flag is not systematically set to zero by the occurrence of an interrupt, as it is in real mode, but the choice of whether to accept further interrupts is left to the user in the selection of the type of descriptor reached by the interrupt number. IF is cleared when an Interrupt Gate is used, and is left unchanged by a Trap Gate.

If the user chooses to permit external interrupts during a particular trap handler, he is, of course, at liberty to inhibit them for certain critical regions using CLI, reenabling them when the region is exited using the STI instruction. In protected mode, these instructions are privileged, and can only be executed if the CPL (Current Privilege Level) is compatible with the current task's IOPL.

The NMI pin is never maskable, but the process of accepting an NMI ensures that NMI interrupts are not serviced reentrantly, any more than in the real mode case. This means that if a second NMI occurs during the servicing of a first, this is noted and the second interrupt is not entered until after the IRET instruction of the first service routine. It is good practice to ensure that NMI is serviced using an Interrupt Gate Descriptor which ensures that IF is cleared, preventing the servicing of INTR signals during the NMI service routine.

The method of generating programmed interrupts and internal exceptions is the same as in real mode; in protected mode, however, the user has again the freedom to choose whether to service the interrupt in the current context or to use a Task Gate to provoke a task switch.

Interrupt Gate and Trap Gate

The single difference between the use of Interrupt and Task Gates is the state in which each leaves the interrupt flag IF. The use of an Interrupt Gate specifies that IF is to be cleared (INTR inhibited) during the service procedure, whereas the use of a Trap Gate leaves IF unchanged, without changing the masking of INTR. Both descriptors cause the interrupt service routine to be run within the context active at the time of the interrupt.

The format of these descriptors (shown in figure 3.4.8) is similar to that of a Call Gate. In particular, the descriptors show the segment containing the interrupt service routine and the offset within the segment of the routine.

The two different descriptors are distinguished by the bit patterns 00110 (Interrupt Gate) or 00111 (Trap Gate) in bits 0 to 4 in the access byte.

The privilege level checking within interrupt handling is a little involved, and takes place using three privilege levels, the current CPL, the DPL in the Interrupt or Trap Gate, and the DPL in the Code Segment Descriptor (indexed using the selector from the Interrupt or Trap Gate). First the Interrupt or Trap Gate DPL is checked to be (numerically) greater or equal to CPL. This ensures that the current task is sufficiently privileged to request this interrupt. Secondly, the Code Descriptor (indexed from GDT or LDT by the selector in the Trap or Interrupt Gate) is examined. The DPL in this descriptor must be (numerically) less than or equal

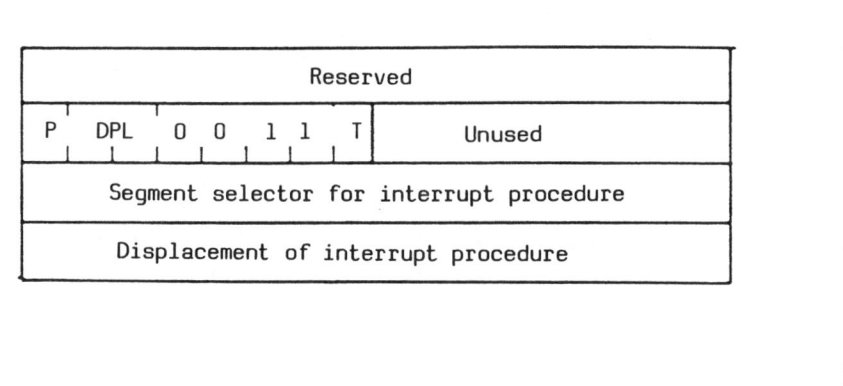

Figure 3.4.8 Interrupt and Trap Gate descriptor format

to CPL. This check ensures that the interrupt service routine is not run at a less privileged level than the interrupted task, ensuring that a less privileged routine never has access to more privileged data.

The Code Descriptor accessed via the Interrupt or Trap Descriptor may specify a "conformant" segment, in which case CPL is not changed and the interrupt handler is run at the same PL as the interrupted task. If the segment is not conformant, PL is reduced to the value specified in its descriptor.

The checking outlined above is of primary value for establishing the validity of programmed interrupts; gates for handling external interrupt or fault exceptions should permit access from any privilege level by having a DPL of 3 and by accessing code at level 0.

When Interrupt or Trap Gates are used, the flags register and a return address are stacked on the current stack. If a change in Privilege Level occurs (via a Gate indicating a non-conformant code segment), a different stack is used as specified in the TSS. Figure 3.4.9 shows the state of the stack after the occurrence of an error exception; it shows that most errors cause a single-word error code to be pushed on top of the return address. The programmer needs to remove this word before executing the IRET instruction at the end of the service routine to return to the interrupted routine.

Two further details are important in the acceptance of interrupts via Interrupt or Trap Gates. One is that the IRET instruction used at the end of an interrupt service routine may cause the alteration of the state of the IF flag, via restoration from the stacked Flags register. This operation is only permitted if the current CPL is less than or equal to IOPL. Secondly, the Nested Task (NT) bit in the Flags register is unconditionally cleared to zero when an interrupt is accepted by one of these Gates.

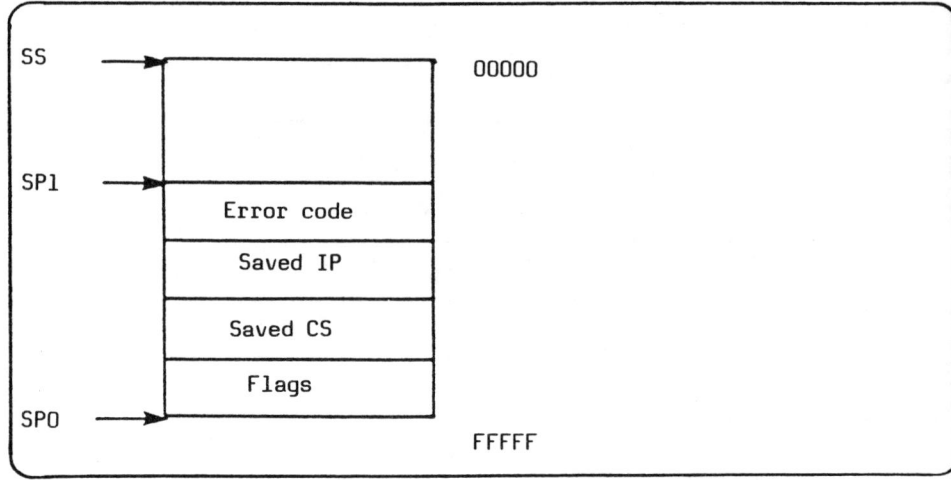

Figure 3.4.9 Stack following an error exception

Interrupts using Task Gates

Task Gates are the alternative mechanism used for accepting interrupts. Using a Task Gate has the advantage of providing the greatest isolation between the interrupt handling code and data and that of the interrupted task, giving the greatest reliability and security in a software system. Handling an interrupt in this way uses a gate of exactly the structure described in paragraph 3.3.4.

A second immediate advantage of this technique is that accepting the interrupt provokes a task switch, thus saving the complete running context of the interrupted task; this is different from the previous cases in which only the flags and the return address CS:IP are saved.

The operations that occur are those of a classical task switch:

- The Task Gate allows the processor to access the TSS of the new task and load its context; the Privilege-related rules of the interrupt are exactly the same as a normal task switch.
- The NT (Nested Task) bit is set.
- The selector of the TSS of the interrupted task is saved in the "back link" field of the new TSS.

The reverse switch (at the end of the interrupt service routine) is carried out automatically by the execution of the IRET instruction.

One significant point of difference is important: because the interrupt causes the resumption of a task, the interrupt service routine is not entered at a fixed point given by the interrupt descriptor table entry, but the task is reactivated at the point following where it last gave up control (probably by an IRET instruction). This means that an interrupt task will be written as a continuous loop, with the IRET at the end followed by a jump back to the start of the service routine.

Operating system programming

The previous section describes how a Task Gate Descriptor can be used to cause a task switch when a particular interrupt is accepted, and how the interrupted task is indicated by a selector of that task's TSS being written into the new task's TSS.

An example will serve to illustrate the difficulties that this mechanism can cause within an operating system: if a scheduler gives control to task "A", this task may be interrupted by (into) task "B". Task "B" may be further interrupted by task "C". If task "C" solicits the intervention of the task scheduler, this will see that it has been called by a different task from the one that it dispatched. In this case (see figure 3.4.10), it is likely that the scheduler will need to follow the backlinks from the current task in order to deduce the sequence of events, and may wish to alter this list in order to resume tasks in a non-nested manner.

The choice between the use of a Task Gate rather than an Interrupt or Trap Gate is left entirely to the system designer. He is likely to have regard to two basic criteria in making his choice:

- The use of a Task Gate ensures that all current context is saved and that maximum protection is preserved, while
- An Interrupt or Trap Gate gives a quicker response to the interrupt, but involves more complex rules regarding the relative Privilege levels of the interrupted and interrupt service routines.

In protected mode, a number of additional interrupt numbers are used when error checks fail:

8: double fault. This exception is generated when a second exception occurs during the processing of a first. For example, if an overflow exception cannot be completed because one of the essential segments is not present in main memory, an interrupt number 8 is generated.

9: the numeric coprocessor has attempted to exceed a segment limit during a read or write of an operand.

10: invalid task segment. This exception is generated when the TSS reached via a Gate descriptor is not valid: this might be caused by the LDT described in the TSS being absent or a failure of the protection rules. This exception should be handled via a Task Gate.

11: an attempt has been made to use a segment which is not present in memory. This exception can be managed by a virtual memory handler which will need to make room for this segment in main memory, fetch it from disk, and mark the descriptor "present" before resuming the interrupted operation. See section 3.5 for a more detailed discussion of virtual memory.

12: stack error. The stack segment is not present or has been exceeded.

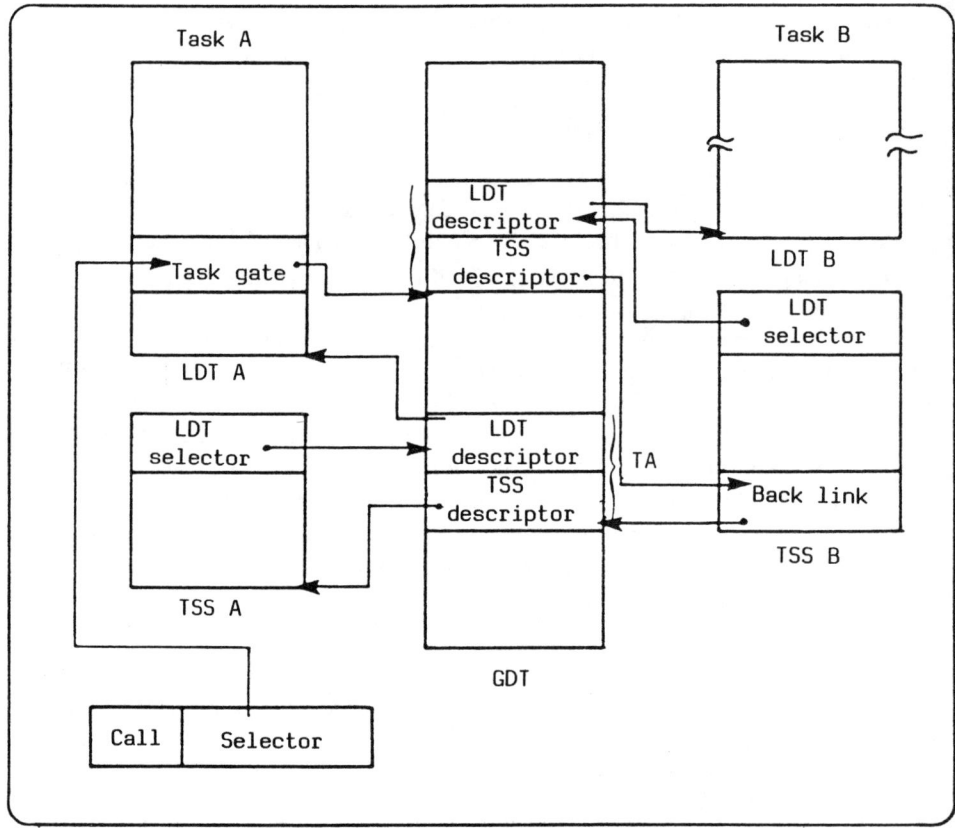

Figure 3.4.10 Relationship between two tasks

13: general protection error. This error arises when a segment bound is violated, or when the privilege level checks for an operation fail.

The complexity and sophistication of these different exception conditions will convince many users that it is best to use the 80286 under some standard operating system when operating in protected mode.

3.5 Virtual Memory

The 80286 has an address bus of 24 bits, permitting it to access 16 megabytes of real memory. The addressing capability of programs, however, can extend to a maximum of about 1 gigabyte (2 descriptor tables, each of 8192 entries, each entry describing a 64 kilobyte segment).

This discrepancy gives rise to the possibility of implementing a virtual memory scheme, in which not all allocated memory space is present in real memory at the same time. This scheme is possible because each segment descriptor has two bits, P and A, for use as follows:

- The P (Segment Present bit) is initialised to a "1" only if the segment described is present in real memory. Any access to a segment with the P bit zero causes an exception, of type 8, 10, 11 or 12, depending upon the exact circumstances of the access.
- The A (Segment Accessed) bit in a segment descriptor is set by hardware every time the processor uses this segment by loading its selector into a segment register. This bit serves two purposes in a virtual memory system:
    - if the memory manager periodically resets this bit, it may gather information about the frequency of access to segments.
    - if a segment is declared as writable, the setting of the A bit may indicate that the contents of the segment have been changed by a write operation. This means that the segment will need to be written back to a disk if its memory space is to be reused.

Together, these two indicators can be used to build a powerful virtual memory management system.

The virtual memory manager is a centrally important part of some operating systems such as UNIX. Its function is to manage a disk space and the main memory of the system, migrating segments from main memory to disk in order to make space to read other segments from disk when required by running tasks. The algorithms for management of space are important in ensuring the efficient running of the system as a whole: "thrashing", an excessive amount of copying to and from the disk, is a well-known consequence of overloading a virtual memory system.

The 80286 virtual memory system uses variable-sized segments as the entity of allocation and movement; this makes the task of the memory management software more difficult than a "paging" scheme which uses fixed-size pages (of perhaps 2 kilobytes) as the unit of allocation and swapping. Chapter 7 explains how the 80386 microprocessor provides paging in addition to variable-sized segments.

3.5.1 Strategy for Managing Segments

The simplest method of managing virtual memory is to perform "demand-driven" actions. This means that if a segment is absent and a task causes exception 11 attempting to access it, the memory manager will try to load this segment into memory. In order to make space for this segment, the memory manager may need to free or to copy back to disk a number of other segments. In order to do this, it will need to:

1. Find a number of free segments, to make a contiguous space large enough to hold the required segment.
2. Free these segments, copying them back to disk if necessary.
3. Read the desired segment into memory, marking its descriptor "present".

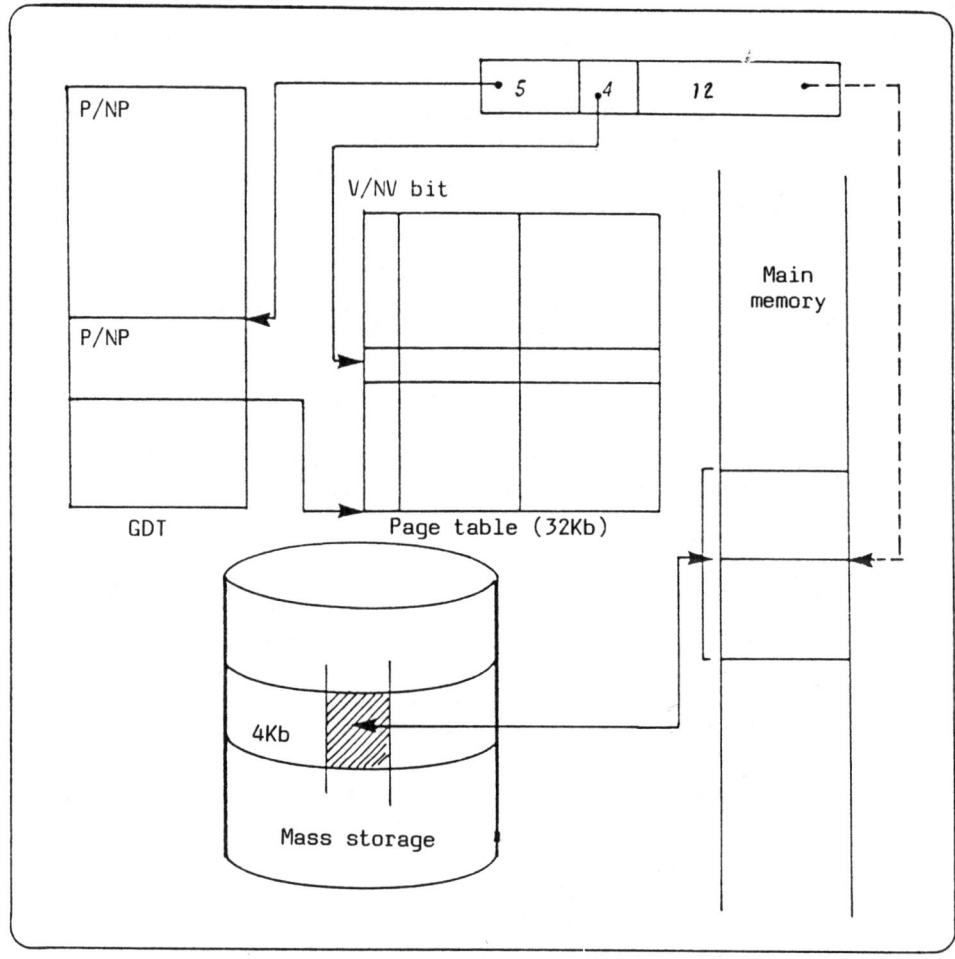

Figure 3.5.1 Virtual memory

Because of the variable-sized segmentation of the 80286, it will be necessary for the virtual memory manager to keep a record of where free segments reside in main memory, together with their sizes. In addition, it is necessary to record where segments which are not present are residing on the disk. This information might be kept in the "physical address" field of the descriptor, since this is unused by the hardware when the Present bit is zero, or might be kept in a separate set of tables corresponding to the GDT and LDT tables.

Segment rejection algorithm

In order to make space for a required segment it will usually be necessary to remove or reject one or more segments currently resident in memory. A number of different techniques are described in the specialist literature on this subject. Interesting methods use statistical and historical information to try to reject the segments which are least likely to be needed in the near future.

One common technique is to reject those segments which have been least-recently used. This can be carried out by having a procedure to keep a note of each active segment, its size and its address, and noting for each when it was last accessed (using information gathered using the A bit as described in section 3.5). This task will run periodically, and will build up a profile of each active segment, identifying candidates for rejection based upon long periods of inactivity. When space in main memory becomes short, these least-recently used segments can be rejected to make additional space free.

3.5.2 Input/Output Management

The virtual memory manager is often called when a new program is loaded, and when a task makes a request for additional memory.

The manager must contain procedures which operate at protection level zero in order to manipulate the descriptors of the segments which it is managing. Consider the case of loading a new task. It is necessary to create a memory segment which becomes the LDT. This needs inserting in the GDT a descriptor to the LDT, then inserting into the LDT the code, data and stack segment descriptors for the new task.

Certain segments must never be rejected from memory. The following segment types fall in this category:

- The GDT
- Task LDTs
- Task TSSs
- Segments containing code and data used by the virtual memory manager
- Segments containing Input/Output code
- Segments containing interrupt and error handling procedures.

Freeing memory

Once the segments to be rejected have been chosen, if any of them have been altered and need copying back to disk, the following steps are necessary:

- The P bit is cleared, indicating that the segment is absent and preventing further accesses.

- The disk address for this segment is determined and remembered, either in the descriptor table or in the parallel structure described above.
- An alias for this segment is created in the GDT to make it readable.
- The segment is written to the disk.
- The space occupied by the segment is freed.
- The alias in the GDT is released.

Loading segments

The inverse operation of loading a required segment from the disk is carried out by reversing this sequence of operations, finishing by marking the segment present by setting the "P" bit.

In larger systems, it will normally be advantageous to use different disks for memory management and normal I/O activity to ensure a reasonable performance.

4 Programming the 80286

4.1 80286 Programs

The 80286 processor in protected virtual mode presents the programmer with a complex architecture. This means that some programs originally written for the 8086 family of devices will need significant changes. However, in order to preserve as far as possible the investment in existing programs, the manufacturer has made available a number of translator and compiler tools which help transition to the new architecture. There is a major difference in the difficulty of porting individual applications or entire systems programs.

4.1.1 Applications Code

If an 8086 application has been written in a high-level language such as PL/M, C, Pascal, even Fortran, it will in most cases be ported to the 80286 simply by recompiling into an 80286 object module. This step will cause the program to use the new instructions of the 80286 and will result in a file in a format compatible with the 80286 link-editor tools. Having recompiled the application, it is linked with a new set of 80286 library routines to form an executable binary program. This procedure is particularly simple using an operating system such as UNIX, which hides the details of the individual steps in the compilation system.

In the case of applications running under Intel's iRMX/286 operating system, the situation is almost identical. Catalogued procedures are provided to perform the link-editing step in 80286 mode, using a link editor called Binder in this environment. The purpose of this program is to take the applications code and descriptions of call gates to the operating system to produce an executable binary file: it is described in section 4.4.2.

If standard products and languages are used, then, there is little difficulty in moving applications from an 8086 system to an 80286 environment.

4.1.2 System Code

A programmer writing an operating system for the 80286, or porting one from the 8086 faces much more difficulty. Operating systems are often written partly, if not totally, in assembly language. In order to use the increased power of the 80286 fully, it is necessary to rewrite parts of the system, identify the user entry points of the system, and introduce totally new code to implement the desired protection schemes. This is a significant task.

This chapter examines the facilities that are available to the assembly language programmer, and describes the software development tools used with the 80286.

4.2 Assembly Language

The assembly language of the 80286 is very largely compatible with that of the 8086, the essential differences relating to the definition of segments and of stacks. The instruction set is a superset of that of the 8086; the reader will find a complete list of the instructions in appendix A.

Since the 80286 processor is designed with a segmented architecture, it is natural to find this characteristic in the assembly language. Programs consist of a number of segments, ranging from the simplest case containing three:

code containing the program

data and

stack

Figure 4.2.1 gives an example of a simple program containing three segments.

```
                NAME        BRESENHAM
;
;------------------------------------------------------------------------
;
; Bresenham's Algorithm is used to draw a straight line on a graphics
; display by using the best pixel approximation.
;
; Works by finding the minimum error for the next point to be drawn
;
; "Algorithm for computer control of a digital plotter", J E Bresenham,
; IBM Systems Journal, Vol 4, No 1, 1965, p. 25
;
; The best results are with lines parallel to the axes or at 45 degrees.
;
;------------------------------------------------------------------------
ECR_PIX         EQU         0C8H
;
DATASEG         SEGMENT     RW
;  Define variable
DELTAY2         DW          ?              ; 2 * Delta Y
DATASEG         ENDS
;
;   Local stack segment
;
STACK           STACKSEG    20
;
;   Code Segment
```

Programming the 80286

```
;
PROG        SEGMENT     EO                      ; execute only
            ASSUME      DS:DATASEG
;
; Set the pixel at (x, y)
;
PRINT_PIX   PROC        NEAR
            ENTER       0,2*2                   ; 2 params
S_S         STRUC                               ; define params
S_BP        DW          ?                       ; old BP
S_RET       DW          ?                       ; return address
S_X         DW          ?                       ; X
S_Y         DW          ?                       ; Y
S_S         ENDS
XR          EQU         [BP-OFFSET S_RET]
            PUSHA                               ; save registers
            MOV         DX,ECR_PIX
            MOV         AX,XR.S_X
            OUT         DX,AX                   ; write X
            MOV         AX,XR.S_Y
            OUT         DX,AX                   ; write Y
            POPA                                ; restore registers
purge       XR
            LEAVE
            RET         2*2
PRINT_PIX   ENDP
;
; First quadrant
;
QUAD        PROC        NEAR
            ENTER       0,2*4
S_1         STRUC                               ; define params
I_BP        DW          ?                       ; old BP
I_RET       DW          ?                       ; return address
I_XL        DW          ?                       ; (XL,
I_YL        DW          ?                       ;       YL) -lineto-
I_XR        DW          ?                       ; (XR,
I_YR        DW          ?                       ;       YR)
S_1         ENDS
XR          EQU         [BP-OFFSET I_ARET]
Err         EQU         DX
;
; Register Usage:
; SI = X, DI = Y, CX = (XR-XL) (DeltaX)
; AX = 2*CX, BX = (YR-YL) (DeltaY)
; DX = Err
;
; Initialise
            MOV         SI,XR.I_XL              ; X
            MOV         DI,XR.I_YL              ; Y
            MOV         CX,XR.I_XR
            SUB         CX,SI                   ; CX = DeltaX
            SHL         CX,1
            MOV         AX,CX                   ; AX = 2 * DeltaX
            SHR         CX,1
```

```
                MOV     BX,XR.I_YR
                SUB     BX,DI           ; BX = DeltaY
                SHL     BX,1
                MOV     DELTAY2,BX
                MOV     Err,BX
                SUB     Err,CX          ; DX=2*DeltaY-DeltaX
; Loop CX times
QUAD_00:
                PUSH    SI
                PUSH    DI              ; Plot x,y
                CALL    PRINT_PIX
; end of line?
                DEC     CX
                JZ      QUAD_99         ; End.
QUAD_10:
; When Err >= 0, make
;    Y = Y+1
;    Err = Err - 2*DeltaX
                CMP     Err,0
                JB      QUAD_20         ; jump if < 0
                INC     DI
                SUB     Err,AX
                JMP     QUAD_10
QUAD_20:                                ; else..
                INC     SI              ; X = X + 1
                ADD     Err,DELTAY2     ; Err = Err + 2*DeltaY
                JMP     QUAD_00
QUAD_99:
purge           XR
                LEAVE
                RET     2*4
QUAD            ENDP
PROG            ENDS
                END
```

Figure 4.2.1 A simple program

4.2.1 SEGMENT Directive - Defining a Segment

A segment is defined using the following construction:

```
MY_SEG          SEGMENT         Attributes
   ; contents ..
   ; .. of segment, code or data
MY_SEG          ENDS
```

The name of the segment (MY_SEG) is obligatory, and is used subsequently to identify individual segments for operations in subsequent compilation steps. Here the assembler is reflecting the segmented structure of the machine.

The attributes of a segment specify two attributes, the type of access permitted and the method of aggregation.

Access permissions permit a segment to be typed and protected in one of a number of different ways, in order to prevent accesses caused by erroneous coding. The following types are recognised:

RO: Read Only. This segment contains only constant data, which may not be altered during program execution.

EO: Execute Only. This segment contains instructions, and access is only permitted using offsets from the Code Segment Register CS.

ER: Execute and Read. A combination of the previous two types.

RW: Read Write. The segment consists of data which may be read or altered during program execution.

Aggregation attributes refer to the link-editing phase of compilation. A number of single segments of the same type defined in assembly language files may be aggregated during the link phase to form a single larger segment when the program is executed. Any segment declared using the PUBLIC keyword may be aggregated; note the inappropriate choice of directive!

4.2.2 Definition of Data Items

There are few variations from the 8086 assembly language, the definition consisting of the form:

```
Name     TYPE    Value
```

The recognised types are:

DB Byte

DW Word

DD Double Word (32 bits), pointer or single precision real number

DQ Double precision real number

DT Extended precision real.

The value may occur in a number of different forms: an uninitialised number is written as "?", and a constant initial value may be written in binary, octal, decimal, hexadecimal or ASCII.

If a number of data items need initialising to the same value, the "DUP" construct may be used as in the example:

```
Flag    DW    3              ; 1 word, value 3
Mult    DD    20 DUP(?)      ; 20 uninitialised pointers
Line    DB    256 DUP(20H)   ; 256 bytes of space characters
```

4.2.3 Initialising Segment Registers

After having defined a segment, the programmer needs to initialise the segment registers, especially DS (the Data Segment register) and SS (the Stack Segment register). CS, the Code Segment register is not directly modifiable, but is changed only by instructions which cause a change of sequence such as CALL, JMP, INT, RET and IRET.

Registers DS and ES need to be explicitly loaded with the base address (or selector) of the segment containing the data to be processed by a particular routine. Two instructions are necessary to do this:

```
    MOV     AX,Data_Seg     ; segment selector into AX
    MOV     DS,AX           ; load selector into DS
```

Access to particular data items can now take place using the format:

```
    MOV     CX,DS:Variable
```

This format is cumbersome for frequent usage, and it is preferable to use the directive ASSUME which simplifies the appearance of the source code. If at the beginning of the procedure the following line is inserted:

```
    ASSUME  DS:Data_Seg
```

the assembler can infer the correct segment register to use when the source line is written as:

```
    MOV     CX,Variable
```

The assembler correctly generates code which will at run-time use the displacement of "Variable" from the selector in DS to access the correct memory location.

Note that loading the segment register is a much more complex operation in the 80286 in protected mode than in the 8086, since the hardware needs to check if the segment exists, if it is present in memory, if the user is sufficiently privileged to access the segment, and so on.

If a particular procedure also wishes to use a second segment, ES can be used in a similar manner by first loading it with a selector for that segment, and using an appropriate ASSUME assembler directive.

Chapter 3 described how switching between stacks defined in the TSS is an integral part of changing privilege levels; the assembler provides a directive for allocating stack segments. For example, to allocate a stack called "My_stk", the following line is necessary:

```
My_stk STACKSEG 50           ; allocate a 50-byte stack
```

Initialising the stack-specific registers may be carried out using the sequence:

```
    MOV     AX,My_stk
    MOV     SS,AX
    MOV     SP,STACKSTART My_stk    ; load the stackpointer
```

Stack segments are automatically declared to be Read-Write and PUBLIC.

4.2.4 END Directive

This directive is used to terminate the assembly of a single module. In a complex program, one assembly language module will become the main body of the program, and the END directive serves to notify the linker how to initialise the base registers when the program is loaded.

This use of the END directive may look like one of

```
END      Symbol1
END      CS:Symbol1,DS:Symbol2,SS:Symbol3
```

These uses of the directive cause the assembler to generate an initialisation sequence in the object code, which will ultimately enable a program loader to perform a far jump to the named symbol in order to start the program running, with appropriate values in DS, SS and SP if the second form is used.

4.2.5 Structure of Procedures

The 80286 assembly language supports structuring programs into procedures in order to handle returns and parameter copying. Two types of calls are available: NEAR, which does not modify the code segment register, and allows a call only within 64 kilobytes, and FAR which allows a transfer to any other address within the address space by altering the code segment register. The general structure of procedures is shown below.

```
Name     PROC     Type    WC(Expr)
  ; instructions
  ; more instructions
         RET      [num]        ; number of bytes to unstack
Name     ENDP
```

The procedure's name is given as "Name".

The Type indicates whether the procedure is accessed by NEAR or FAR calls. The RET instruction is coded as a Near or Far return according to this Type.

WC indicates the number of parameters (in words) passed when the procedure is called. This value may ultimately be used to construct a Call Gate descriptor.

Procedures normally begin with the ENTER instruction and leave via the LEAVE instruction. Accessing parameters and local variables is normally carried out using an offset from the BP register.

4.2.6 Structures, Records and Macro Instructions

The 80286 assembly language supports a data definition STRUCT which allows the definition of composite data items which are addressed via a base register (BX, BP, SI or DI), giving a similar facility to that found in high-level languages. Figure 4.2.1 contains an example of the usage of this directive.

The RECORD directive permits the definition of bit-fields within a byte or word, and the definition of methods of individual access to these bits.

Lastly, the 80286 assembler is a powerful macro-assembler with a structured control language, in which it is possible to define the most powerful of macro-instructions containing parameters and conditionals.

4.3 Modular Programming in Assembly Language

As an ideal, it is desirable to partition a large program into a number of separate modules of compilation or assembly, calling them modules. For example, a particular application might be divided in the following manner:

- A Main program, defining the principal procedure, in a code segment, and a stack segment.
- A Subroutines module, containing input/output utilities.
- A number of task modules, one module per task.
- A Data Module, consisting of constant data, variables, and external parameters.

In addition, one can define the manner in which inter-module calls are carried out, and the overall size of the system. At least two options are possible: the small model and the large model.

In the small model, a program consists of a single code segment, so that all procedure calls and returns are intra-segment and can be effected without changing the segment selector. The total size of the code cannot, however, exceed 64 kilobytes. Similarly, all data, variables and constants are contained within a single segment, which also contains the program's stack. Figure 4.3.1 shows the layout of the system tables for a small model program, showing that all references within the program can be made simply using offsets.

With the large model, full access is given to the full 16 megabytes physical address space of the 80286; this requires each reference to a subroutine or a data item to be made via a two word pointer, containing both a segment selector and an offset. In this model, all items are relocatable in main memory, since selectors and offsets do not need to change when segments are moved in memory. Figure 4.3.2 shows a large model program running.

These options are more flexible than the equivalent facilities in the 8086, and it is possible to mix the models within one application. One reasonable case would be to consider a multitasking system which used extended addressing to set up a number of tasks. Once each task was started, it might execute completely within one segment of code, processing one segment of data using the small model. The size of the overall system might, however, significantly exceed the 64 kilobyte limit.

Access to system procedures in both models is made using Call Gate descriptors, so system calls must always be made using far calls using two word pointers.

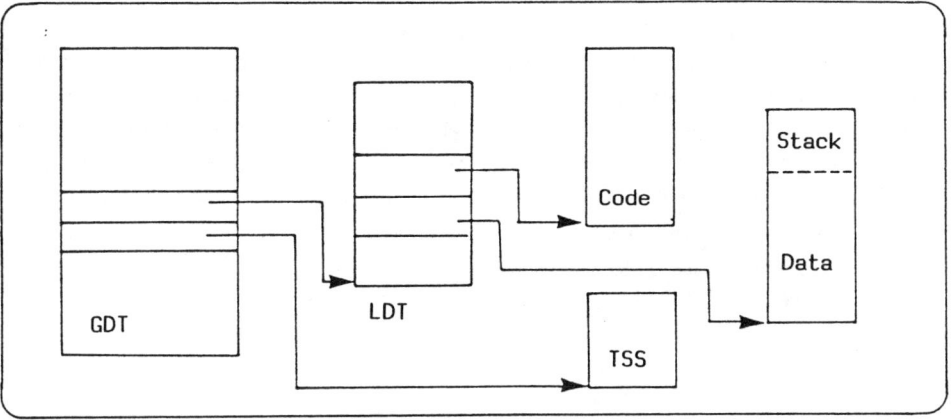

Figure 4.3.1 Small model

The following sections will consider the means provided by the 80286 assembly language to resolve the differing requirements of the two models. These facilities are relatively straightforward, and largely follow the methods used in 8086 assemblers.

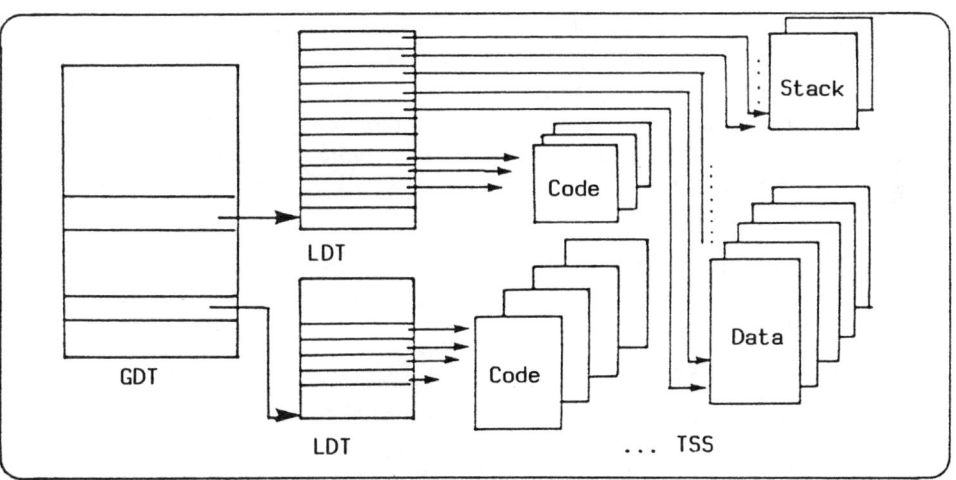

Figure 4.3.2 Large model

4.3.1 Segment Sharing

The first problem to resolve is that of sharing segment information between several compilation units. This is resolved by associating the "PUBLIC" attribute with the sharable segment. The shared segment must be given the same name in all the compilation modules, but must also be given the same access attributes. Once these conditions are realised, the link editor has the job of combining the segments from a number of object file into one logical segment in the running program.

For example, in the example below, the data areas defined in each of the source files are concatenated by the link editor to form a single logical segment with sixteen successive memory locations.

```
DataSeg SEGMENT RW PUBLIC      ; in file 1
        DW      0,1,2,3,4,5,6,7
DataSeg ENDS

DataSeg SEGMENT RW PUBLIC      ; in file 2
        DW      8,9,10,11,12,13,14,15
DataSeg ENDS
```

Note that although the segment is declared as "PUBLIC", the symbols defined within it are not themselves externally visible; to achieve this, each of them needs itself to be declared "PUBLIC".

4.3.2 PUBLIC Data and Procedures

A procedure or data item which needs to be visible outside a module is defined again using the PUBLIC keyword, in the same way as in the 8086 assembler.

To access procedures or data which have been declared PUBLIC in one module from another, it is necessary to declare them using the "EXTRN" directive. This needs a certain amount of care in its use. For example, to reference a procedure defined elsewhere, one writes:

```
        EXTRN       Proc_Name:FAR
```

replacing FAR with NEAR if the code is to be in the same segment as the current code. Once the declaration is made, the procedure is called by using the same syntax in either case:

```
        CALL        Proc_Name
```

This means that the declaration must agree with the way in which the program is linked.

For data items, the same keyword is used, but the type of the data must also be specified, for example:

```
        EXTERN      Data_Name: BYTE
```

where BYTE may be replaced by WORD, DWORD, etc. The assembler can thus check that the correct type of access is made to the data. These specifications are more useful to the programmer than to the assembler, since it is very easy to commit an error of one type or another. There is, of course, no harm in declaring a procedure as "FAR" even if it is reachable via a NEAR call.

One additional problem concerns the exact positioning of the EXTERN directive in the source program.

Two different cases exist: in the first, the programmer knows the name of the segment within which the variable that he wishes to access is defined. In this case, he places the EXTERN declaration in a pseudo segment with the same name and attributes as the definition segment, ensuring that at the moment of access, a segment register is correctly loaded to access this segment. For example:

```
Data    SEGMENT PUBLIC
        EXTERN  Var:WORD
Data    ENDS

        ASSUME  DS:Data
...
        MOV     AX,Var          ; using DS
```

In the second case, if the programmer does not know in which segment the data item is defined, the EXTERN declaration is placed outside any segment definition and the data item is accessed using ES, which can be explicitly loaded with the correct selector. For example:

```
        MOV     AX,SEG Variable
        MOV     ES,AX
        MOV     DX,ES:Variable
```

This is more complex since loading the ES register is a more expensive operation on the 80286 than on the 8086.

4.3.3 Invoking the Assembler

The assembler is executed under an operating system using the command line:

`ASM286 file [options]`

The file argument supplies the name of the assembler source file, and the options can be placed on the command line (except the INCLUDE option) or within the file, prefaced by a $(Dollar) sign. The options available are:

DEBUG: put debugging symbols in the object file
PAGELENGTH: length of pages in the listing file
PAGEWIDTH: width of pages in the listing file
XREF: request a cross reference listing
$INCLUDE: include other files in the assembly process
TITLE: title the listing pages
TYPE: type of data in the object

The assembler produces an object file (with an extension of ".OBJ") and a listing file (".LST").

4.4 Development Tools

Largely because of the number of different software structures that can be built around the 80286, a number of different tools are provided to help in the generation of binary programs.

4.4.1 Builder

Builder is a tool whose purpose is twofold: it is used to create a memory image for systems with fixed memory usage, and to provide the initial environment for a dynamic system. As its name implies, its function is to build the essential system tables (GDT, IDT, LDT and TSS) for an executable task.

For a dynamic system such as a real-time monitor, Builder will create the environment for the initialisation task, whose function is to bring the system into full operation, possibly creating additional tasks, initialising their LDT and TSS and creating appropriate additional entries in the GDT.

In the case of a static system, the application may run completely within the initial task and no other task manipulation may be necessary.

How Builder is used

Figure 4.4.1 gives a diagrammatic representation of the use of Builder. It reads a configuration file and a number of object files, either compiler or assembler output files, libraries of routines, or the output of a previous Builder run, and outputs binary files in one of a number of formats as well as map and export information.

Using Builder in system development

The following scenario suggests how the overall design of a software system based on the 80286 in protected mode might proceed:

1. The privilege levels of different program modules and their data is defined.
2. The inter-module and inter-level calls are identified.
3. The interfaces between subsystems and the visibility of software between levels are defined.
4. The individual modules are all compiled or assembled to produce 80286 object code files.
5. The different object files are combined using the Binder link-editor. This utility is capable of producing segments at only one level of protection.
6. Builder is used finally to create the system tables and to install the segment descriptors in them.

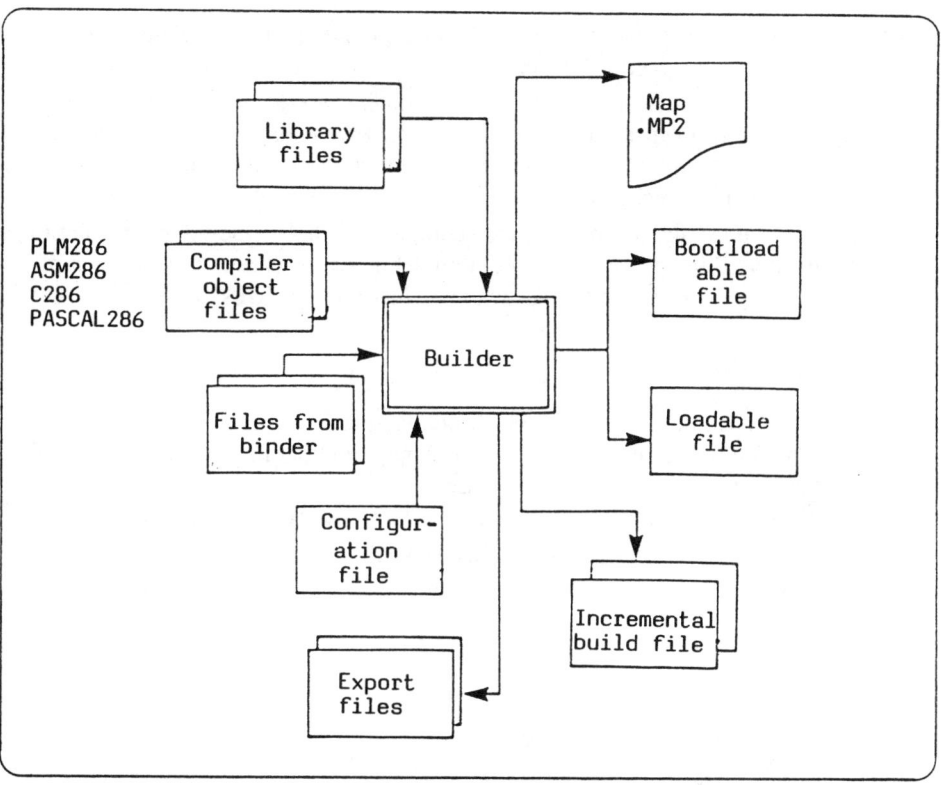

Figure 4.4.1 Using Builder

The different privilege levels of different parts of the system and the interfaces between them are defined in a configuration file input by Builder. This is a text file, created with a text editor, and contains information on:

Segments: A definition of the protection level and the access rights of individual segments.
Gates: Which routines are accessible by Gate descriptors; from what privilege levels these are visible; what WC (word count) value to insert.
Tables: Entries for the GDT, IDT, and each LDT and TSS.
Exports: Information for the Exports file; this is output by Builder, and can be linked with applications tasks to define system entry points.
Aliases: Description of aliases of system tables.
Memory: Allocation of segments in memory. Memory can be reserved, allocated, or assigned to a particular segment.

In all of these areas, Builder is capable of initialising descriptors in the finest of detail: the user can individually specify the present bit, the protection level, the access rights, the base and the limit of every segment. Sensible defaults are used to avoid the need to specify this detail for every individual segment.

Builder is capable of producing binary files in two different formats; "boot-loadable" files are ideal for programming into PROM for use when a system is powered on. This format is very simple, in that it consists only of memory images of the constituent segments and system tables.

The "loadable" file format is more complex in that it includes information about the external interfaces of the program. This format is used in loading applications tasks by operating systems such as iRMX286 and XENIX/286.

Builder configuration file

Builder reads a configuration file which defines the contents of the tables that it creates. The file is read in a single pass, and may not contain forward-references: every item must be defined before it is used.

Each part of the configuration file is introduced by a key-word: comments are introduced by a double minus sign -- (as in Ada!).

A complete Builder configuration file for ETR_286 is included in appendix C.

Gate definition

```
GATE {
  ENTRY = entry-point name
  WC    = value
  DPL   = privilege level (0..3)
  Type
  Present Bit, etc } ;
```

In this definition, the fields contain:

ENTRY: The identifier of the entry point, either a PUBLIC procedure or the name of a task's TSS (defined earlier in the file).

WC: For call gates only, indicating the number of words passed as parameters.

TYPE: Chosen from CALL, TASK, INTERRUPT, TRAP.

Table definition

```
TABLE {
  Name (
    BASE     = 24-bit value
    LIMIT    = 16-bit value
    DPL      = 0..3
    RESERVE  = (slota..slotc, ...)
    LOCATION = identifier
```

```
            Attributes = present or not
            Alias of table
            ENTRY      = (list of entries) };
```

Name: is IDT, GDT or an LDT identifier.
BASE: is either an absolute physical address or a PUBLIC identifier.
RESERVE: is used to prevent Builder using certain table entries.
LOCATION: instructs Builder to place the base and limit of the table at a particular location. From here, the table can be the subject of LGDT or LIDT instructions.
ENTRY: a list of entries in the form (index:entry). Possible entries are:
- Segment
- GATE
- TSS
- LDT

Task definition The TASK section allows a TSS to be statically defined for a task. The information in the TSS is extracted from the module in which the task code appears, or may be specified in the Builder configuration file.

```
TASK {
  Name_TSS (
    BASE     = 24-bit address
    CODE     = module name
    LDT      = LDT name
    OBJECT   = module
    DPL      = 0..3
    DATA     = module
    STACKS   = module
    LIMIT    = 16-bit value
    Presence bit
    INITIAL  -- or NOT INITIAL
    FLAGS ) };
```

Even if no TASK is defined in the configuration file, Builder creates a TSS for the initial task from information contained in the file holding the main program. This default TSS is given the name TSS?.

CODE: Defines the task's entry point.
LDT: Identifies the task's LDT.
OBJECT: The name of the module containing the code of the task.
DATA: The module containing the initial state of the task's DS.
STACKS: Definitions for stacks for all privilege levels.
INITIAL: Indicates that this is task executed on start-up.

LIMIT: Specifies the TSS size.

FLAGS: Specifies the IOPL of the task and the IF bit when the task runs.

Builder is run using a command line:

`BLD286 CF(cfile) BF(bfile) [options]`

The configuration file is contained in the "bfile", while the "cfile" may contain a list of the object files which are to be linked.

The options available are:

BOOTLOAD: Generate an absolute loadable file.

BOOTSTRAP: Generate a JMP instruction at 0FFFFF0H.

DEBUG: Place debugging code in the output.

TYPE: Data types are included in input.

TITLE: Heading for output pages.

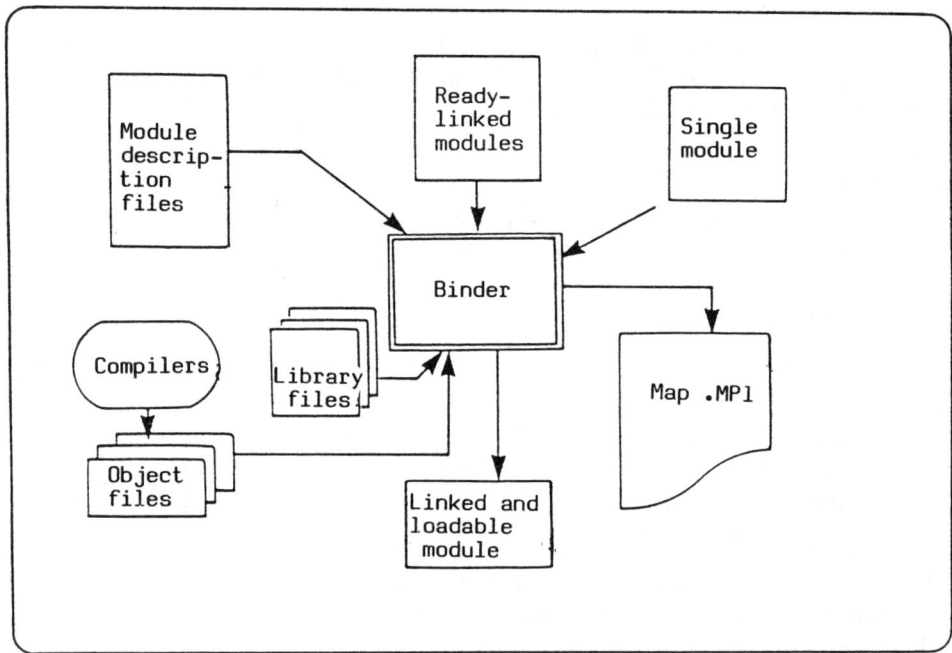

Figure 4.4.2 Using Binder

4.4.2 Binder

Binder is a tool which links object files, resolving (perhaps partially) their inter-module references, creating either a loadable file or an intermediate file suitable for further Binder or Builder runs. Its primary function is to combine PUBLIC segments at the same protection level into single segments and to fix-up the EXTRN references from one module to the PUBLIC declarations in another. Figure 4.4.2 shows how Binder is used.

Binder operates on object files generated by 80286 Assembler or by one of the Intel compilers for PL/M, C, Fortran and Pascal, and on library files and files produced by an earlier incremental bind operation.

Binder can produce output files containing multiple tasks (called Variable Task Loadable, VTL files), or only a single task (Single Task Loadable or STL).

Binder is invoked by the command line:
BND286 [list of modules] [CF(conf.file)] [options]

The list of modules to be linked is given directly or in the configuration file, specified with CF. Options are provided to define the size of the LDT, the privilege level of the task's TSS, and whether the result is to run on XENIX/286 or iRMX286.

The map file, with MP1 extension, output by Builder gives the names of all segments that have been combined, with their privilege levels and access rights.

4.4.3 Mapper

Mapper is a very useful utility which reads the binary file written by Builder or Binder and prints a map of the physical memory used by the program, identifying the following information:
- List of modules
- Map of tables
- Map of segments, identifying Gates, symbols, PUBLIC segments, and tasks
- Cross reference listing of variables and procedures.

4.4.4 LIB286 Librarian

The librarian LIB286 is a tool to manage the object files created by the assembler and different compilers. It has the following functions:
- Library creation
- Insertion and deletion of routines in library
- Listing the contents of library
- Version number management.

4.4.5 OVL286 Overlay Manager

Since the 80286 can address a very large memory indeed, one might think that overlays might have reduced in importance over earlier architectures with much more limited addressing. Unfortunately, software always seems to grow to exceed the space available, so overlays are still provided and used, even though they complicate individual programs and their operating systems and loaders.

As in most overlay schemes, OVL286 is used to define a "root" segment of a program in memory, permitting it to make calls on other parts of the program by loading them into memory as needed, so that not all parts are present at the same time.

4.5 PLM/286

4.5.1 PLM/286: A High-Level System Language

It will be evident to the reader that using the 80286 presents a number of problems for the assembly-language programmer, particularly in the area of segmentation. In addition, we have stated that the addressing modes of the processor are particularly well adapted to implementing the complex addressing needed by accesses to the structured data items used in high-level language. The 80286 is a significantly faster CPU than its predecessor, and can therefore execute high-level languages with a good performance.

A number of high-level languages are available for systems and applications programming on the 80286. PLM/286, C, Ada, Modula-2 are oriented to systems programming, while Fortran, Cobol and Pascal are oriented to applications. It is possible to build 80286 systems which have a very high proportion (over 95%) of high-level language, with only a small number of specialist routines, often concerned with input/output, or very frequently used, time-critical procedures being written in assembler.

This section introduces the PLM/286 language which is provided by Intel for system programming.

The characteristics of a systems programming language are designed to replace the need for assembly-language programming in most cases. From the point of view of its specifications, PLM/286 is a modern block structured language, providing procedures and simple data structuring facilities. Compared to well-known languages such as Pascal it is less comprehensive in its facilities, and lacks type-checking features and array access checks. On the other hand, it is a more flexible language because it gives the programmer total access to the structure of the machine, input/output ports, interrupts and addresses. In addition, it allows the use of the instructions in 80286 protected mode which are not available from standard languages.

4.5.2 Variables and Constants

Scalar data

Five types of scalar data are defined in the language: Integers (signed and unsigned), Reals, Pointers and Selectors.

Unsigned integers may be declared to be 8, 16 or 32 bits long, using the BYTE, WORD or DWORD keywords, whereas integers, declared using the INTEGER keyword, are 16-bit signed items. The keyword REAL declares a 32-bit single precision IEEE format floating-point variable, while POINTER declares a 16- or 32-bit address of another variable or a procedure. A SELECTOR is the segment part of a pointer, used to select an entry from a Descriptor Table, GDT, LDT or IDT.

The DECLARE keyword is used to introduce the name of a new variable, and a semicolon is used in PLM to indicate the end of a statement, so a declaration looks like:

```
DECLARE Name Type ;
DECLARE Tax INTEGER ;
DECLARE Address POINTER ;
```

The initialisation of variables may be carried out by the program or within the declaration. In the latter case, two modes are possible, one a "hard" initialisation using the DATA attribute, in which case the variable is a constant and will never be changed, or alternatively using the INITIAL keyword, which indicates that the variable has the specified initial value, which may be changed at run-time.

```
DECLARE V WORD DATA(5);    /* Read-Only Constant */
DECLARE W BYTE INITIAL(7); /* Initial Value -- ..ay be altered */
```

Structured data

Structured data items are constructed using collections of scalar data, grouped into either a vector or a structure.

Vectors are used to collect a number of identically typed scalar items, accessible using indices of 0 to N-1. The declaration has the form

```
Declare Name(Count) Type ;
```

For example, the declaration below declares Temp to be a 20 element vector of words:

```
DECLARE Temp(20) Word ;
```

Access to a particular item within the vector is carried out using a subscript, which may be a constant, a scalar variable, the result of a function, or an expression. The compiler does not check the validity of the index value.

Structures are used to group together data items with different types into a single entity. The declaration of a structure takes the form:

```
DECLARE Name STRUCTURE (
  Field1 Type,
  Field2 Type,
  ...
  Fieldn Type ) ;
```

For example, the example below may contain a structure to keep relevant information about a star together.

```
Declare Star      STRUCTURE (
        Name(20)    BYTE,
        Brightness  REAL,
        Coord(2)    WORD);
```

As in this case, vectors can be elements of structures, and it is possible to declare vectors of structures, but structures may not contain other structures. Access to fields within structures is made using a full stop to separate the field name from the structure name; for example, to access the first character of the name in the above structure, the construct `Star.Name(0)` is used.

4.5.3 *Program Structure*

PLM/286 is a block structured program, blocks consisting of complete procedures or blocks of statements. The outermost block is called the "Module Block". As for other block structured languages, the declaration of variables in a block gives the variables a scope equal to the block itself and any blocks it may contain. Variables may be redeclared within inner blocks (with the same name but a different type), but this practice may give rise to confusion and is not recommended. Figure 4.5.1 gives an example of block structure.

4.5.4 *Arithmetic and Logical Operators*

Traditional arithmetic operators (+, -, *, /, MOD) are provided. The operations must be carried out between data of the same type, with the exception that BYTE, WORD and DWORD operands may be mixed.

Relational operators (>, <, =, <>, <=, >=) are also provided, giving a BYTE result of "00" for false and "FF" for true. Again, the comparisons must take place between equal operand types. Pointers may be compared, but not altered by arithmetic operations.

Logical operators (AND, OR, XOR, NOT) operate on the unsigned types BYTE, WORD and DWORD.

Assignment statements are written as:

```
Variable = expression;
```

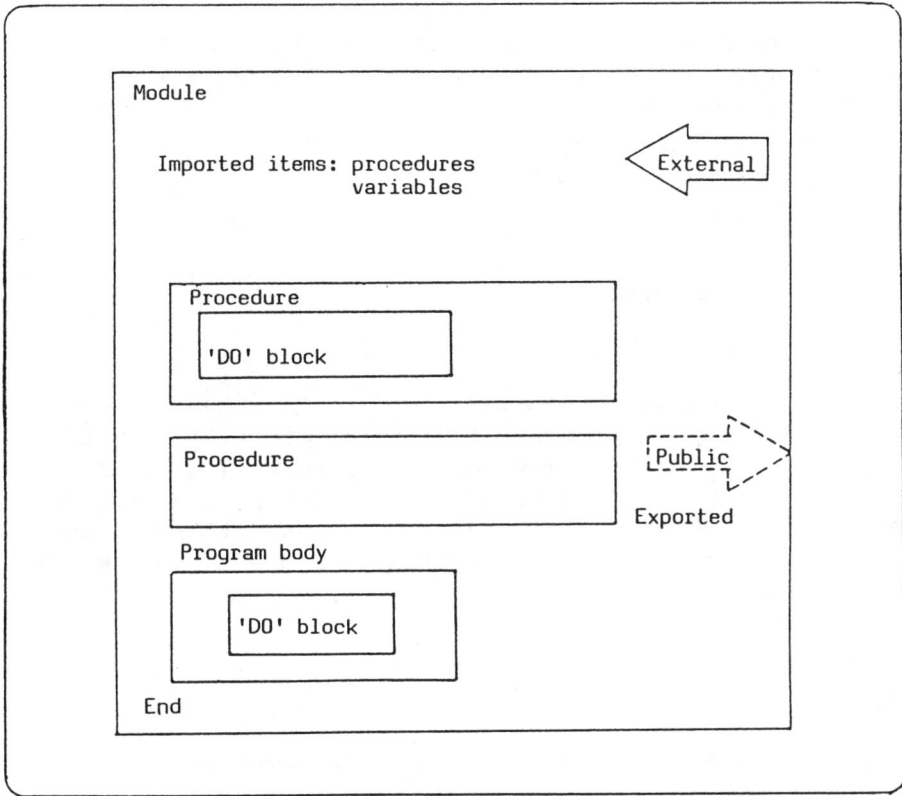

Figure 4.5.1 Block structure in a PLM/286 program

Expressions are written in the conventional manner, with the usual operator precedence, the use of parentheses, and function calls all being provided.

Constants are immediate values, expressed with the aid of different numeric bases, indicated by a letter suffix, for example

67H	Hexadecimal
67	(or 67D) Decimal
34Q	Octal
010B	Binary
'Alasdair'	String
+2.35E-16	Real value

One common way of using constants is to use literal constants which replace a literal value by a mnemonic name, for example:

DECLARE Address LITERALLY 'Waterloo Place';

These constant values are substituted in the source program by a preprocessing phase of the compiler. This feature is very useful in creating readable programs using fictitious types, for example:

```
DECLARE TRUE LITERALLY 'OFFH' ;
DECLARE BOOL LITERALLY 'BYTE' ;
DECLARE FLAG BOOL ;
```

4.5.5 Control Constructs

Simple DO block

The simple DO Block is used to sequence a number of statements between the DO and END keywords. The statements in the block may themselves be simple assignments, or they may be structured statements containing further blocks. When blocks are embedded within other blocks, it is common to present the program in an aesthetically pleasing manner by indenting the text of each block to show the structure. It is also possible to declare variables within a block. Since a DO block may take the place of a simple statement, "Statement" in the examples below may be replaced by a DO Block.

Testing

The IF statement evaluates a boolean expression and executes one of two supplied statements depending on its value. For example:

```
IF ((A > B) AND (I <= IMAX))
THEN DO;
     C = C / 7;
     D = E;
END;
```

Repetition

Two forms of repetitive statement are available, depending on whether the number of iterations is known before the loop is started.

The DO Loop performs a fixed number of repetitions of a block of statements. For example, in the case below, J must be an integer type (BYTE, WORD or INTEGER), and Min, Max and Interval must be of the same type. If the "BY Interval" is omitted, the implicit step is 1.

```
Sum = 0;
DO J = Min TO Max BY Interval;
     Sum = Sum + X(J) ;     /* sum a part of a vector */
END;
```

The WHILE Loop repeats a sequence of statements until some condition becomes false. For example, the loop below finds the first occurrence of a zero value in a vector.

```
Try = 0;
DO WHILE ((Try < Size) AND (Vec(Try) <> 0));
     Try = Try + 1;
END;
```

Multiple selection

The last form of control instruction is a variation in test function, and implements a multiway branch. It is used to select and execute a statement or group of statements depending upon an index variable which may take a value between 0 and K-1, where K different statements are supplied.

```
DO CASE Variable;
   Statement0;          /* Executed if Variable = 0 */
   Statement1;          /* Executed if Variable = 1 */
   Statement2;          /* Executed if Variable = 2 */
   Statement3;          /* Executed if Variable = 3 */
END;
```

The implementation is simple-minded, and the compiler does not test to ensure that the expression lies within acceptable bounds. For this reason, it is often suggested that the statement be preceded by a preliminary test.

4.5.6 Subprograms

Two different types of subprograms are defined in PLM/286, procedures and functions which can return a scalar value.

Declaration of subprograms

In the example declaration below, the arguments of the procedure are optional, and must all be scalar items. If passing structures or vectors is required, they may be passed by reference by passing a pointer to the structure. TYPE is also optional, meaning when present that the subprogram is to return a value. ATTRIBUTE specifies the non-exclusive attributes of a procedure: REENTRANT, INTERRUPT, EXTERNAL or PUBLIC. For example:

```
Name: PROCEDURE (Arg1, Arg2, Arg3) TYPE    ... ;
```

After the procedure heading is defined, the type of each argument must also be defined. These declarations will be followed by a declaration of the procedure's local variables, followed by the actual code of the procedure.

Return from a procedure is effected automatically on reaching the end of the procedure. In addition, it is possible to cause an explicit return from anywhere within the procedure using a return statement, which can also indicate the value to be returned from the function:

RETURN expression;

Figure 4.5.2 shows the general layout of a function.

```
HCF:    PROCEDURE(x, y) INTEGER PUBLIC REENTRANT;
        /* Declaration of arguments */
        DECLARE x INTEGER;
        DECLARE y INTEGER;
        /* Declare local variables */
        DECLARE Temp WORD;
        /* Body of subprogram */
        DO;
             . . . .
        END;
        RETURN Temp + 1;
        END HCF;
```

Figure 4.5.2 General layout of a subprogram

Calling subprograms

Depending on their type, subprograms are called using the CALL statement, or by including their name in an expression. The values of the actual parameters supplied in the call replace the formal parameters mentioned in the subprogram definition. The compiler checks both the number and the types of the parameters. The following example shows both a procedure and a function call:

CALL Cv_Hex(P_Zone, N);

RESULT = (Func(3) * Func(N)) * 5;

It is convenient to place the subprograms within the source file before their usage. Procedures are permitted to contain further procedure definitions within themselves, in the customary block-structured manner.

Included procedures

A number of pre-defined procedures and functions, called "built-ins", are available to perform operations which otherwise would need to be written in assembly language. These are:

MOVB/MOVW Transfer a string of bytes or words
FINDB/FINDW Find first matching value
CMPB/CMPW Compare strings
SKIPB/SKIPW Find first non-matching value
SETB/SETW String initialisation
XLAT Table translation
LENGTH Size of a table (in number of elements)
LAST Index of last element in a table
DOUBLE Conversion of BYTE into WORD or WORD into DWORD
LOW Returns the low-order half of a BYTE, WORD or DWORD
HIGH Returns the high-order half of a BYTE, WORD or DWORD
FLOAT Converts INTEGER into REAL
INT Converts BYTE or WORD into INTEGER
FIX Converts REAL into INTEGER
SIGNED Conversion of WORD into INTEGER
UNSIGN Conversion of INTEGER into WORD
ABS Absolute value of REAL
IABS Absolute value of INTEGER.

4.5.7 BASED Variables

As mentioned above, PLM/286 does not permit passing structured arguments into subprograms, and the only way of returning a value is to have a function return a scalar. It is necessary, then, to provide a means for a subroutine to access structured data and to enable it to modify such structures. The notion of a BASED variable provides one solution to these problems.

The caller passes a pointer to the required structure (or to a scalar), using an "@" sign in front of the parameter name.

In the called routine, a single pointer parameter is available, containing the address of the designated scalar, structure or vector. Within the routine, a fictitious variable is declared to be BASED on the pointer parameter, forming a pro-forma for the variable. A BASED variable, then, is characterised by the two declarations:

Pointer: address of actual data

Fictitious variable: description of data item.

In the example below, Ptr_Df is the formal parameter in the procedure header, and Df is the definition of the structure to which this pointer leads:

```
DECLARE Ptr_Df POINTER;
DECLARE Df BASED Ptr_Df STRUCTURE (
  C WORD;
  P POINTER);
```

The type of the fictitious BASED variable is not checked to be consistent with that of the actual parameter, so care is needed when coding using this facility.

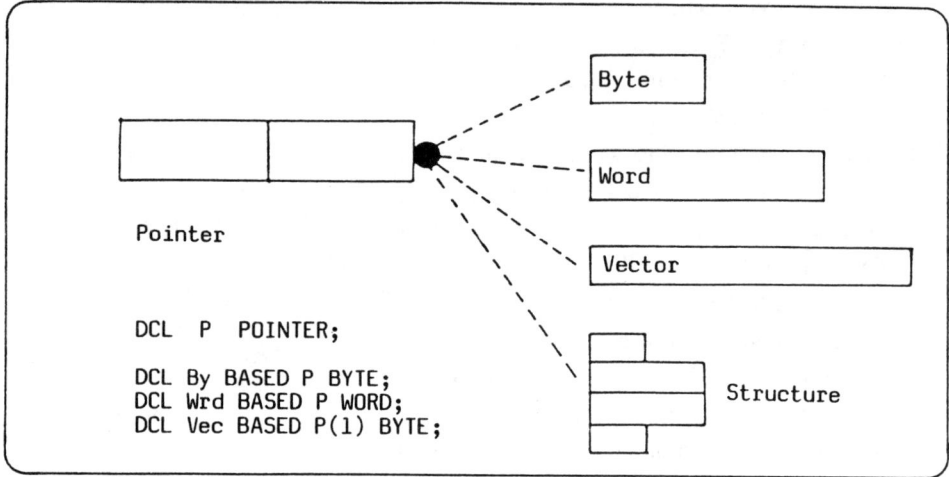

Figure 4.5.3 BASED variables

This technique can also be used when it is required to operate on a number of real structures which all share one definition.

A number of Built In operations are available to manipulate pointers:

BUILDPTR concatenates a selector and an offset to create a pointer;

SELECTOR$OF returns the selector of a pointer;

OFFSET$OF returns the offset part of a pointer.

4.5.8 Modular Programming

PLM/286 supports modular programming by allowing the use of both variables and procedures from outside their defining module.

Variables may be shared between modules by placing a PUBLIC definition in one module, and an EXTERNAL definition in all others, using the same name and types in all modules. For example:

```
DECLARE Tax_Rate WORD PUBLIC;   /* in defining module */

DECLARE Tax_Rate WORD EXTERNAL;
         /* in all other modules accessing variable */
```

These PUBLIC and EXTERNAL declarations must be made in the outermost block of the module.

PUBLIC subroutines and functions are declared in the obvious manner; in order to use such a procedure from within a second module, this module must contain an EXTERNAL procedure declaration, which declares the types of formal parameters and contains no code. This is demonstrated in figure 4.5.4.

```
                        Definition:
p1: PROCEDURE(a1, p) PUBLIC;
   DECLARE a1 WORD;
   DECLARE p POINTER;
   DECLARE b BASED p WORD;
   ...
   ... /* procedure code */
END p1;

DECLARE X(20) BYTE PUBLIC;
   ...
                        Usage:
p1: PROCEDURE(a1, p) EXTERNAL;
   DECLARE a1 WORD;
   DECLARE p POINTER;
END p1;

DECLARE X(20) BYTE EXTERNAL;

   ...

   CALL p1(2, @v)
```

Figure 4.5.4 Accessing variables and procedures from other modules

4.5.9 System Programming

Interrupt service routines are declared in PLM/286 by nominating them using the INTERRUPT n declaration, where n is the interrupt number to be served. As defined by the hardware, interrupt procedures may not have parameters. The use of this directive causes the compiler to generate code for saving and restoring the register state on entry to and exit from the procedure. The interrupt descriptor table is built by the Builder program, or by the program loader in a dynamic environment.

The built-in operation WAIT$INTERRUPT causes the IRET instruction to be planted. This permits the coding of interrupt tasks which need to be structured as infinite loops awaiting the occurrence of their interrupt.

The REENTRANT attribute in a procedure declaration causes the compiler to allocate space for the procedure's local variables dynamically on the stack, so that every invocation of the procedure has a separate copy of its variables. Reentrance allows PLM/286 procedures to call themselves recursively or to be used in a number of different contexts, such as two different tasks or within two nested interrupt procedures.

Input/output is directly possible in PLM/286 by using the INPUT or OUTPUT built-ins. It is possible to carry out byte or word operations, and to perform a repeated operation on a string of operands. The underlying hardware will continue, of course, to prevent direct access to input/output ports if the tasks priority level is inconsistent with its IOPL bits in the flag register.

Lastly, variables may be redefined, to permit the same data item to be interpreted in one of a number of different types, using the AT keyword. For example, if the same memory word were to be used sometimes as a segment selector and sometimes as an unsigned value, the following declarations might be made:

DECLARE S Selector;

DECLARE W WORD AT(@S);

4.5.10 System Management

The system aspects of the 80286 chip may be directly accessed from PLM/286 using more built-in operations. Once again, these operations are privileged, and their use will only be permitted by the hardware if the task is running at privilege level 0.

TASK$REGISTER is a variable which makes the selector of the current TSS available. It may be read or written.

SAVE$GLOBAL$TABLE and RESTORE$GLOBAL$TABLE may be used to manipulate the Global Descriptor Table Register, and SAVE$INTERRUPT$TABLE and RESTORE$INTERRUPT$TABLE may be used to save or alter the value of the Interrupt Descriptor Table Register.

A variable LOCAL$TABLE, of type selector, is used to contain the selector of the Local Descriptor Table. Again, it may be read or written.

A number of procedures are built in to permit the manipulation and interrogation of segment descriptors.

GET$ACCESS$RIGHTS(Selector) returns a WORD which contains the access rights or permissions of the selected segment. In the same way, GET$SEGMENT$LIMIT(Selector) returns the limit of the selected segment in a WORD. In both cases, the ZERO variable, representing the state of the 80286 Z flag, is set to indicate whether the segment is visible.

SEGMENT$READABLE and SEGMENT$WRITABLE are BOOLEAN functions provided to indicate whether the relevant access is permitted to a particular segment.

The WORD variable gives the value of the MSW of the 80286 CPU.

Lastly, ADJUST$RPL(Selector) adjusts the RPL of a segment in order to request a less privileged permission.

4.5.11 Compilation Modes

The compilation of a PLM/286 module generates a number of sections in the object module:

- A CODE section contains the instructions and the register initialisations for the module.
- A DATA section contains most variables, apart from parameters and those defined as constants.
- A STACK section will contain the area destined to provide the stack segment for the running code, and may be contained within the DATA section.
- A CONST section will contain the values of all variables initialised using the DATA keyword. Depending on whether RAM or ROM options are selected, this section will ultimately appear in the CODE or DATA segment of the program.

Depending upon the eventual size of an application (in terms of the 64 kilobyte segment limit), the user will choose a memory model (SMALL, MEDIUM, COMPACT or LARGE), and the compiler will generate the appropriate code to manage segment registers and pointers. The default model is LARGE.

PLM/286 offers the concept of a sub-system. This is a useful means of optimising system size, and means that while each task may be implemented in SMALL mode, communications may be carried out among tasks and between a task and the underlying operating system using the LARGE model.

4.5.12 Invoking the Compiler

The compiler is invoked using a command line that specifies a file and optional switches.

`PLM286 file [options]`

Options are also available (some exclusively) from within the module text using, for example, the form $DEBUG. Common options available are:

SMALL Use Small compilation model
MEDIUM Use medium compilation model
COMPACT Use compact compilation model
LARGE Use large compilation model
DEBUG Include debugging code in object file
OPTIMISE(n) Specify level of object optimisation permitted

RAM/ROM Specify where constants are to be placed
XREF Require a cross-reference listing
TYPE Specify type of data in object file
$IF/$ENDIF Conditional compilation
INTERFACE Specify calling-sequence compatibility with C
$INCLUDE Include other source file.

The PLM/286 programs in this book (particularly in chapter 5) were compiled on an IBM PC model XT with 512 kilobytes of memory and a 10 megabyte hard disk.

5 Operating Systems

The operating systems that run on the 80286 fall into two broad classes, real-time operating systems and operating systems for applications and development. In this chapter, we consider one standard operating system in each class, and discuss aspects of the design of special-purpose operating systems with the aid of a substantial example.

5.1 Real-time Operating Systems

The most widely known operating system in the real-time category for the 80286 is iRMX/286, developed by Intel from iRMX86 on the 8086. It is a transition product, as its principal innovation is to provide an address space of 16 megabytes while preserving the primitives present in iRMX86. New primitive operations have been introduced to cope with memory management, and small modifications to the iRMX86 primitives have taken place. The major functional difference in the system is that the tables defined in the 80286 CPU protected virtual mode are managed and system accesses via gates are permitted.

As an operating system, iRMX286 uses some of the additional features of the 80286. Only two privilege levels are provided, level 0 for the system and level 3 for all applications. With this protection, the system is much more robust than is possible on the 8086 processor, and since the 80286 system can cope with a greater range of errors, it can be used to implement high-reliability products.

The primitives which have changed most from iRMX86 are the kernel procedures, other layers remaining largely unchanged.

5.1.1 Memory Management

Memory is addressed throughout using segments, and segment selectors do not point directly to real memory, but act as indices into the system tables. The segmentation management routines allow an application to request contiguous memory in sizes up to 16 megabytes.

5.1.2 Object Management

The iRMX286 system supports the management of up to about 8000 objects, each of which appears as a reference within the GDT. Objects are protected since the system controls their availability, using the underlying hardware to cause a protection error exception on any unauthorised access. Applications can ask the system to alter the access bytes of their own objects, such as memory segments, to "Data segment" or "Code segment", or to alter their "conformant" state.

5.1.3 Descriptor Management

The system provides routines for the application to create descriptors in the GDT. These descriptors may describe pre-allocated memory areas, and may then have their access rights altered by the application. This mechanism is used to create aliases to data segments, and when creating segments for memory-mapped input/output areas.

Descriptor creation requires a physical address and a size and allocates the descriptor by incrementing a "high" marker in the GDT. The system returns a selector which is used for further manipulations of the segment. For example:

```
desc = rqe$create$descriptor(addr_24, size, @err);
```

The descriptor created thus has read/write access. It can be used to declare BASED variables in PLM/286, for example:

```
DECLARE desc SELECTOR;
DECLARE buffer BASED desc (1024) BYTE;
   ...
buffer(1) = val;
```

5.1.4 Exceptions

Programming errors in the 80286 are handled by interrupts which cause entry to a routine indicated by an entry in the IDT. Within iRMX286, individual exceptions can be defined to cause entry to a system procedure, to a user-specified routine, or to be ignored.

5.1.5 Extensions to Operating System Primitives

The final point of interest in iRMX286 is the way in which additional facilities may be added to the operating system. Extra routines are introduced by adding CALL GATE entries into the GDT, using an interactive configurator program. Figure 5.1.1 shows how a new system call could be added.

The user notifies the operating system of additional gates by calling the new primitive routine rqesetos$extension. In the following example, 350 is the number of the GATE which is reserved for enhancing the system.

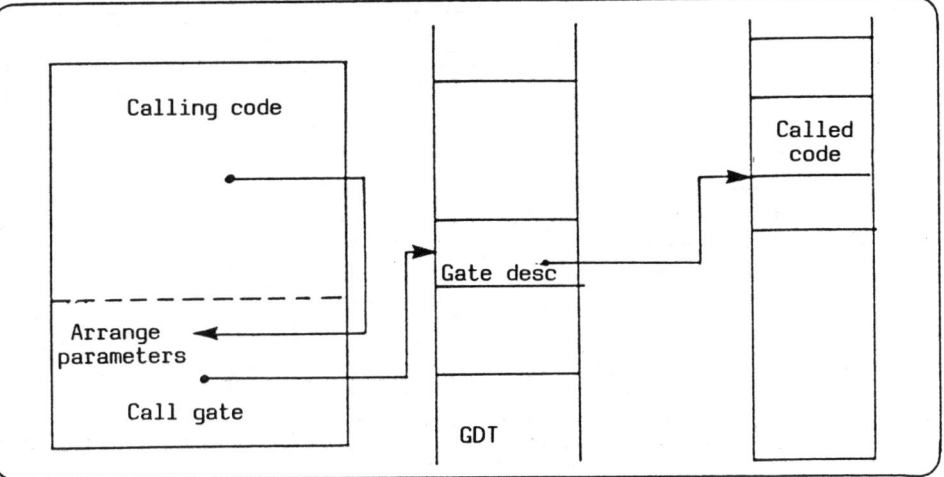

Figure 5.1.1 Adding iRMX286 primitives

```
proc$350: PROCEDURE (p1, p2) EXTERNAL;
  DECLARE (P1, P2) WORD;
END;

CALL rqe$set$os$extension(350, @proc$350, @err);
```

5.2 XENIX/286: A Development Environment

A second standard operating system to consider is Xenix/286. As for iRMX286, Xenix has been enhanced from the 8086, the changes being confined to the kernel of the system, substantially preserving its external interfaces.

The key element of the implementation is again the GDT which contains pointers to the central elements of the system and the kernel code and data.

For each process (in the UNIX sense), a TSS and a LDT is defined. These define the UNIX "u" structure which contains information relevant to a running process, such as its memory allocation, the state of its open files, and pointers to the process's entries in various system tables. Figure 5.2.1 shows the system tables within a Xenix/286 system.

5.3 Operating System Design

This chapter cannot cover the complete design of a full operating system, but discusses some important concepts and the way in which the hardware and software

118   *80286 and 80386 Microprocessors*

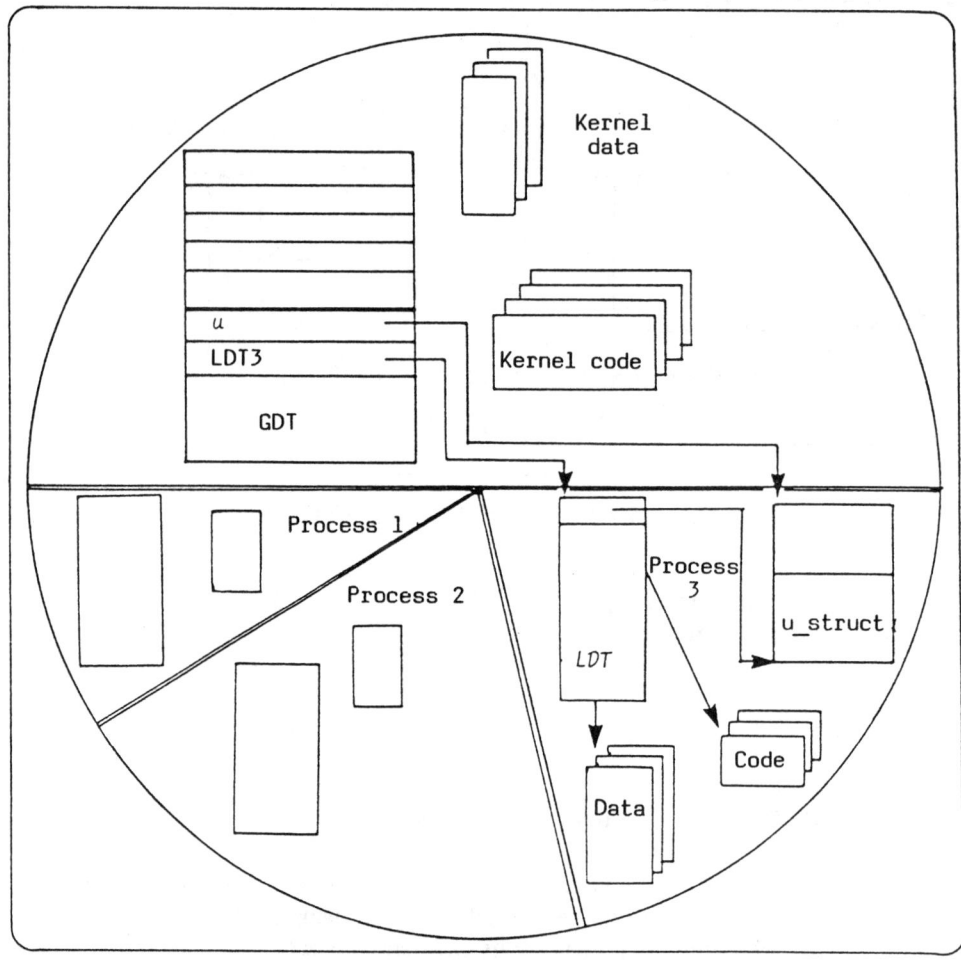

Figure 5.2.1 Xenix/286 organisation

facilities of the 80286 can be used to implement these ideas. The aim of the presentation is to give a flavour of the thought which went into the design of the 80286 CPU, and to persuade the reader that operating system tools can be designed upon a firm foundation. It is important to realise that since this processor breaks new ground in the facilities which it provides, the best use of the CPU will come in those systems whose software best exploits these facilities.

An operating system can be defined as a structure consisting of a number of layers of software, whose purpose is to offer the user a convenient means of using a computer system, and managing the full set of system resources, both physical and logical.

The functional characteristics of an operating system depend heavily on the designer's overall conception, on the types of applications envisaged, and the demands that they will make. For example, is the system to be single-user, multitasking, or multi-user? Must the task structure be altered dynamically, or can it be built once, statically? What sort of input/output devices (what performance, synchronous, async, novel) must be supported?

Many more questions need to be examined in the design of a full system, but a certain number of standard functions have been defined and are found in most current operating systems:

- A scheduler allocates one (or more) processor to executable tasks or programs.
- Synchronisation and communication between tasks is provided.
- Internal and external interrupts are handled.
- Standard interfaces to input/output devices are provided to the application by input/output drivers software.
- A numeric coprocessor (if present) is handled transparently.
- A manager allocates real memory.
- Virtual memory, or overlays, are handled.
- Programs are loaded and run on demand.

Looking back at the description of the 80286 hardware facilities, we see that the whole design of the processor is suited to implementing these software concepts in hardware, permitting the user to create an elementary operating system kernel providing these facilities.

5.3.1 Tasks

A task is commonly defined as the execution of a sequence of operations in a particular context. As opposed to a program which may have a number of different representations, such as the source, the object file, its state in execution, and so on, a task is defined as the code which is being executed by the machine at a particular instant. The important point of this definition is the word "context". 80286 tasks, iRMX tasks, and UNIX tasks differ from one another in the sense that the context in each case is different.

The word "task" is used in a multitasking system, in which a number of different programs can execute in turn, each associated with a set of register contents, a priority, a memory allocation, each protected from any possible malfunction in another program.

A runnable program is created using either a high-level language compiler or an assembler. Creation of a task, consisting of associating the code with its own resources, is done by reference to the information stored in the program file describing its requirements and initialisation. This information is stored in the program by configuration tools, link editors, Builder or Binder.

The memory segmentation provided by the 80286 acts as the primary focus for task construction. The partition of an application into logical segments, for code, data or stack, provides a straightforward means of grouping objects that belong to one specific task.

The task concept is fundamental to the 80286 architecture. Perhaps the most explicit example of this is the Task State Segment (TSS), which contains the hardware context (general registers, LDT, privilege levels, and stacks) defining the code and data for a running task.

One of the primitive hardware operations of the 80286 is its rapid switching between tasks, using task gates. Figure 5.3.1 shows a system with 4 tasks, showing how each task has a different set of segments, each described by an entry in the task's own LDT.

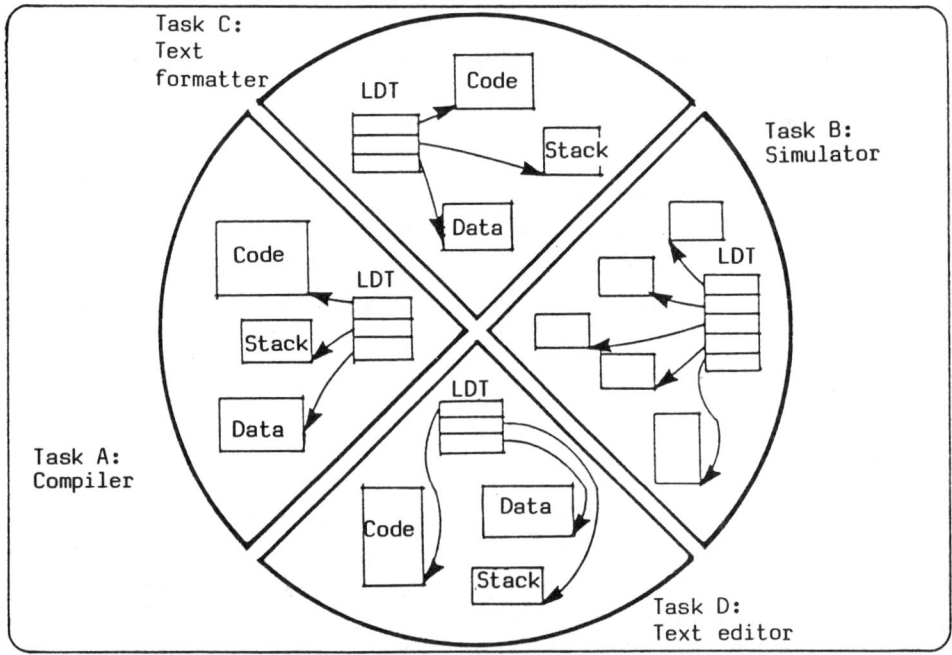

Figure 5.3.1 Separation of data between tasks

Figure 5.3.1 also shows clearly how the separation or isolation of one task from another is achieved; figure 5.3.2 show how data and code can be shared between a number of tasks using descriptors in the GDT rather than the LDT.

5.3.2 Levels of Privilege

Privilege levels are used within a task to protect trusted procedures, and to ensure that they suffer no interference from other software running in the task. This is a

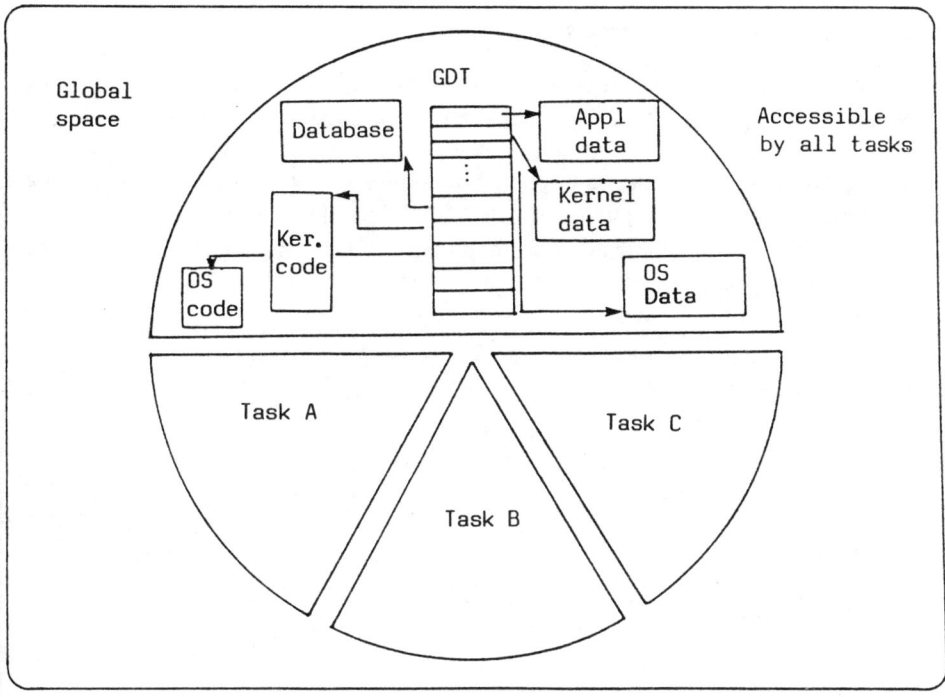

Figure 5.3.2 Sharing information between tasks

valuable function, but it is even more valuable to consider protection in a system in which applications programs are running under an operating system. In this type of system architecture, any procedure within any of the tasks is free to make requests of the operating system. The operating system facilities thus appear as part of the context of all the active tasks.

This idea gives us a typical configuration in which a number of procedures are known to be reliable and critical in the sense that they access sensitive data such as control blocks, semaphores, and so on. The use of different privilege levels is useful to add reliability, by protecting system data areas and ensuring that they are only altered by the appropriate procedures within the operating system. This type of protection will mean that operating system procedures execute at a more privileged level (that is, with a lower privilege number, in the 80286) than applications code.

Figure 5.3.3 shows an example of the levels of privilege at different layers of a system. This particular example has four levels, with the applications program running at the outermost, least privileged level.

5.3.3 Structures of Programs

Figure 5.3.3 shows a system structure illustrating how the operating system forms a part of an applications task, protected by the privilege mechanism. In this type of structure, the individual tasks are seen as concurrently-running processes. In a large system, some tasks may contain activities solely related to the operating system, such as input/output tasks, while others run applications code.

For many years, mainframe systems and minicomputers have provided at least two levels of privilege, "user" and "system" mode.

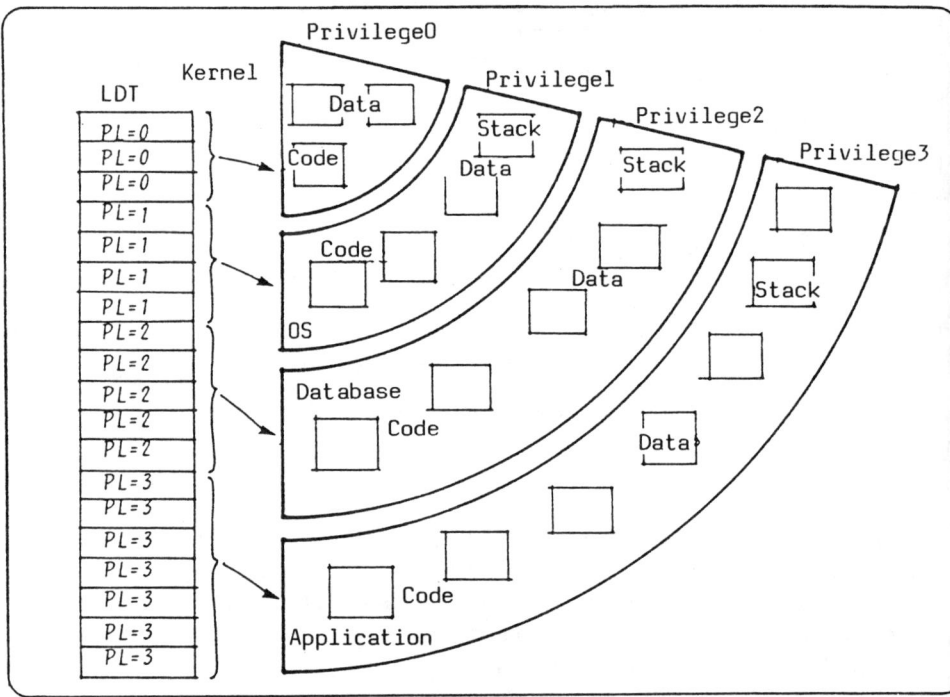

Figure 5.3.3 System with four privilege levels

5.3.4 Configuring Software Systems

When constructing an application or a stand-alone operating system, the developer needs to specify his configuration and real memory usage. Figures 5.3.4 and 5.3.5 show how the Builder and Binder programs are used in construction of static or dynamic systems. A dynamic system is capable of loading applications dynamically, and needs to contain code for task creation and memory management; a static system, in which the task structure is fixed at load-time, can be much simpler.

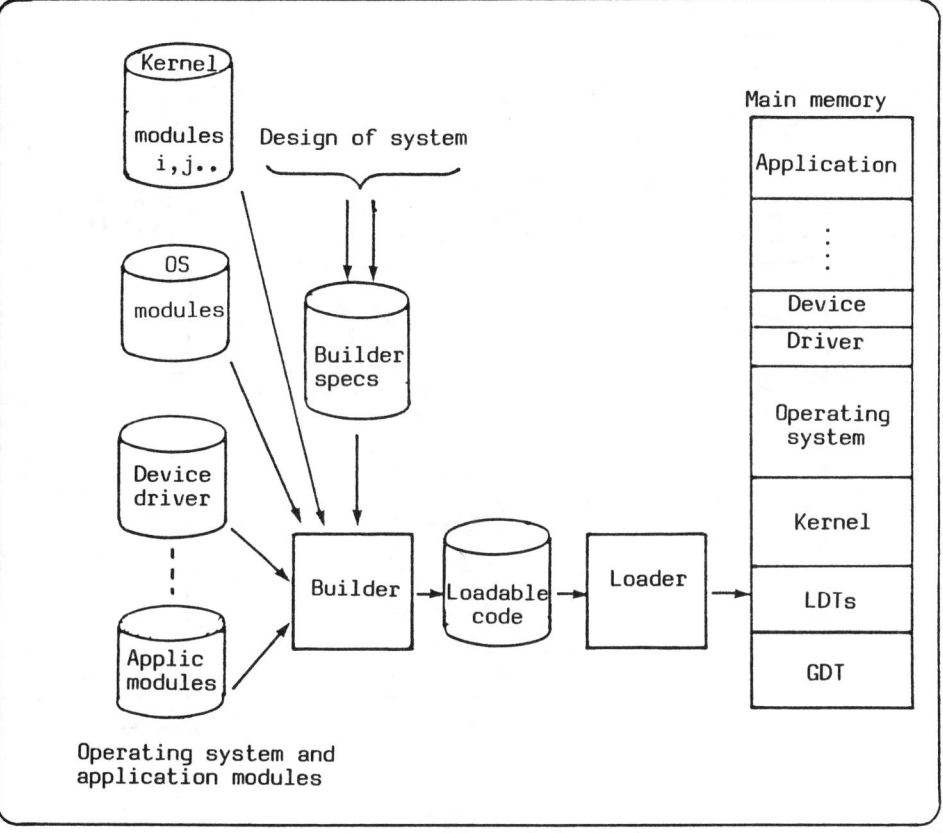

Figure 5.3.4 Constructing a static system

This section has introduced some of the decisions that need to be taken in the design of an operating system: we illustrate the application of some of these principles by introducing the design of a real-time executive ETR_286.

5.4 ETR_286: A Real-Time Toolbox

The aim of this section is to show how a real-time executive is specified, and how it may be written. We discuss the specification of ETR_286, the implementation of some of its modules, link editing and configuration using Binder and Builder, and some directions for future enhancement.

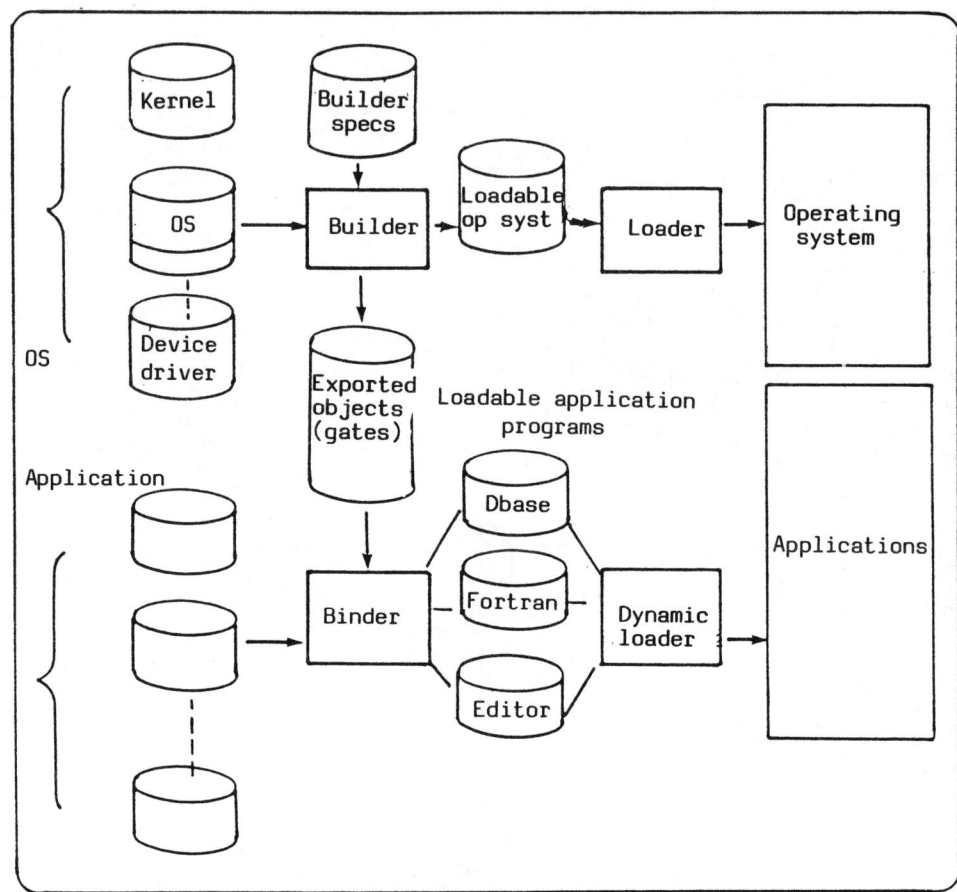

Figure 5.3.5 Constructing a dynamic system

5.4.1 Specification

The aim of the executive is to act as a simple demonstration of real-time mechanisms and their implementation on the 80286 CPU. ETR_286 is a single-processor monitor capable of supporting a number of concurrent tasks.

ETR_286 is non-preemptive, which means that a task continues running until it makes an explicit request. Other types of system may preempt running tasks on clock interrupts or when higher-priority tasks are unblocked.

ETR_286 has very simplistic error handling: on the occurrence of an exception, the error number is printed; no attempt is made to remedy the situation, and a HALT instruction is executed.

ETR_286 does not contain peripheral drivers, although it provides a framework within which these can be implemented.

ETR_286 manages the following object types:

- Tasks (to a maximum of 32)
- Events (maximum of 12 per tasks)
- Messages and a mailbox specific to tasks
- Memory areas (allocated by a "Buddy" system)
- Timeouts and task timing.

A set of global semaphores are to be implemented in a future version.

ETR_286 is configured by a descriptor file which specifies the tasks, their entry points, and the size of a message-arrival list. Another section of the configuration file describes input/output drivers.

From the applications viewpoint, code runs at privilege level 3 and uses call gates to access system routines. These gates appear in level 3 and contain the usual Word Count field specifying the count of parameters for each procedure. ETR_286 code itself runs at privilege level 0.

A selection of the ETR_286 source listings is included as appendix C: these may be read in conjunction with the descriptions in this chapter. In particular, the listings *etrt0*, *etrt1*, and *etrtf* show three simple tasks which exercise the monitor's facilities.

5.4.2 Task Scheduling

A scheduler is a procedure which allocates the processor to a particular task. In ETR_286, this procedure is called whenever the current task relinquishes the CPU, either by an explicit timeout call, or by invoking another primitive which cannot complete, such as attempting to receive a message which has not yet arrived.

In this version, ETR_286 manages 32 tasks, each of which has an implicit priority, its task number. The task with the lowest number has the highest priority, with tasks 0 to 7 being reserved to service the 8 interrupts possible from a single 8259A Priority Interrupt Controller. The initial task initialises the monitor and its tables. The *etrinit* listing gives the code for this process. The background task is the last to be declared. It is active when no other task is ready to run.

A number of Static Task Descriptors (STD) are defined, one per task. Each task accesses its own descriptor using the variable name vx_std_nn, where nn varies from 0 to 31. A pointer vx_std points to a table of addresses of each individual descriptor. The *etrcnf* listing initialises these STD structures, in the format declared in the *etrstr.h* listing: each contains the following information:

- task number
- priority (same as task number)
- size of the level 0 stack

o size of the fifo structure for messages awaiting delivery: -1 if no fifo is required.
  o name of task (8 bytes).

The system maintains a double word vx_tready containing the state (ready or blocked) of each of the 32 tasks, 1 bit per task, with "1" indicating ready. The scheduler's task is to run the highest-priority task that is ready, which is the task with the rightmost "1" in this variable. Finding this task is accomplished by the routine sx_fnd_tready in the *etrut* module.

Switching between tasks is performed in the only assembly language module, *etrsched.s86*, using the procedure SEG_SWITCH_TSS. This jumps to the virtual address of the new TSS, using a descriptor fabricated in a double word on the stack. To aid this process, the TSS of each task has a descriptor in the GDT.

5.4.3 Task Descriptor

Each running task is described within ETR_286 by a structure called the Operational Task Descriptor (OTD), declared as dx_otd in the *etrstr* declarations, containing the following fields:

num: task number

prior: priority of task (= task number here)

status: state of task (ready, waiting, etc.)

event: task's pending events

ce: scheduling counter

ctick: number of clock ticks in this task

p_fifo: pointer to the list of pending messages

p_otd: pointer to task's own OTD

next: pointer to next OTD, if linked (suspended by timeout)

prev: pointer to previous OTD, if linked.

The state word of the task gives information on the state of the task, indicating if the task is suspended, waiting for an event or a message, and if so whether the wait can timeout.

Within the GDT, there exists a sequence of 128 task-related entries, starting with segment 50. There are four entries for each task, the entries containing:

LDT: the LDT of the task

TSS: the task's TSS

OTD: an alias for the task's OTD

FIFO: an alias for the task's message fifo.

The procedure sx_create_task, in the *etrmain* listing, is used to create a task. The procedure creates the different memory areas by calling sx_get_memx which returns the address of a block of memory. Once the memory segments have been created, the two alias descriptors are entered in the GDT, with read and write access, and pointers to these zones are placed in the OTD.

Note that the TSS and LDT entries are created statically by the Builder program (see the *etr286.bld* listing), although it is still necessary to reserve the areas for the ODT and the timeout list. Figure 5.4.1 shows the principal tables in ETR_286.

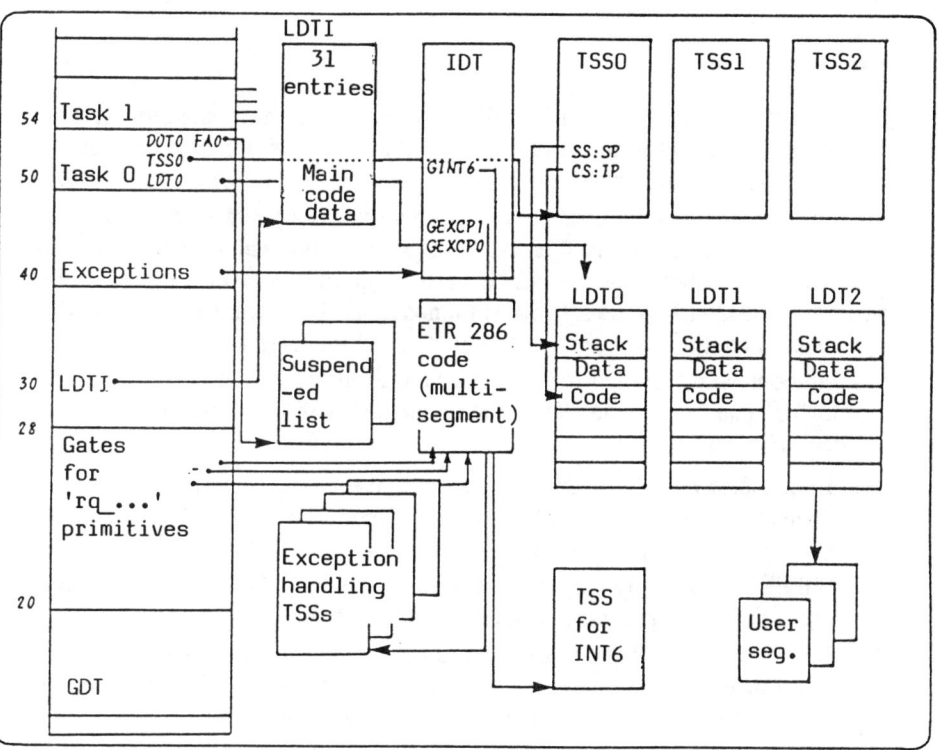

Figure 5.4.1 Principal ETR_286 data structures

5.4.4 Timer Manager

ETR_286 uses interrupt signal 0 from an 8259A PIC interrupt controller to manage its own internal timing. The clock interrupt rate ("tick rate") can be configured between 10 to 500 ms, and on every interrupt, two actions are carried out, updating the time, and handling timeouts. The code for the clock interrupt handler is shown in the *etrto* listing.

Updating the time

ETR_286 keeps a notion of the current time in two variables, one a 64-bit binary representation of run-time in clock tick units, the other a dx_clock structure (see *etrstr.h*) for ready conversion into an ASCII character string, with the format:

DD/MM/YY HH:MM:SS

Timeout handling

ETR_286 offers two forms of timeout facilities, in that a task can request a pure suspension, or can set a maximum limit on the time it is prepared to wait for a message or an event to arrive.

Pure suspensions are requested by a task calling the rq_timout routine (see the *etrprc* listing for declarations of user-level task requests), which suspends the task for a specified number of clock ticks. If a task is running when the timeout expires, of course, a task will not be scheduled immediately; this means that a task which requests a timeout must be prepared to be delayed for longer than it requests.

A timeout on a message read or an await_event operation is specified when the relevant request is made. The time parameter with these operations can ask for three different actions:

- Immediate, encoded using the value lx_notimout, implying that the task wants to be resumed immediately even if there is no message or event waiting (in this case an error status is returned).
- Infinite, encoded by the value lx_waitto, in which the task is not resumed until the event or message arrives, no matter how long this takes, and
- Bounded, in which a timeout period is specified in clock tick units. If the event or message arrives in time, it is passed to the task, but if the period elapses first, the task is resumed with an error indication.

In the interests of efficiency, a dynamic data structure links together all the tasks which are currently waiting for a timeout. The head of this structure is defined as the structure dx_timeout in the *etrstr.h* listing. The "next" entry points to the first task's OTD; subsequent tasks are linked using the "next" and "prev" fields in their OTD. The list is kept ordered by timeout time, so that timeouts occur in the same order as OTDs occur in the list. The head structure contains the time until the first timeout occurs in "ctick"; the 2nd and subsequent OTDs in the list contain a "delta" value, which is the amount by which their timeout expiry time is later than that before.

This means that only the head of the list needs to be examined on every clock tick, and other operations on the list are implemented conveniently: insertion and deletion are efficient since the list is doubly-linked.

These data structures are manipulated by the internal routines sx_init_to, sx_timeout, sx_cancel_to, and sx_dequeue_to in the *etrford* listing. The

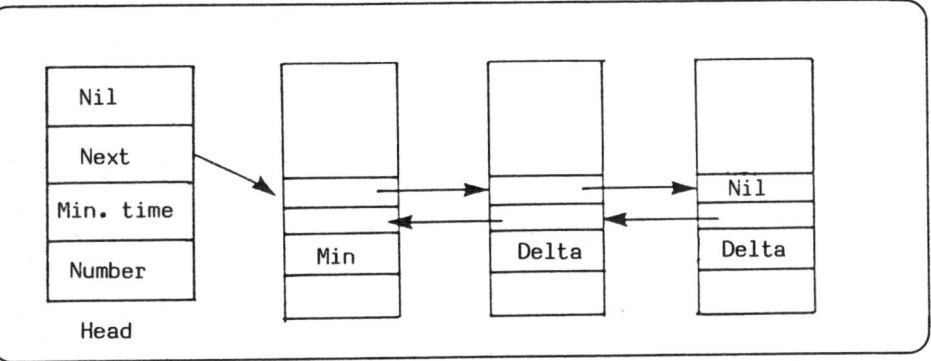

Figure 5.4.2 Data structures for timeouts

sx_cancel_to routine is used when a message or event arrives and the timeout is superfluous, and sx_dequeue_to when a timeout period has expired and the task (or tasks!) at the head of the list can be made ready to run.

5.4.5 Message Queue

Messages between tasks are handled using a circular buffer for each task, declared in *etrstr.h* as dx_fifo. The size of the buffer is specified when a task is initialised, and each entry in the buffer may contain a pointer to a message which has arrived but has not been read. The user requests rq_send_msg and rq_read_msg are declared in the *etrprc.h* listing, and are implemented by the procedures sx_read_msg and sx_send_msg routines in the *etrevms* listing. These procedures use the internal utility procedures sx_enqueue_fifo and sx_dequeue_fifo shown in the *etrfifo* listing.

5.4.6 Semaphores

A future version of ETR_286 will implement 16 global semaphores, which allow tasks to collaborate while preserving mutually exclusive access to specific critical regions. Two operations are possible on a semaphore, Take and GiveBack, and any attempt to Take a semaphore that is already Taken causes the task to be suspended until it is GivenBack.

The example shows how semaphores are used.

```
Take(SemX)    /* Example showing use of semaphores */
    .
    .   Critical Region of Code
    .
GiveBack(SemX)
```

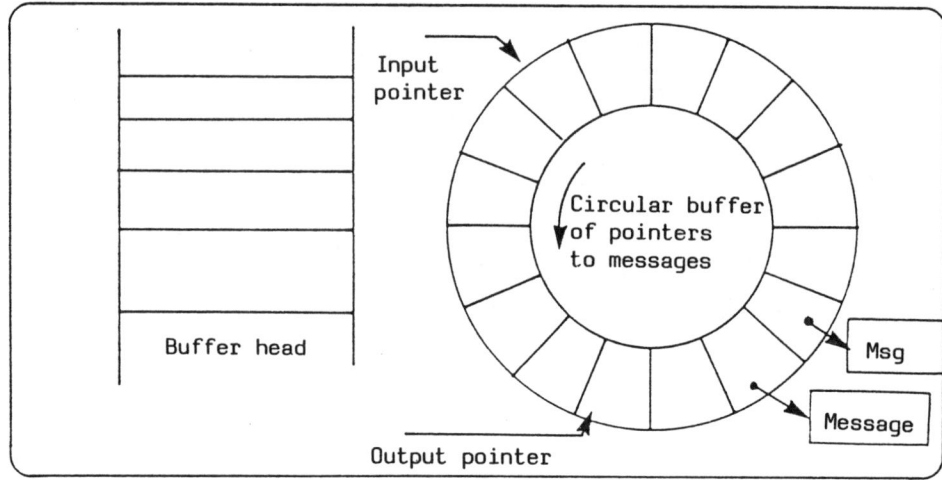

Figure 5.4.3 Message queue

5.4.7 Events

Each task has a number of events, which can be caused by different tasks using rq_send_event (see *etrprc.h*), and interrogated using rq_await_event. The await_event primitive waits for *any* event to arrive: since a number of events may arrive while a task is suspended waiting for a message, or a second event may arrive before the task is scheduled, rq_await_event always returns the full set of events that have arrived.

As for messages, the user may specify a timeout time when waiting for an event, and the task will regain control after this time even if no events have been received. Alternatively, the user may call rq_await_event with a timeout value of lx_notimout to test whether events are present without waiting.

The listing *etrevms* shows the code which implements events.

5.4.8 Memory Allocation

ETR_286 provides two memory allocators, one for internal use and one for user tasks.

Internal memory allocator

The internal memory allocator supplies memory at protection level 0 only, and is used by ETR_286 routines for all their dynamic memory allocation needs. This allows system tables to be allocated in exactly the sizes required, depending upon the number of active tasks and their precise requirements.

Operating Systems

The allocator, which provides only one entry point, sx_gmemx, is shown in the listing *etrinit*, and operates by returning areas from a segment statically allocated in *etrmemx*. Once internal memory has been allocated, there is no way of relinquishing it.

External memory allocator

Allocating memory for use by user tasks is accomplished using a different request, rq_get_memu, which allocates memory from a free list in such a way as to permit it to be returned (by rq_free_memu) and reused for subsequent requests.

The allocation is performed using a "buddy" system in order to permit freed blocks to be coalesced for future allocation; in place of the normal binary division method, ETR_286 implements a fibonacci size system, in which blocks are split in the manner:

$$sz(n) = sz(n-1) + sz(n-2)$$

This algorithm has the effect of reducing the amount of memory fragmentation over the classical buddy implementation.

The user memory allocator is shown in the module *etrbud*.

5.4.9 Input/Output Management

The ETR_286 input/output management routines are based around an 8259A PIC interrupt controller. Interrupt 0 is reserved for the clock interrupt, numbers 1 to 7 being available for other peripherals.

Eight entries in the Interrupt Descriptor Table are allocated from 32 upwards: each entry contains a Task Gate which references 8 system tasks, one for each interrupt level. The interrupt task TI0 is used to field the clock interrupt, and TI1, TI2 ... TI7 are available for other peripherals.

Input/output is managed using three tables within ETR_286, defined in the *etrstr.h* declarations as dx_ioconf, dx_iodesc and dx_iostate.

I/O configuration

Each I/O driver is described in the *etrcnf* file using a dx_ioconf structure, which gives the name of the driver, its logical number, and the interrupt level which it uses. As for the static task descriptors in this file, there is also a table of pointers called vx_ioconf to the individual ioconf structures.

Driver description

Once a driver is initialised, it is managed using a dx_iodesc structure. This contains:

- pointers to the six procedures offered by each driver (attach, detach, open, close, read and write)
- the interrupt level used
- a pointer to the current dx_iodesc structure (see below)
- the number of the task currently using the driver
- a fifo to queue driver requests, and
- a busy flag to indicate activity.

The pointers to the 6 driver entry-points are initialised in the source file of the driver, and are found using a table vx_driver which points to all the io_desc structures.

I/O requests

Input/output requests are carried out using a dx_iostate structure, one per active request. These structures must be allocated by the user, perhaps dynamically using rq_get_memu, and contain fields for

- an error code
- a status
- a task number
- a function number, to indicate which of the seven driver routines to call
- an event number to be sent to the task when the I/O operation is complete
- a logical driver number
- the interrupt level used by the driver
- an index and a pointer to the data area for the transfer, and
- a boolean to indicate that the transfer has finished.

Figure 5.4.4 shows the relationship between the different driver structures.

An I/O driver is attached using the procedure rq_iomanager(p_iostate), with the function code in the iostate structure indicating an attach request, and the name of the desired driver in the data area. This causes the I/O manager to search the *ioconf* structures for the driver with the correct name, allocate an ioconf structure and initalise it, put an entry into the vx_ioptr table, copy the pointers to the driver entry points, and return the logical driver number. The user task can then make calls to the driver's open routine to initialise the device, and carry out his input/output operations by making calls to the driver's read or write routines.

The generic I/O handling code and an embryo serial line driver are both shown in the listing *etrdrv*.

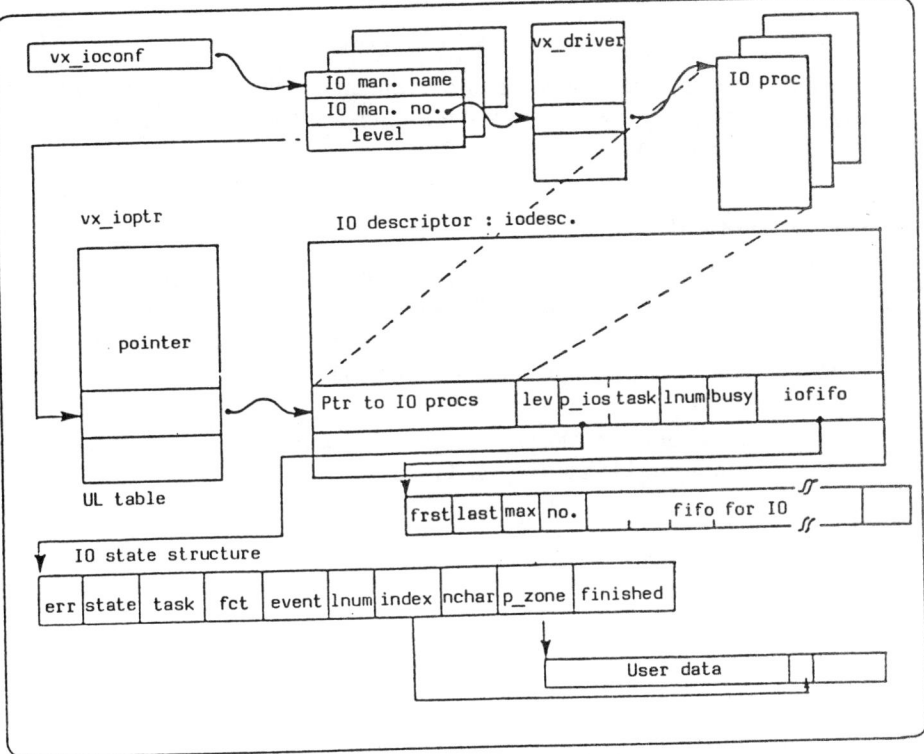

Figure 5.4.4 ETR_286 Input/Output structures

5.4.10 Extensions

ETR_286 implements two facilities, both in the scheduler, specifically for debugging: a history of the last 512 tasks scheduled is kept in the table vx_histo, and a count is maintained for each task, incremented every time the task is scheduled.

A number of other debugging facilities are desirable, and might be usefully added. These include a limit on the run time of every task: the clock interrupt routine might cause a task which overran its time to be killed, or might stop the whole system, and access to internal structures from the console. In particular, it would be useful to be able to study the OTDs, the timeout list, and the state of the memory allocator interactively on a live system.

5.4.11 Exceptions

As the listing *etrexp* shows, error handling is the simplest possible; each possible exception prints an error code and halts the system.

5.4.12 Utilities

The listing *etrut* includes a number of convenient utilities, concerned with task ready-state management, allocation and manipulation of GDT entries, and sundry conversion and indexing operations.

5.4.13 Creating an Absolute File

Once all the individual components of ETR_286 have been compiled, they are linked using the Builder program with the configuration file *etr286.bld*. This defines the segments used, the gates for user entry points, the LDT and TSS segments for the individual tasks, the interrupt table, the GDT and the real memory usage of the final system.

Using this configuration file, an absolute boot-loadable image is formed. This can be loaded into suitable hardware and run.

6 Input/Output and Networking

6.1 Physical Management of Input/output

When we talk about a "powerful" computer, we mean one which can handle large quantities of data rapidly. In previous chapters, we have explored the aspects of the 80286 which contribute to its power, although the most widespread use of the processor has been in the IBM PC/AT and its "clones", which do not fully exploit the more advanced 80286 facilities. Another way of gauging the power of these machines is by assessing their communications abilities. Workstations built using the 80286 need to communicate with other similar machines, in general using Local Area Networks, with departmental machines of moderate power, and with large centralised database machines using either local or remote networks. These requirements give rise to the idea of heterogeneous networks connecting computers of different sizes and in different locations. Communication may be by either private, local networks, or using public networks. One of the current major growth areas in telecommunications is that of "Value Added Networks" or VANs.

This chapter gives an overview of the aspects of the 80286 architecture which contribute to creating a networked environment.

6.1.1 Hardware Aspects

It is a general principle in all but the simplest computer system that the main processor is used as little as possible for the demanding functions associated with input/output and networking. One technique that is often employed is to leave the main processor handling the simplest input/output devices, such as a serial console port. Chapters 2 and 3 contain information on input/output bus cycles and interrupts; since driving these devices is a real-time activity, the relevant software will make use of the real-time features of the 80286. With more complex input/output devices, and especially with networks, it is common to introduce another processor to the system to cope solely with that interface. A version of the IBM PC/AT is available, for example, complete with MAP interface containing its own processor.

6.1.2 Software Aspects

In order to use the simpler devices, the software will use an interrupt gate to accept the interrupts from a serial line driver (8274 or 8251A), and associated read and write procedures will be used.

The input/output procedures in a protected system might be placed in a privilege level, for example level 1, above the kernel code, and might be entered using a task gate to activate the input/output task itself. The response time to an interrupt causing a task switch is approximately 167 clock ticks (including saving the old state and loading new register state), or 21 microseconds at 8 MHz, short enough to handle the majority of simple devices.

Once the interrupt has been dealt with, the services of the underlying operating system will be used to send a message or an event to the relevant application to signal that the operation is complete or to send it the new input data.

The input/output instructions are privileged, under the control of the two IOPL bits in the machine state word. These two bits indicate the maximum (numerical) privilege level that a task may run at and still use the IN, OUT, INS, OUTS, STI, CLI and LOCK instructions.

The INS and OUTS instructions are new in the 80286, and cause a serial transfer of data between an 8- or 16-bit port and a vector in memory.

If any of these instructions is used in a task with a (numerically) higher privilege level than IOPL, a "General Protection" error (13) is caused.

6.1.3 Local Area Networks

It is common to implement a local area network connection by providing an interface complete with its own processor and software, capable of communicating with the main processor using a high-level interface. One of the commonest types of network interface used is the CSMA/CD type first used in Ethernet. Figure 6.1.1 shows how a network interface, built using the 80186 microprocessor driving an 82588 interface chip, could be assembled as a complete subsystem to be interfaced to an 80286 system.

The 82588 is a single-chip interface which implements a CSMA/CD (Carrier Sense Multiple Access with Collision Detection) network connection using Manchester encoding, at a speed of up to 2 megabits per second (5 megabits with an external data encoder/decoder). It implements levels 1 and 2 (physical and link level) protocols of the IEEE 802.3 specification, although its speed restrictions prevent it being used in true Ethernet systems which operate at 10 megabits per second.

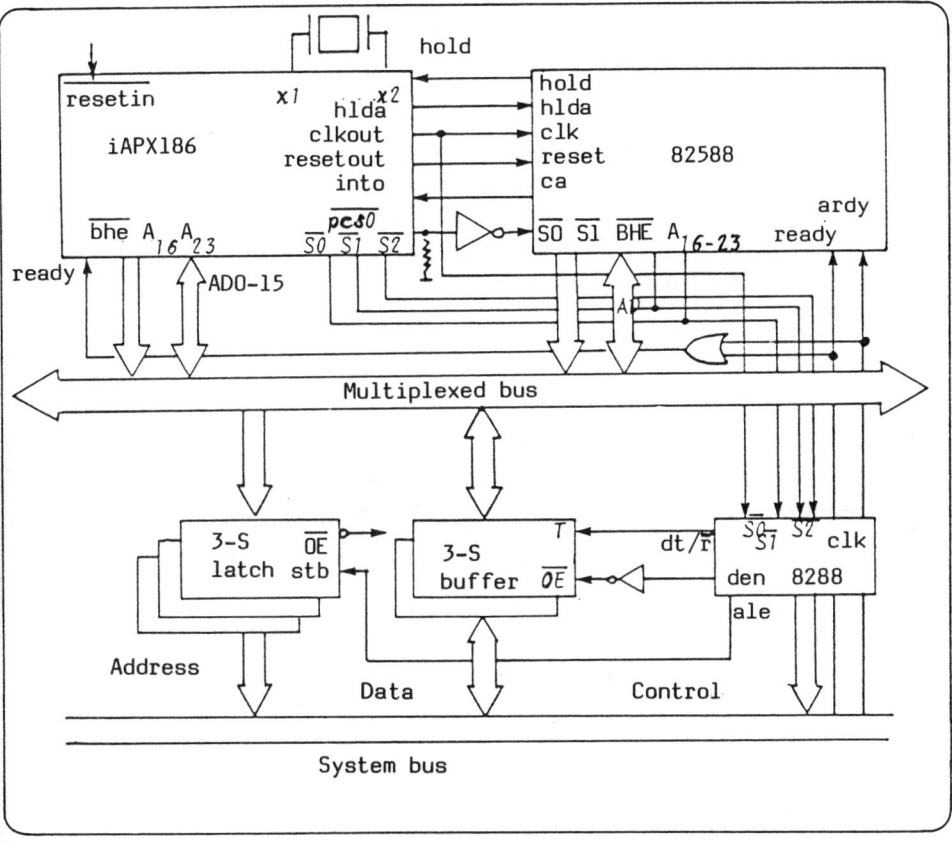

Figure 6.1.1 Network subsystem using 82588

Packet transmission

In order to send a packet, the CPU creates a command block, as shown in figure 6.1.2. When this is created in memory, the CPU initialises the DMA controller (the 82588 contains two DMA channels; typically one is used for reception, the other for transmission).

The parameters are transferred from memory to the 82588 which transmits the packet on the network interface, filling in the correct fields at the front and rear of the data block.

The 82588 recognises a number of types of addresses, which may be up to 6 bytes in length. These allow an individual station address, the address of a group of stations, or a broadcast address to be used.

The data portion of a packet will, in general, be initialised by the high-level protocol modules. The CPU initialises the DMA controllers with the address of

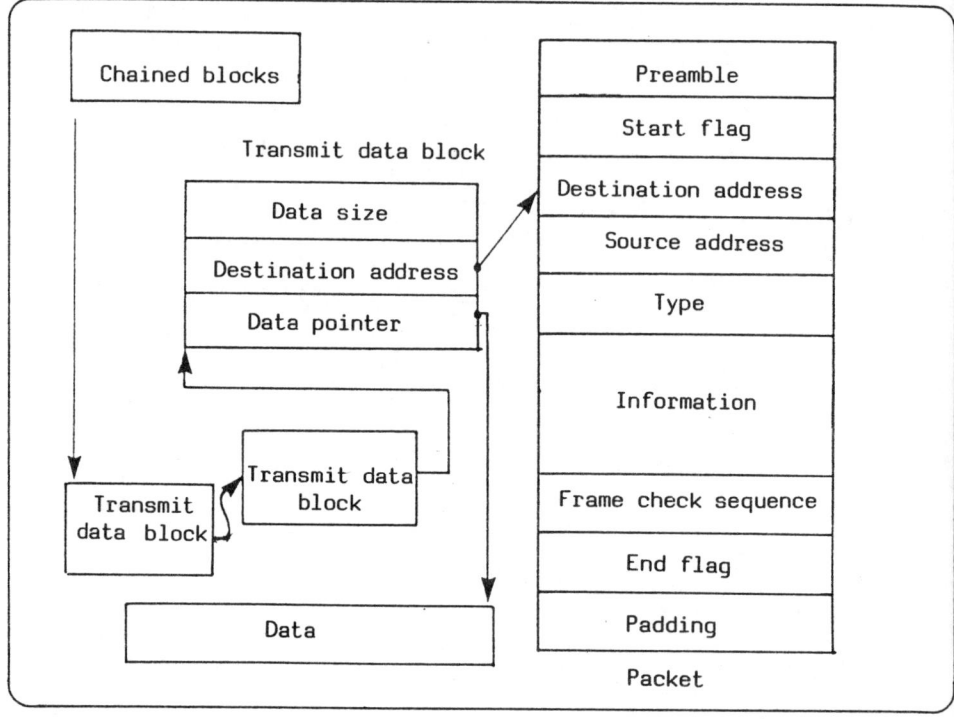

Figure 6.1.2 Data structures used by the 82588

the data field in memory, then sends a "transmit" command to the 82588. Once the command is issued, the 82588 reads the first two of the block to find the data block length, waits for the network connection to become free, then sends the packet, beginning with the preamble bits and the flag, which are both generated by the chip itself. While sending the packet, the data bytes are fetched from memory in 16-byte blocks, using an internal FIFO to buffer the different speeds of the bus and the network. The destination address is sent next, followed by the source address (which is set up during the device's initialisation phase). Following the data field, a CRC is transmitted, again calculated by the 82588.

If a collision between two messages is detected during transmission, sending is abandoned by both stations, both send a "jamming" pattern to ensure each network station realises that an error has occurred, and each interface reports a transmission error, causing the controlling software to back off and retry the transmission.

Packet reception

The interface chip monitors the network state continuously, and starts to receive a frame as soon as it recognises the destination address (be it individual, a group address, or a broadcast address). Transferring the data into memory takes place using DMA. Before the packet arrives, the CPU needs to supply the chip with a packet receive buffer. The number of bytes received in the packet is made available to the CPU in registers, the frame status is appended to the packet buffer in memory, and an interrupt is sent to the CPU.

If the packet size used is unknown, or highly variable, the CPU can pre-allocate a number of buffers, chained together by programmed linkage structures. When the receiver starts to use one buffer, it interrupts the CPU to ask for another buffer address. This technique means using both DMA channels for frame reception.

Managing the physical connection

The 82588 LAN Controller follows the standards of IEE 802.3. It constantly monitors the network connection, detecting activity or inactivity. If activity is detected, packet transmission is delayed for a programmable "inter-packet" time. If a collision during a frame is detected, the transmitting station sends a 32- to 48-bit jamming pattern (all "1"s), in order to ensure that all receivers notice the collision. Retransmission takes place (under CPU control) after a delay which is calculated using an IEEE specified algorithm. This delay is a multiple of a "unit delay", which is the time taken for a frame to traverse the longest network path. The retransmission delay is a randomly chosen value, uniformly distributed between 0 and 2^k, k increasing by one for each retransmission, up to a maximum of 10. The number of retransmissions is programmable between 0 and 15, a count of the number of retransmissions being kept by the 82588.

6.2 High-Level Protocols

In a system, such as an IBM PC/AT, with a network interface, the network processor may implement the low-level protocol layers for Ethernet or X.25, while the higher-level protocols may be managed by networking code integrated into the operating system on the main processor. Current higher-level protocols do not always respect the layering suggested by the OSI seven layer model; some currently-used protocols are shown in figure 6.2.1.

6.3 Open Net

This software, supplied by Intel, can be used with Intel's networking hardware to implement an Ethernet network to connect a range of heterogeneous machines, such as IBM PC/XT and PC/AT, the 86/310 processor, and DEC VAX computers. The operating systems supporting this network are MSDOS3.1, XENIX286, iRMX286 and VMS.

7 Application	X.400 Message Handling		T.73 Document Handling
	FTAM File Transfer		VTP Terminal Protocol
	MAP (industrial)		TOP (office)
6 Presentation	X.409 Coding		IS 8825
	NAPLS: North American Presentation Level Syntax		
5 Session	IS 8237		T.62 Teletex and Fax
	BCS BAS BSS		CCITT X.225, X.215
4 Transport	ISO 8073		CCITT X.224, X.214
	(Classes 0 to 4)		Intel iNA960
3 Network	ISO 8473		CCITT X.25
	Internet		
2 Data Link	802.2, 802.3, 802.4		X.25, LAP, LAPB
1 Physical	Ethernet, Token Ring		X.21, V.21, V.24

Figure 6.2.1 OSI and CCITT protocols

Open Net provides a number of primitives in the context of a "session": Open initiates a session, waiting for a connection if necessary; Close terminates a connection; Status returns the state of a connection; Send and Receive transfer data, and Abort forces a premature termination.

This software is a standard implementation of a class 4 transport protocol. This protocol layer provides a full-duplex connection between two entities on different systems. In addition, there is a "datagram" service provided. The client entities are identified by two numbers, a network address and a Transport Service Access Point (TSAP). Two types of connection are provided, the Virtual Circuit (VC) and Datagram. A virtual circuit establishes a logical connection in which data is reliably delivered, even if the underlying network is slightly error-prone. The Datagram service is a connection which is established for an individual packet, offering a lower certainty of delivery, but less complex. Data sent by datagram may arrive out-of-order, or may not arrive at all!

In a virtual circuit, data is delivered at the destination in exactly the same order as it is sent, without error, duplication, or loss. A number of processes may use the services of a single virtual circuit to send messages of variable sizes without any risk of confusion.

6.3.1 Open Net Under iRMX286

Consider the interaction between an applications program running under iRMX/286 and the network driver iNA960. The application uses memory segments containing requests for transmission or reception (or auxiliary services). These requests have a fixed header format, containing the size of the data buffer, the mailbox to reply to, the identity of the sender, and so on.

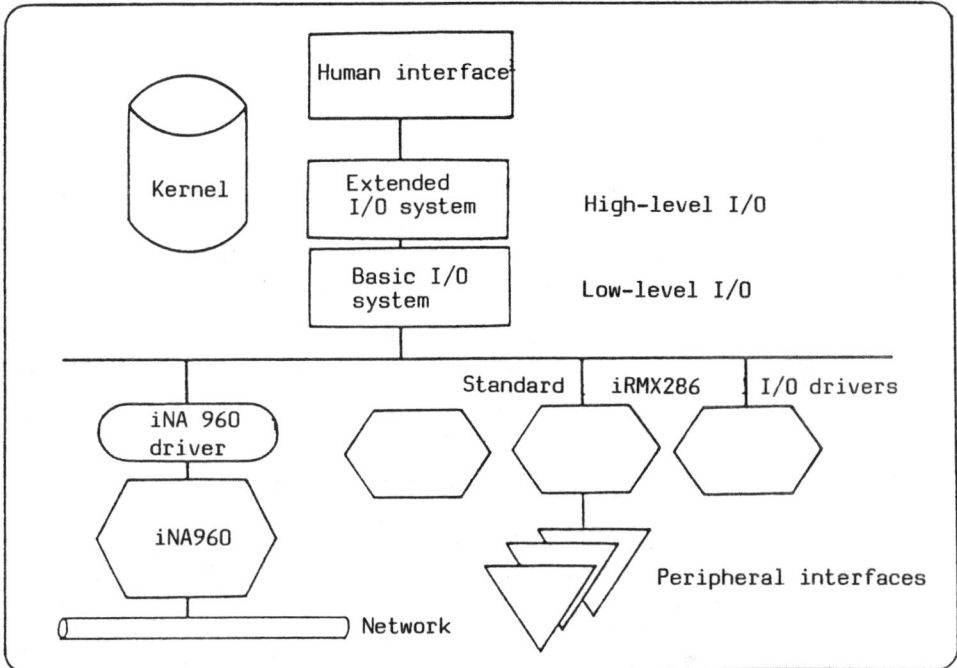

Figure 6.3.1 *iNA960 under iRMX286*

Intel offers a file transfer program, compatible between XENIX and MS/Net (under MS/DOS), as an applications protocol, corresponding to layers 5, 6 and 7 of the ISO Reference Model. Under iRMX286, this software is called iRMX/NET. The software is a server and requester of files, and remote file access takes place over the network.

Figure 6.4.1 shows the relationship between the layers of iRMX286 and the file handling protocol layers.

A user of one iRMX286 system can "see" the file systems of other networked systems using the remote file system facilities. Figure 6.3.2 shows how this is implemented by extending the conventional hierarchical description of one system's filestore, introducing the notion of a virtual "super root" which appears above the root of each individual file system.

The file system services in all networks are configured with their own interface program. When the user opens a file which is not stored locally on his system, a request message is broadcast, and the server recognising its own name replies with its own network address, thus enabling a virtual circuit to be set up.

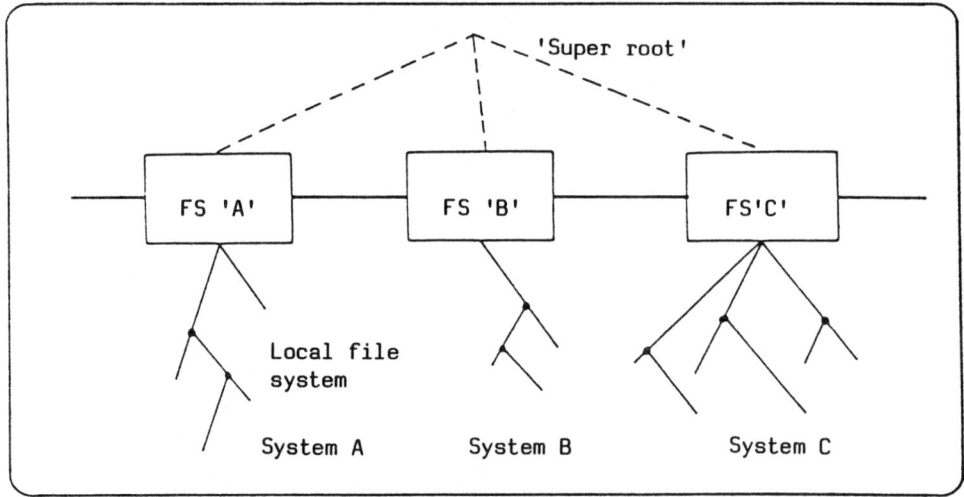

Figure 6.3.2 Open Net file systems

The user command to access a remote machine, under iRMX286 is:

`attachdevice machineB as :MB: remote`

This command establishes a virtual circuit with "machineB", permitting further network requests. Following this stage, the command "`DIR :MB:`" lists the top-level directory of machine B, and a file can be copied from machine B to the local machine using the command:

`copy :MB:file to /usr/local/file`

6.3.2 Usage Under XENIX/286

Under XENIX, the protocol is implemented under the XENIX file system and access to remote systems is made via a "super root" which is notionally one level above the file system roots of all of the networked machines. In order to access a remote system, a slightly different syntax from normal UNIX system file naming is used, specifying "//machine" as the first component of the name, as in:

`more //mach1/etc/passwd   : browse a different system user list`

6.3.3 PC/NETWORK

Version 3.1 of MS/DOS contains networking functions, compatible with Microsoft's MS/NET, called NETBIOS. IBM's own network is PC/NETWORK, and may use CSMA/CD interface cards (possibly with the 82588 chip) or IBM's own Token Ring hardware.

7 The 80386 Microprocessor

As will be seen in the following description, although the 80386 differs from the 80286 in some quantitative respects, such as its word length and its overall performance, it is built upon many of the same principles, and adopts many of the same system-level design solutions as its predecessor. In particular, its logical addressing, memory management, and protection facilities are very similar to those provided in the 80286.

7.1 General Characteristics of the 80386

7.1.1 Software Aspects

The 80386 is Intel's first 32-bit microprocessor offering. Other manufacturers have launched 32-bit products before the availability of the 80386, and it has become apparent that the general trend in these 32-bit CPUs is to provide larger and larger address spaces, supporting ever more powerful operating systems.

The 80386 is a true 32-bit CPU: it has a 32-bit external data bus, a number of 32-bit general registers, and its operations act upon 32-bit data items in a single operation. The performance that it offers is impressive, and can be expressed relatively straightforwardly: it has a physical address space of 4 gigabytes, managed using the same scheme as the 80286, offers a logical address space of 64×10^{12} or 64 terabytes, and its raw performance is somewhere between 3 and 4 MIPS using an 8 MHz clock. (Clock speeds of 12 and 16 MHz are likely to be available in the future.) This power is supremely suited to running a full-function operating system, much more sophisticated than is common on 16-bit microprocessors. In particular, the 80386 runs a UNIX multitasking multi-user operating system well, and it is possible to consider the implementation of a VM style of "hypervisor" supporting a number of different operating systems simultaneously.

In addition to its raw power, the machine offers an extremely high level of compatibility with earlier Intel processors, with the ability to run 8086 code in a virtual environment, and preserving the same protection mechanism, objects and instructions as the 80286. This compatibility gives rise to the possibility of integrating two or more different operating systems into the same environment: systems offering both MS/DOS and UNIX concurrently are now available. The value of this facility is that it allows the use of a large range of applications software already written for the 16-bit machines, while permitting the development of larger, more demanding applications which exploit the full power of the underlying hardware.

The implementation of 32-bit registers is not a straightforward doubling of the 80286 register width: two enhancements have been made. One is that certain instructions operating on BIT type addresses have been provided, and the other is that the orthogonality principle which allows any general register to be used with any instruction has been greatly extended. Many of the 80386's predecessors (even the 80286!) limited some instructions to operating on certain registers, and restricted addressing modes to certain address registers. The full set of interchangeable registers on the 80386 introduces a greater flexibility in programming and can significantly improve the code produced by both an assembly language programmer and the code generator of a compiler.

Two concepts within the 80386 will be readily familiar to the reader, because they so resemble the 80286 facilities described previously: the memory management system and the protection system.

The virtual memory management system is segmented, in the same way as in the 80286, and uses the same "segment absent" type of interrupt to permit the operating system to migrate segments between main and secondary memory.

The protection mechanism is exactly the same as in the 80286: there are 4 privilege levels, with a ring-type hierarchy of data and code segments; there is strict separation of the address spaces of different tasks; each segment is given an access permission parameter; and certain instructions (input/output and state-modifying instructions, for example), are only permitted in a privileged mode.

All of these enhancements are described in the following sections.

7.1.2 Hardware aspects

In this section, we will consider some of the technological requirements necessary for the implementation of this type of circuit.

The technology used to fabricate the 80386 is Intel's CHMOS III using a double metallisation. The geometry used has a line width of 1.5 microns, and about 275000 transistors are present on the chip. The speed of this technology will permit the fabrication of 12- and 16 MHz devices. On the chip, a 32 x 32 bit multiplication takes between 9 and 41 clock cycles, depending upon the address mode used, or an average time of perhaps 3 microseconds in the initial 8 MHz part.

The internal architecture of the chip has had to be adapted to offer the user full use of the vast address space. Six functional units have been connected in a "pipeline", permitting the optimisation of the use of the external bus by anticipating its usage and overlapping the physical address calculations. A memory management is integrated on chip, optimising the implementation of segmentation, paging and protection.

The 80386 Microprocessor

Outside the processor chip, two different means of enhancing the overall system performance are envisaged: coprocessors and cache memory.

The CPU chip provides the means of interfacing a numeric coprocessor in a straightforward manner, implementing real arithmetic at an impressive speed.

In addition, facilities are provided to interpose a cache memory between the CPU and main memory; this offers the potential for greatly improving the overall speed of the system and will be described in more detail later. The requirement for a cache arises fairly naturally: an 80386 system will usually be built with an extremely large main memory system, which would be expensive and power-hungry if built entirely out of the fast memory devices necessary to keep the CPU operating at full speed. The compromise is to build main memory out of slower, cheaper devices whilst attempting to keep the most frequently accessed data and instructions in a fast cache memory, local to the CPU.

7.2 80386 Structure - the Applications View

The 80386 programmer needs to manage the use of a number of resources: the memory and the CPU registers are all 32 bits wide. Users of the 80386 CPU need to be aware of the processor's capabilities from two points of view: the applications view and the system view. In a design team, it will be necessary to have people primarily concerned with the systems part of the overall software, and others concerned with the applications programming. Systems aspects of the CPU are described separately.

7.2.1 General Registers and Flags

General registers

The general registers are very similar to those present in the two preceding generations of processors: the 8 familiar registers AX, BX, CX, DX, SI, DI, SP and BP are provided. These registers contain the data which is most frequently manipulated by both assembly-language and high-level language programs.

The fundamental difference comes from the fact that the width of each has been doubled: there are eight 32-bit registers, given the names EAX (Extended EAX), EBX, ECX, EDX, ESI, EDI, ESP and EBP. Figure 7.2.1 shows this bank of internal registers; it is convenient to add to this set the 32-bit instruction pointer, EIP.

Figure 7.2.1 shows the use made of the register names that were provided in the 8086 and 80286 machines. The user is able to use 8 and 16-bit fragments of the 32-bit registers by using these names, one aspect of the compatibility with earlier CPUs provided by the 80386.

The programmer therefore has available eight 32-bit registers, eight 16-bit registers (e.g. AX, BX) and four pairs of 8-bit registers (e.g. AH–AL, BH–BL).

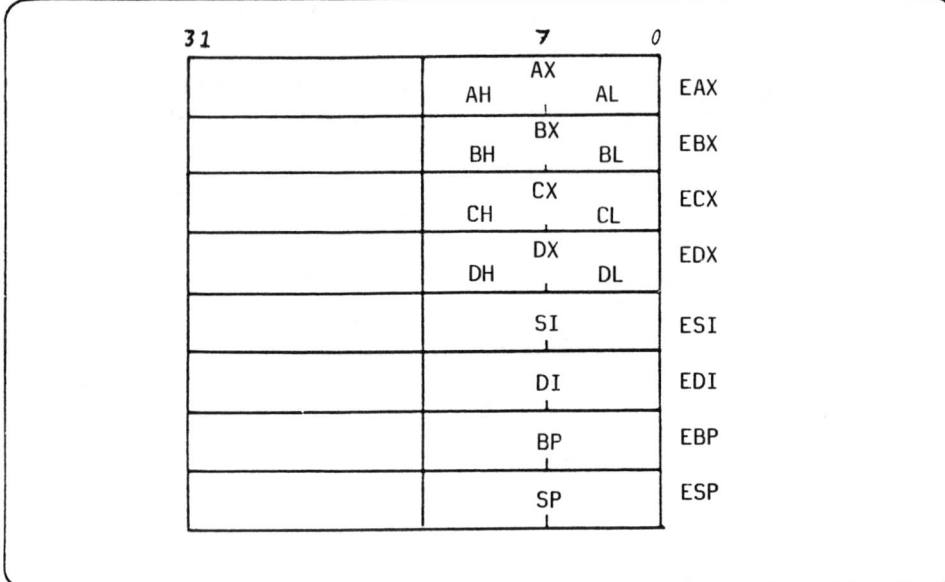

Figure 7.2.1 General registers

This facility is exploited by the machine in its native mode to give the ability to manipulate data of different lengths.

We will see that these registers are almost completely interchangeable, particularly when it comes to implementing different addressing modes. Only two of the registers are dedicated to specific purposes: ESP is the stack pointer, and EIP is the instruction pointer.

In any program, all other registers may be used without distinction, and if it happens that certain conventions for register usage are common, these arise simply from a requirement for some standardisation in coding practice, to improve the efficiency of code that is produced, or to maintain compatibility with the usage practices (particularly procedure calling conventions) of some high-level language compiler.

Flags

The flags register is a privileged machine resource in the 80386 as in the 80286 CPU. This is necessary as it contains bits which affect the overall operation of the machine. Figure 7.2.2 shows that this register has a structure and a bit-allocation

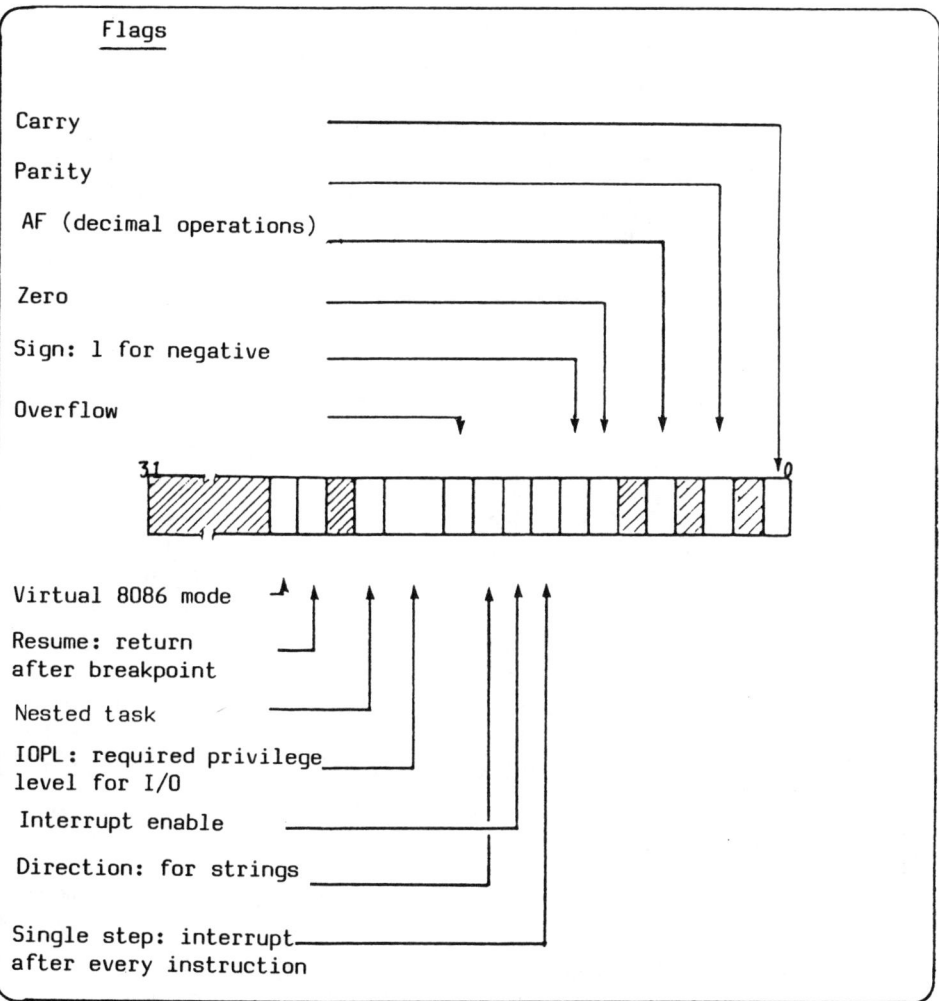

Figure 7.2.2 80386 flags register

which is very similar to that of the 80286. In particular, the state bits showing the results of a calculation (Zero, Carry, etc.) are identical.

This register contains four indicators which describe the overall system state:

IOPL is the Input/Output Privilege Level, which is the (numeric) maximum privilege level at which I/O operations may be carried out without causing a privilege level exception.

NT, or the Nested Task bit, indicates that the current task has been chained or activated by a previous task. This bit and the IOPL field perform an identical function on the 80286 CPU.

VM indicates "Virtual 8086 Mode". This bit is used by the operating system to provide a virtual execution mode in which to run an 8086 program. When this bit is set, the program is permitted to manipulate the segment registers as if it were being run on an 8086 CPU.

RF indicates that an operation has been partially completed, and needs to be resumed when the task is rescheduled. The Resume Flag is set when a debugging breakpoint set in one of the machine's debugging registers is encountered.

7.2.2 Numeric Coprocessors

The extension of the capabilities of the 80386 by the addition of a numeric coprocessor is carried out in the same way as with the 8086 and the 80286. One difference is that the 80386 is capable of using the 80287 coprocessor as an alternative to its own 80387. The machine state register is used to identify which type of coprocessor is connected. The effect of adding the 80387 coprocessor is as beneficial as was the case with previous CPUs, and the ease of use by a programmer is preserved, especially using high-level languages. As with the 80287 coprocessor, extended integers, decimal operands, both packed and unpacked, and reals, both single and double precision are supported by the 80387 coprocessor. The general register bank in the CPU is augmented by eight 80-bit registers in the coprocessor, which also contains two registers for control and state information.

7.2.3 Memory and Addresses

The physical address space of the 80386 is extended to 4 gigabytes by providing a 32-bit external address bus.

With this size of address space, it is inconceivable that programmers will access all data items with a single physical address, and it is therefore normal to use a logical or symbolic addressing scheme. It is at this point that the needs of a systems engineer and of an application programmer will diverge. The programming techniques used in the 80386 follow those which were followed with the 80286: in particular, the management of addresses is based upon the notion of segments.

Segments in the 80386

The 80386 translates logical program addresses into physical buses at the time of executing instructions. The user sees memory as consisting of a collection of segments, each with a size and usage defined when they were created. As in all segmented machines, a broad distinction between different types of segments can be made: segments may contain executable code, data, a stack, and so on.

One of the differences from the 80286 is in the possible sizes of segments: in the 80386 they may have a size varying from 1 byte to 4 gigabytes. There is nothing to prevent a system being created to use just one or two 4 gigabyte segments, but this would be to the detriment of the flexibility and protection facilities of this machine.

As in the 80286, the segmentation scheme allows each segment to be characterised by its access rights (read-only, executable, or read-write), by its protection level, and by its size, accesses lying outside this limit being prevented by a hardware check. These attributes and the real base address of the segment are specified in a segment descriptor, which is used to check and to translate every segment access.

Logical addresses

A program may be accessing a number of segments at a particular moment. Every access, to a data item or a procedure, specifies a particular segment, the item itself being uniquely identified by its address within the segment. In this way, every memory access is characterised by two address components, a selector and an offset. The segment selector is a 16-bit quantity used as an index into a table of segment descriptors, permitting the appropriate descriptor to be fetched to find the segments attributes and its physical address, and the offset (or displacement) is a 32-bit quantity giving the location of the item within the segment.

Figure 7.2.3 shows that the 80386 CPU address translation is logically identical to the 80286: the segment selector is converted into a 32-bit physical base address (24 bits on 80286), to which is added the 32-bit displacement (16 bits on 80286).

One distinction between the 80386 CPU and the 80286 is the number of segment registers usable by the programmer: the 80386 is provided with 6, rather than the 4 on the 80286. Figure 7.2.4 shows the 80386 segment registers: CS, SS, DS, ES, FS and GS.

The two additional registers, FS and GS, are normally used as pointers to data areas. One possible use of the six segment registers is to have one pointing to the current code segment, one pointing at the stack segment, and the remaining four pointing to different data segments. This usage improves the performance of the running code, as it lessens the number of times segment registers need saving and restoring over an 80286 program. As is the case for the general registers, it will normally be convenient to develop a standard way of using the segment registers, particularly if interfacing to high-level language programs.

When any of these segment registers is altered, an internal cache circuit within the machine is loaded with the descriptor which describes the new segment. This means that the address translation circuits have the information present to check every access for size and rights permission on-chip.

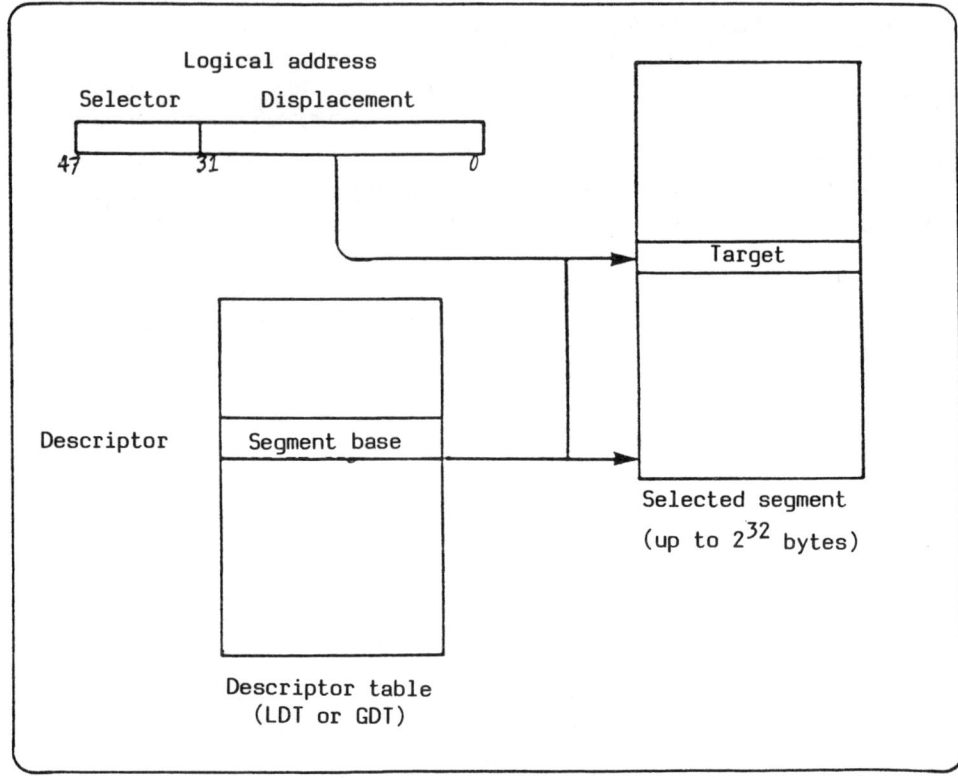

Figure 7.2.3 Translating logical addresses

Addressing modes

The addressing modes usable by the 80386 programmer are a superset of those available on the 80286. Figure 7.2.5 shows the structure within which eleven different types of modes are available:

- Register, in which the operand is contained in a register;
- Immediate Address, in which the value of the operand is contained within the instruction;
- Direct Address, in which an operand displacement of up to 32 bits is directly encoded in the instruction;
- Indirect Address, in which the effective address of the object within a segment is contained within any one of the eight general registers:

  ```
  MOV [ECX],EDX   ; address contained in ECX
  ```

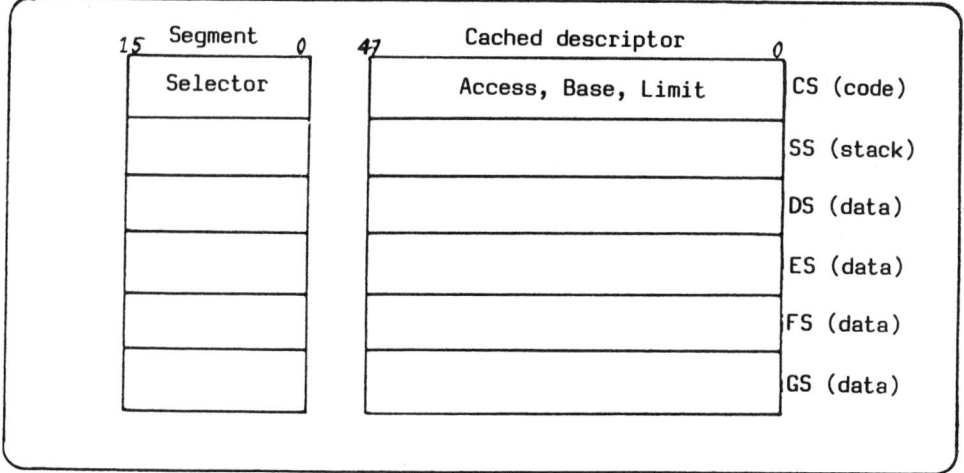

Figure 7.2.4 Segment registers

- Based Address, in which the contents of a general register are combined with a displacement expressed as an absolute value:

  MOV ECX, [EAX+35]

- Indexed Address, in which an index register (any except ESP) is used to index an area or a vector referenced by its name:

  SUB ECX, Zone[EAX]

- Scaled Indexed Address, in which the effective index is obtained by multiplying the value contained in an index register by a scale factor, which is normally the size of one of the table entries:

  IDIV ECX, Table[EDI*4]

- Indexed Base Address, in which the effective address is obtained by adding the contents of a base register and an index register:

  MOV EAX, [ESI][ECX]

Three further addressing modes are obtained by combinations of the previous modes:

```
MOV ECX, [EDX*8]              ; Scaled Indexed Base Addressing
ADD EDX, [ESI][EBP+00FFFF0H]  ; Indexed Base Addressing
                              ;   with Displacement
MOV EAX, Table[EDI*4][EBP+80] ; Scaled Indexed Base Addressing
                              ;   with Displacement
```

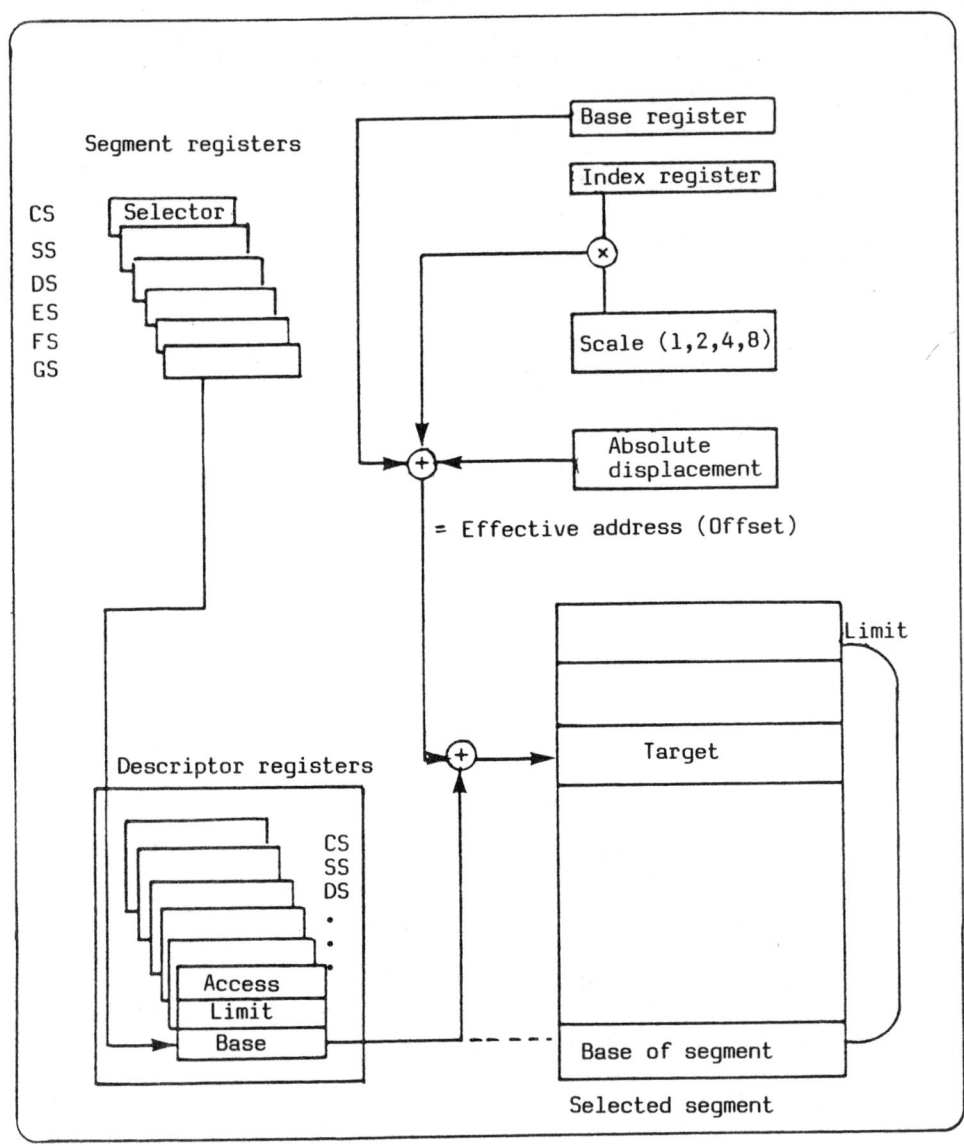

Figure 7.2.5 Address mode summary

Data types

Modern microprocessor hardware is developed to provide facilities for using the devices in the widest possible applications areas, enabling the development cost to be amortised over an extended lifetime. The 80386 follows this principle by providing a particularly flexible, high-performance architecture. In addition, the processor has been designed to promote the use of high-level languages to provide the highest programmer productivity and to ensure the portability of applications. This means providing support for the data types used in these applications, enabling the code generated by compilers to be optimised. In general, the more mumerous the different types of data that are accessible from a machine's instruction set, the better will be the code generated to act on different data. The 80386 extends the range of data types processed over those available on the 80286: the full set is:

- bit
- bit field: a contiguous group of bits extending to 32 bits with a byte, word or double word
- bit string: contiguous string extending up to 4 gigabits (see the description of the IBTS instruction in appendix B)
- byte: unsigned 8 bits
- signed byte
- signed integer: of 16 bits
- long integer: 32 bits signed
- word: 16 bits unsigned
- double word: unsigned 32 bits
- signed quad word: 64 bits
- offset: 32-bit displacement
- 386 pointer: the combination of a 16-bit selector and a 16- or 32-bit displacement
- character: ASCII valued byte
- character string
- Binary Coded Decimal: packed (4 bits per digit) or unpacked (8 bits per digit).

Assembly-language facilities are provided to manipulate each of these data types.

For example, there are instructions which test a combination of flag bits, allowing the programmer to determine whether the result of the last subtraction was "negative, assuming that both operands were signed values".

In the same way, there are instructions provided to test, to complement, to insert or to extract a bit field with a word or longword.

In addition to these data types, there are a number of data types implemented by the numeric coprocessor. These are the same as the data types supported by the 80287 coprocessor.

7.3 System Aspects of the 80386 Structure

The system aspects of the 80386 CPU will not be immediately relevant to the applications programmer, but need to be understood by the system programmer. These system facilities fall under two broad headings: there are a number of system registers, and there are hardware facilities for supporting kernel functions.

7.3.1 *System and Task Registers*

The system aspects of the architecture are concerned with the overall structure of the software, the sharing of machine resources between a number of applications programs, managing a number of tasks and their associated data, handling protection requirements, such as the access to each data class, and permitting programs their relevant privileges. In this area, the facilities of the 80386 resemble very closely those of the 80286. Only one major facility has been introduced in the 80386, the concept of paging, which gives an additional flexibility in the management of memory space by an operating system, particularly valuable with the large segments that are possible with the 80386.

System registers

The segment registers are described above: as in the 80286, these registers contain segment selectors, which index a descriptor table (GDT or LDT) to access the characteristics of a designated segment.

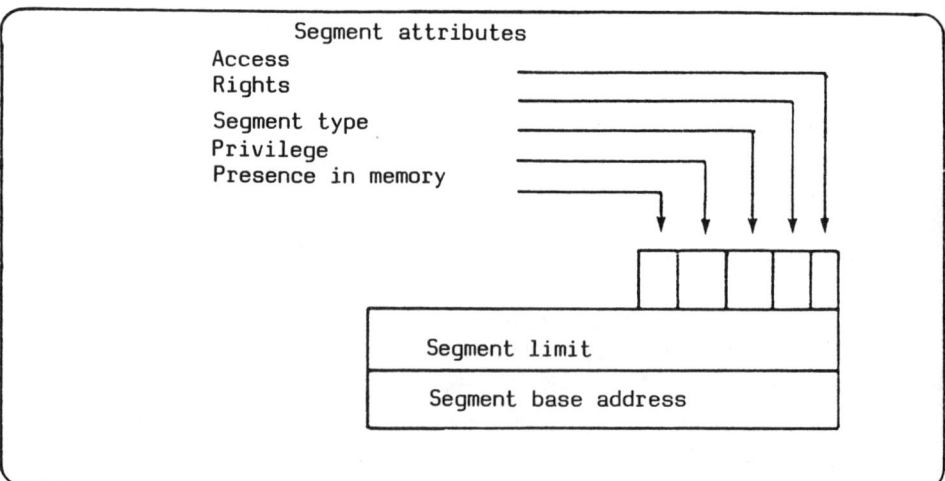

Figure 7.3.1 Descriptor fields

The 80386 Microprocessor

It will be apparent that the 80286 and 80386 descriptors are different owing to the size of physically accessible memory and the permissible size of a segment. An 80286 segment may not exceed 64 kilobytes, whereas the 80386 segment may be up to 4 gigabytes. The base address of a segment is expanded from 24 to 32 bits in the 80386, and the limit or size field has grown from 16 to 20 bits. The size field is associated with a "granularity" bit in the descriptor; if this bit is clear, the size is interpreted in bytes, allowing any size of segment from 1 byte to 1 megabyte. If the granularity bit is set, however, the size is interpreted in units of 4 kilobytes, giving a maximum segment size of 4 gigabytes.

These extra bits in the descriptor do not increase its overall size over 80286 descriptors: use of the "reserved" fields is made to maintain its size at 64 bits.

A second difference between 80286 and 80386 descriptors is in the area of the segment "type" fields. Since the 80386 can emulate the 80286, the type field needs to specify whether individual system descriptors refer to 80286 or 80386 segments or gates. Figure 7.3.2 summarises the principal fields of 80386 descriptors.

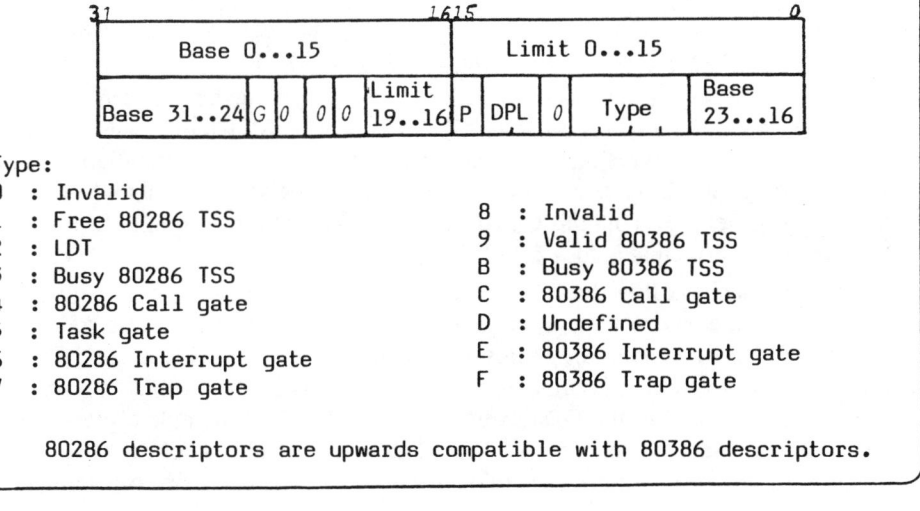

Figure 7.3.2 System segment descriptors

In the same way as in the 80286, the 80386 keeps a copy of the descriptor for each currently accessible segment in a descriptor cache. This cache entry is loaded whenever the programmer changes the selector in a segment register, enabling the address translation and the protection checks for each access to be carried out at maximum speed. The 80386 descriptor cache has six entries, one for each segment register, rather than the four present in the 80286.

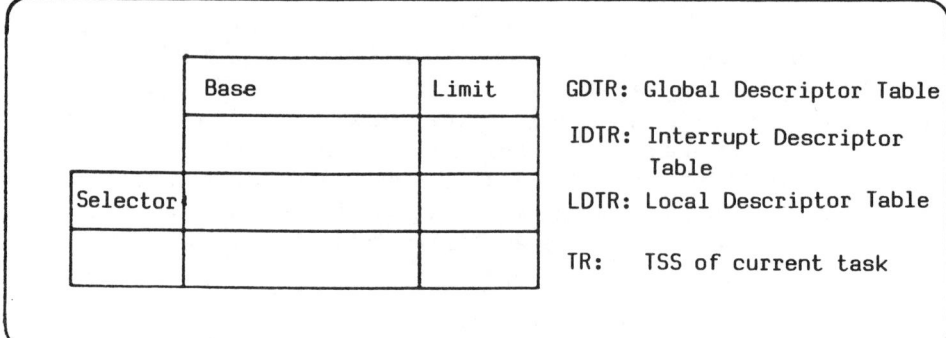

Figure 7.3.3 System segment descriptor registers

The 80386 provides four segment registers to point to the current system structures: these registers are shown in figure 7.3.3.

Task management registers

The concept of a "task" is used with the notion of the "context" within which a particular program is executed in a concurrent environment.

In the same way as in the 80286, a task is described in memory by a particular data area called the Task State Segment (TSS). The size of the TSS is at least 100 bytes. Both the operating system and the hardware use the information in this segment to manage the execution of tasks properly. A register internal to the CPU, the Task Register (TR) contains the address of the TSS of the current task. Figure 7.3.4 gives the principal fields of the TSS.

In particular, note how the TSS contains a selector which identifies the (global) segment which contains the current task's Local Descriptor Table: this address, represented by a complete descriptor, is available to the hardware in the LDTR register while this task is being executed. The address of the Global Descriptor Table is always held in the GDTR register in the CPU. To complete the set of segment descriptor registers, the IDTR register gives the address of a table of Interrupt Descriptors, which are used to define the response to each one of a number of different interrupts.

The list of control registers is completed by four special control registers, CR0, CR1, CR2 and CR3. Shown in figure 7.3.4, these registers implement similar functions to those performed by the Machine Status Word (MSW) in the 80286. Their functions are:

CR0: contains information on the use of paging, on the presence and type of coprocessor (80287 or 80387), and on the operation of protection systems in the current mode of operation. CR0 contains the global state of the machine, as in the 80286 MSW.

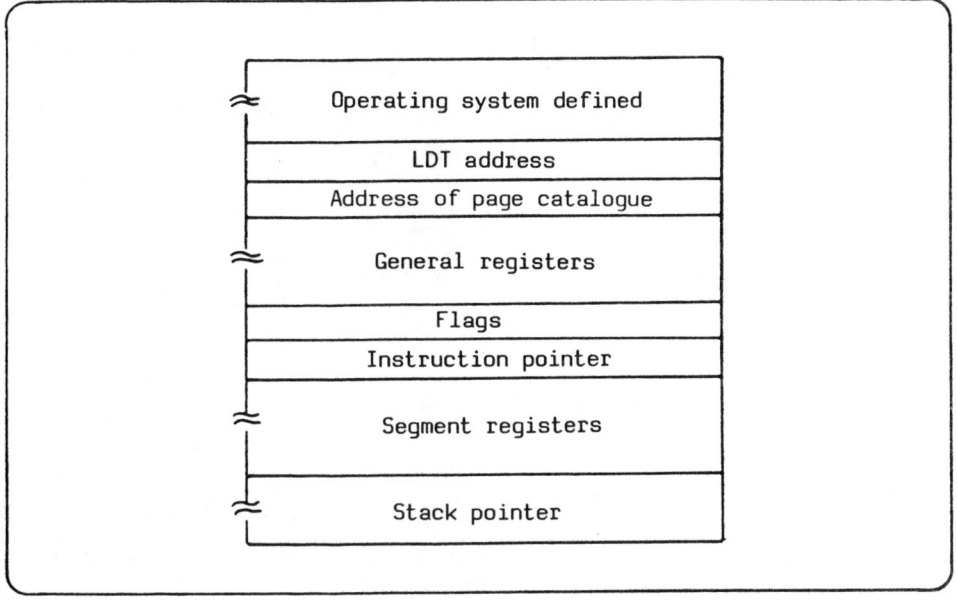

Figure 7.3.4 Principal TSS fields

CR1: is reserved, without function, for functions on future Intel processors.

CR2: contains the address causing an exception during a page translation operation.

CR3: contains the address of the master page table used when the paging mechanism is in use.

These status and control registers are managed by the operating system, ensuring correct overall operation.

Debugging registers

The 80386 designers have provided testing facilities built into the CPU to make the task of debugging systems even more simple. These facilities encompass both test registers and debugging registers. During processor testing, the EAX and EDX registers reflect the result of the various tests.

The 80386 implements 6 debugging registers, which can cause a breakpoint to occur when any one of 6 different variables is accessed. This is a powerful mechanism which ensures that if a particular variable gets accidentally overwritten, the CPU hardware interrupts the operation immediately. This is a particularly useful facility when transient or intermittent bugs are investigated.

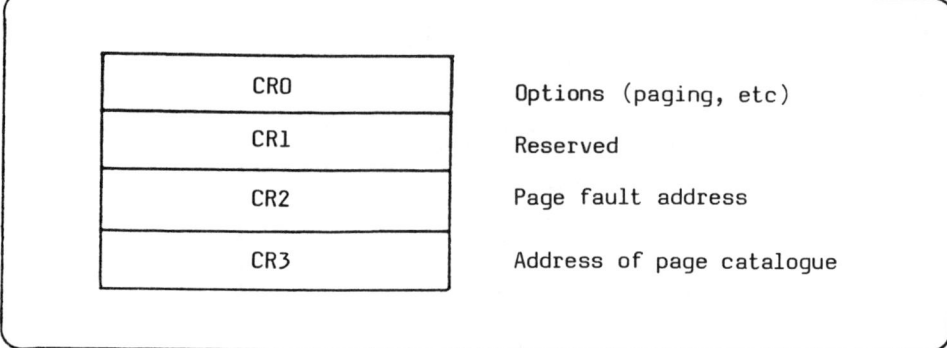

Figure 7.3.5 Control registers

7.3.2 Memory Management

Previous sections have covered the way in which logical addresses are formed and translated into physical memory addresses. This section will complete this description by introducing the concept of paging, and showing how the concept is implemented in this system.

Two new concepts are included in the 80386 memory management facilities:

- A "page" is a fixed-size area of memory, 4 kilobytes in length. Physical memory may be visualised as a collection of fixed-size pages.
- A "paged segment" is a segment which is divided into a number of pages, in the same way as the entire virtual address space is divided into a number of segments.

Figure 7.3.6 shows the general principles of calculating a physical address. The top part of the diagram shows the calculation of a "linear address" in the same way as an 80286 physical address is formed. The lower part of the diagram shows how this linear address is converted into a physical address when paging is enabled in the CR0 Control Register. The paging system introduces an additional indirection step in the address formation.

The purpose of introducing this extra indirection is that it increases the flexibility provided to the operating system in allocating memory: physical memory can be allocated in fixed sized units in a paging system, rather than the variable sized blocks needed in a purely segmented system.

The paging mechanism uses three main components, the repertoire, the page tables, and the pages themselves. Using this mechanism, the linear address obtained from the descriptor table using the selector and offset of the original reference does not represent a direct physical address as is the case in the 80286 segmentation scheme, but is divided into three fields used with the paging system components.

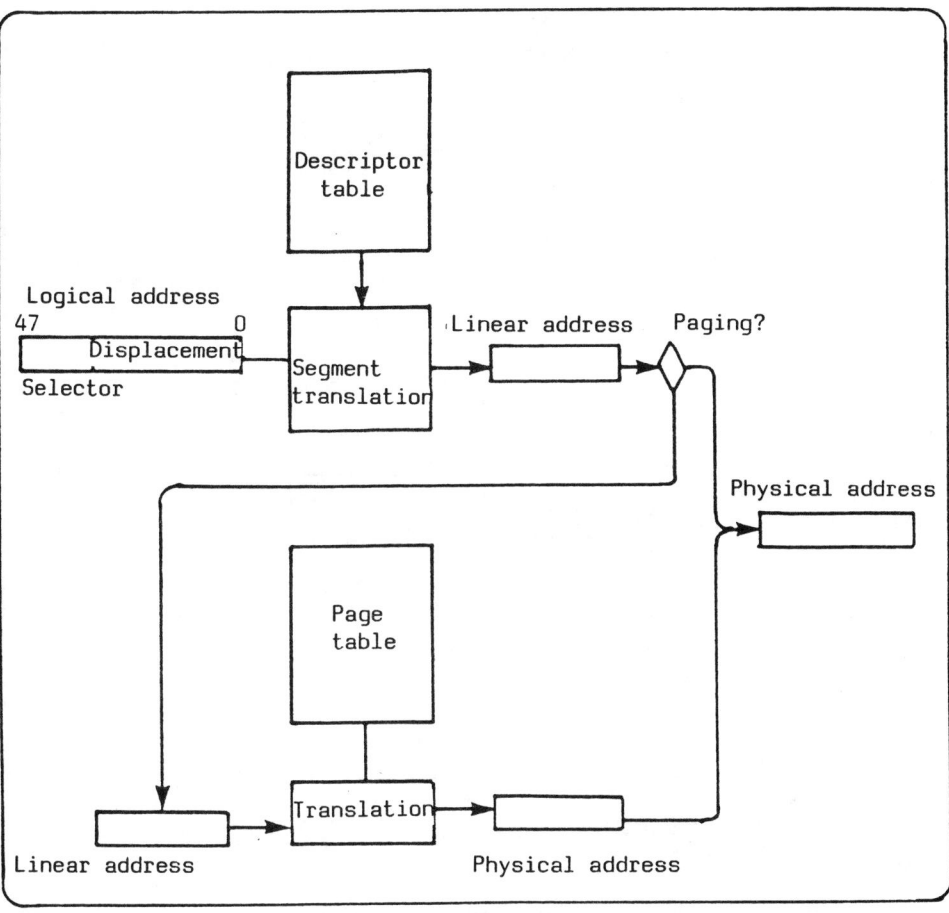

Figure 7.3.6 Address translation with paging

The repertoire is a single page of 4 kilobytes containing 1024 entries. Each entry describes a paging system, that is the address of a page table and the attributes of that table. The address of the repertoire is taken from the CR3 register.

The individual page tables are also 4 kilobyte pages containing the base addresses of the pages which the table describes. Any combination of the pages described in a page table may be present in main memory, or absent, swapped out onto secondary storage. In the page table, each entry is 32 bits long, with 12 bits reserved for the characterisation of the page properties and its protection.

Figure 7.3.7 shows the manner in which the physical address is obtained using the additional indirections introduced by the paging scheme.

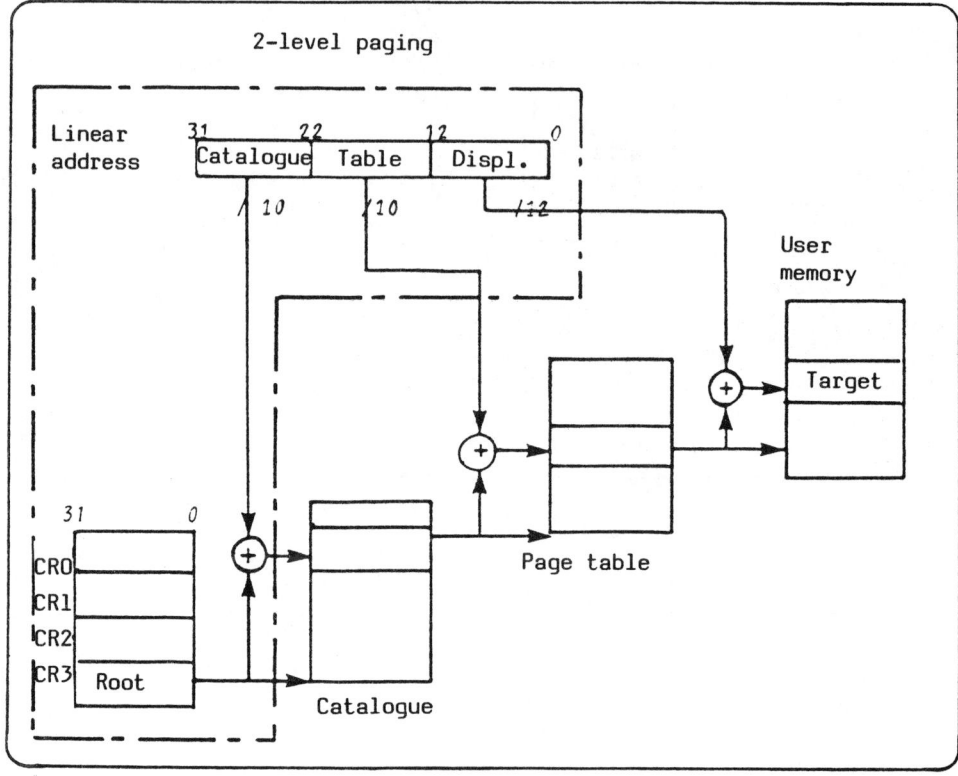

Figure 7.3.7 Paging mechanism

This paging scheme is very similar to that implemented on modern minicomputers and on mainframes, and is oriented towards operating systems which support the scheme.

In this architecture, each task possesses not only its own LDT describing the ensemble of segments which it owns, but also its own repertoire of pages. This enables the protection which comes from the isolation of one running task from another to be preserved. In addition, the CPU automatically implements the switching of repertoires during task switching by hardware, since the repertoire address is present in the TSS attached to each task. As paging is local to a task, two tasks which operate with the same set of linear addresses can operate on quite different physical addresses. This enables two "virtual 8086" tasks to coexist, each operating within the classical linear address space of the 8086, the lowest megabyte of virtual address space.

This additional indirection might slow down the operation of the CPU when accessing main memory, but the hardware design contains facilities to prevent this by including storage on-chip for the most recent 32 page translations. On each memory access, a rapid search of these translations in the Translation Lookaside Buffer (TLB) is made, and only if no translation is stored does access need to be made to the repertoire and the page table. Experience shows that all programs spend all or most of their time accessing relatively limited memory areas, and a statistical calculation shows that, with the TLB, hardly any slowing of the processor due to paging occurs.

7.3.3 Virtual Memory and Protection

Virtual memory

Since the virtual memory principles of the 80386 follow those of the 80286 so closely, this section will not repeat the previous descriptions.

The motivation for providing virtual memory systems comes from the desire to run applications which handle large quantities of information, data or instructions, without the need for the entire application to be present in memory at the same time.

In order to implement a virtual memory system, certain particular indications need to be provided by the underlying hardware. These facilities are all provided by the 80386 CPU.

First, a presence bit is provided in each segment descriptor and in each entry in a page table. This bit is handled by the software which copies pages to and from secondary storage.

Secondly, the hardware checks that every segment and page needed for a particular operation is present in main memory before the operation is allowed to complete. In the 80386, this check is carried out during the address translation phases which use the segment descriptors and the page table.

In this manner, the virtual memory management facilities are provided within the CPU hardware, enabling the software to take decisions on the actions to follow when access to an absent segment or page is made. This software, and the routines to swap specific memory blocks (pages or whole segments) between memory and secondary storage, will generally form part of the operating system which manages the complete operation of the system.

Protection

In the area of protection, the 80386 again offers exactly the same facilities that have been described previously for the 80286 CPU.

The basic mechanisms for protection use four different concepts associated with the memory area to be protected, be it code or data.

- o The privilege level: a program may not access any segment which has a more privileged level than the program itself.

- The segment limit: access to a particular segment is only permitted within the size defined in its descriptor: the system is protected in this way against any accesses outside defined areas, as a task is prevented from overwriting data above or below the area allocated to a particular segment.
- The type: as segment descriptors identify the segment as containing code, for example, or data, the hardware prevents inappropriate accesses to each segment. It is impossible, for example, to execute a data segment inadvertently.
- The access rights: all segments are characterised by definitions in their descriptors, as read-only, read/write, or read and execute, for example, and this characterisation is interpreted by the hardware on every access to the segment. As in the case of the 80286, code segments can be marked "conformant", executable at any privilege level, or "non-conformant", to be executed at a specific privilege level.

In the case of the 80386, pages as well as segments are protected by an attribute system: each entry in a page table contains the attributes of the page which it addresses. Only two privilege levels are implemented, providing the normal distinction between "system" and "application" that is found in minicomputers, rather than the four levels found in the segment protection scheme. In this case, privilege level 3 corresponds to "application" level privilege.

With large segments, the size is given in units of 4 kilobytes, so that a segment may be slightly larger than the data or code that it contains. This means that real memory space for large segments should be allocated in 4 kilobyte units, which may waste some small amount of memory.

7.3.4 Changes of Sequence

As in the 80286, the principal structure used for altering privilege levels is the gate, call gates being used for voluntary calls on operating system functions, and interrupt or trap gates being used to handle interrupts and exceptions. Task gates may be used with CALL instructions to cause out-of-process procedure calls. Interrupts are accepted by using the CPU IDTR register to point to a table of interrupt descriptors, and indexing a particular entry using the interrupt number, in exactly the same way as in the 80286.

7.4 Cache Memory

Previous sections have described the features of the 80386 CPU which affect the software running on the machine: cache memory is a common hardware feature of particular hardware systems, and is almost completely transparent to the software.

The need for cache memory arises very naturally with the 80386 processor: the chip has a 32-bit address bus which permits access to up to 4 gigabytes of real memory, and with its high clock speed and pipelined internal structure, it demands a very short main memory access time. It would be expensive to provide a large main memory with a uniformly fast access time: apart from cost, building a large main memory out of fast RAM chips would result in a physically large and a power-hungry system.

What is needed is a scheme for maintaining the high speed of the processor, while using a large main memory built using the cheapest dynamic RAM components.

This is possible since it is observed that most programs spend most of their time accessing a relatively limited set of instructions and data. In a loop, for example, the same instructions are executed over and over again; within one routine, a program accesses the same data items repeatedly. This observation gives rise to the idea that it might be possible to simulate the effect of a large, uniformly high-speed memory using a small high-speed memory and a large slower memory, provided that at any moment the most frequently accessed instructions and data were held in the faster memory and that accesses to the slower, larger, cost-effective and less power-consuming main memory are infrequent.

Cache memory was first used in 1960s mainframe computers: it appeared in 1970s minicomputers, and is now widely used with the 1980s microprocessors.

7.4.1 Definition of a Cache

A cache memory is a relatively small fast memory, situated between the processor and the large main memory. Hardware is provided to keep copies of the most frequently used memory areas in the cache at any moment.

Cache sizes are limited by cost, circuit area, and electrical fan-out, but a cache needs to contain only the items which are being used or are shortly to be used by the current program. It is reasonable to hope that a program may make several accesses to a particular location during its execution.

The principle and implementation of a cache is quite simple: when the processor needs to fetch a word from main memory, this word is copied into the cache; on the next and subsequent accesses to the same address, this word will be accessed from the fast cache, with no time penalty.

Naturally, in order for this system to perform effectively, it is necessary to determine the optimum size of the cache and to choose algorithms to determine which words are present in the cache and which in main memory. The goal is to optimise the ratio of cached accesses to slow memory accesses. There are a number of different ways of implementing the hardware of a cache.

7.4.2 Cache Design Criteria

The first observation is that the larger a cache is, the more information can be stored in it, and thus the greater the chance of increasing the "hit" rate.

A second constraint is that particular mappings between main memory locations and cache locations can cause excessive copying as different data items compete for access to the same cache locations.

7.4.3 Cache Structures

Cache memory is composed of two parts, a data memory and an address store (or tag store) which identifies which main store locations are present in the cache at any time.

The simplest cache organisation to describe is a "direct-mapped" cache.

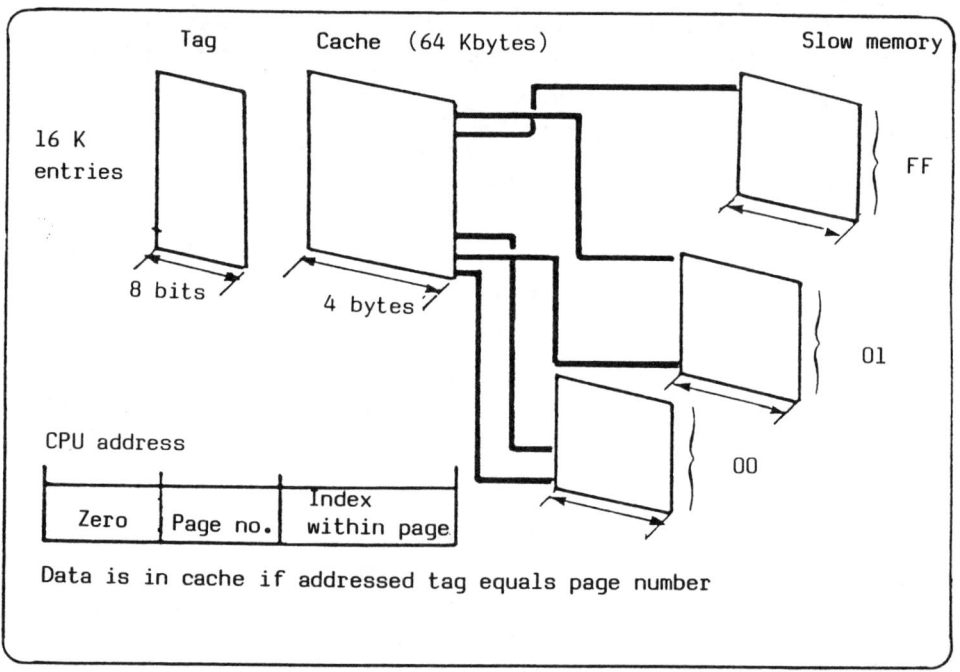

Figure 7.4.1 Direct-mapped 64 kilobyte cache

Figure 7.4.1 shows a cache of 64 kilobytes (or 16K 32-bit words). On every CPU read access, one line in the cache is selected using bits 2–15 of the CPU address: an 8-bit value is read out of the tag store at that address, and if it is equal to the value of bits 16–23 of the CPU address, the required word is present in the cache. If the comparison fails, the word is fetched from memory, stored in the cache, and the current value of bits 16–23 of the CPU address is written into the tag store at the current line.

This cache can cope with a main memory size of up to 16 megabytes (256 x 64K); in an 80386 system, the top 8 bits of the CPU address might be decoded to distinguish between main memory accesses and those to memory mapped peripherals, which must not be cached.

Figure 7.4.2 shows how this cache would be interposed between the CPU and main memory.

It is possible to predict a fairly simple case which gives rise to a poor hit rate with this organisation: this occurs when the current program makes repeated accesses alternately to two memory areas which have the same low-order address bits. The likelihood of this may be low, but if accesses alternate between the two areas, every cache access results in a bad comparison, and each access needs to be handled by main memory.

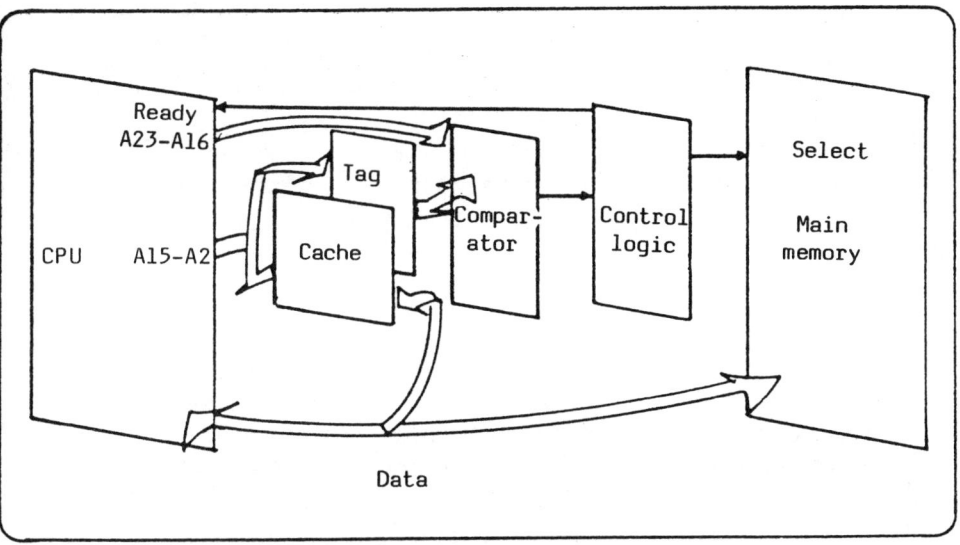

Figure 7.4.2 Direct-mapped cache hardware

Other cache organisations can be envisaged to avoid this drawback. Figure 7.4.3, for example, shows an organisation described as two way set-associative. The direct-mapped cache is the most simple cache organisation, and any more sophisticated structure involves an additional cost in extra hardware. In the two way set-associative cache, for example, two tag stores and two data stores need to be provided, but the advantage is that the cache can cope with memory accesses in two different areas with identical low-order address bits.

Cache architectures can be greatly complicated, but it seems likely that one of the two alternatives outlined will be most commonly used with the 80386, since they offer a reasonable compromise between cost and performance.

So far, the discussion of the cache has only mentioned read cycles. Write cycles from the CPU also need to be studied, and different strategies of dealing with them are possible.

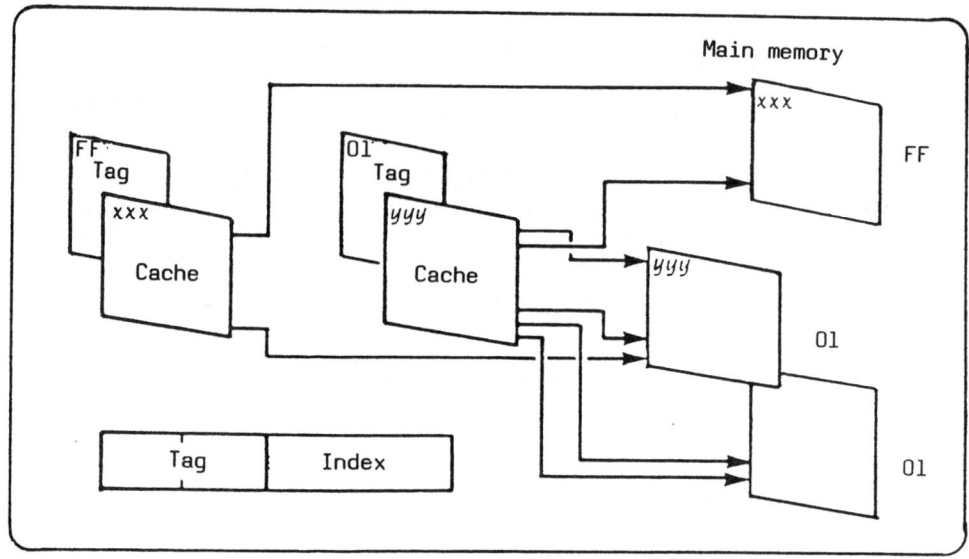

Figure 7.4.3 Two-way set-associative cache

The first alternative is to decide that every CPU write cycle will cause a write cycle in both main and cache memory. This is known as a "write-through" policy. This decision gives rise to difficulties when byte or word operands are written to a 32-bit wide cache, particularly if the relevant word is not present in the cache. The designer might take the decision not to update the cache in this case, but to do so when the operand written is 32 bits long or if the operand were already present in the cache.

The second approach is an obvious optimisation, and introduces a (small) number of buffers into the system, so that when a write is started, the CPU can continue without waiting for the write to finish.

A third alternative is to omit the main memory cycle for writes, just updating the cache, and to maintain a bit for each cache line to identify "dirty" locations, which hold more recent information than the corresponding main memory locations. This scheme is known as "write-back", since each dirty location must be written back to memory before the cache line can be reused. Write-back can result in a reduction of main-memory bandwidth for writes, since a number of successive write operations to a dirty cache line will normally occur before the location needs to be written to main memory.

The discussion of cache memory and its implementation here is intended purely as an introduction and to suggest its value in 80386-based systems. A number of problems remain for the implementor, particularly in the areas of the interaction of cache memory and input-output operations, virtual memory, and task switching.

7.5 Using an 80386

The power of the 80386 architecture, and its range of possibilities are astonishing when considered in the light of the primitive microprocessors of ten years ago. Two questions arise when considering the chip:

- What sort of hardware systems will it be used in?
- What software will these systems use?

The internal structure of the 80386 and its potential uses offer a very powerful 32-bit machine with capabilities matching and exceeding those of the superminicomputers of just a few years ago. The 80386 allows a number of widely varied and very demanding applications to be envisaged, such as robotics, office management, scientific processing, graphics work, workstations, and so on.

Hardware development with this processor will represent a greater investment than using the 80286 or the 8086, perhaps more appropriate to the traditional computer companies than to the individual developer who has a particular requirement. This means that many applications will depend upon standard board-level components, rather than the design of a special-purpose circuit board.

The problem of operating systems is still not resolved. Standard microcomputer operating systems (especially MS/DOS) can be used, but it is obvious that the current versions of these are not capable of exploiting the resources of a large 80386 system efficiently. It is worth asking whether a computer built around the 80386 is worth considering as a "micro" at all; even if the size is small, the power is enormous, and is accompanied by the necessary complications essential to enable the construction of large and flexible systems.

The new product OS/2 provides multitasking on both 80286 and 80386 systems, but few applications are currently available.

Windows/386, from Microsoft, provides a multitasking environment, in which a number of DOS applications can coexist.

Unix is an operating system widely used on minicomputers and now available on single-user workstations, but the complexity inherited from its time-sharing origins may prevent it from becoming very popular on 80386-based PCs.

The very best software environments are those in which the advanced facilities of the 80386 are made available and in which a number of existing 16-bit applications can be run simultaneously, thus preserving the enormous investment in PC software.

Appendix A *80286 Instruction Set*

The full set of 80286 instructions is given in alphabetic order. Each description gives the instruction mnemonic, the addressing modes, and the flags that it modifies.

Each flag bears one of the letters:

u: the instruction leaves the flag undefined
m: the instruction modifies the flag
i: the instruction leaves the flag in its initial state

The permissible addressing modes are indicated in the following manner:

RR,RM,RI: Register. The instruction operates between a register and a second register, a memory location, or an immediate value.

MM,MI: Memory. The two operands are both in memory, or one is an immediate value.

PC: Relative to IP, the instruction pointer.

AA: Absolute Address.

Memory is addressed by one of a number of addressing modes:

- Absolute, where the displacement is in the instruction
- Indexed, [SI] or [DI]
- Based, [BP] or [BX]
- Based Indexed, [BX+SI], [BX+DI], [BP+SI], or [BP+DI]
- Based Indexed with Displacement, for example displacement[BX][SI]

AAA – ASCII adjust for addition

Flags:	S	Z	A	P	C	Ov	TF	IF	DF
	u	u	m	u	m	m	i	i	i

This instruction is used after an ADD instruction to correct the result for ASCII number representation.

Example:

```
ADD    AL, BL    ; AL=32H, BL=33H
AAA              ; AL=35H
```

AAD – ASCII adjust for division

Flags: S Z A P C Ov TF IF DF
        m m u m u u   i   i i

Makes an adjustment to the value in the accumulator so that a subsequent divide by an ASCII coded value produces the correct result: AL is left with the value $10 \times AH + AL$.

Example:

```
AAD              ; AL=32H,AH=33H --> AX=17H
```

AAM – ASCII adjust for multiplication

Flags: S Z A P C Ov TF IF DF
        m m u m u u   i   i   i

Executed after a MUL instruction to produce a correct result in ASCII, by making $AH = AX/10$ and $AL = AX\ MOD\ 10$.

Example:

```
AAM              ; AX=62H -> AH=39H, AL=38H, or 98 BCD
```

AAS – ASCII adjust for subtraction

Flags: S Z A P C Ov TF IF DF
        u u m u m u   i   i   i

Executed after a SUB instruction to correct the result for ASCII.

Example:

```
SUB    AL, BL    ;AL=37H, BL=33H
AAS              ; AL=34H
```

ADD/ADC – Add 8- or 16-bit values

Flags: S Z A P C Ov TF IF DF
        m m m m m m   i   i   i

Operates on RR, RM and RI operands. Both operands must be of the same length. ADC takes the state of the carry flag into account.

Example:

```
ADD    AL, BL    ; AL := AL + BL
ADC    AX, Var   ; AX := AX + (Var) + CF
```

AND – Logical AND between 8- or 16-bit values

Flags:	S	Z	A	P	C	Ov	TF	IF	DF
	m	m	u	m	0	0	i	i	i

Operates on RR, RM and RI operands. Both operands must be of the same length.

Example:
```
AND    AL,BL    ; AL := AL AND BL
AND    Var,AX   ; (Var) := (Var) AND AX
```

ARPL – Adjust Request Privilege Level of a selector

Flags:	S	Z	A	P	C	Ov	TF	IF	DF
	i	m	i	i	i	i	i	i	i

If the RPL field (the 2 least-significant bits) of the selector is lower than the RPL field of the register, the Z flag is set and the RPL field of the selector is raised to that of the second operand. This instruction is provided to help avoid a violation of the ring-structured protection rules. It is used by interface routines in more privileged code to raise the RPL fields of descriptors passed from user-level code to that level. For more detail, see the explanation in chapter 3.

Example:
```
ARPL   SEL,AX   ; Z = 0 or 1
```

BOUND – Check the limits of a table

Flags:	S	Z	A	P	C	Ov	TF	IF	DF
	i	i	i	i	i	i	i	i	i

This instruction verifies that the first operand (which must be a register) is within the limits expressed in the second, which is a double word giving minimum and maximum values. If $R \leq min$ or $R \geq max$, exception 5 is generated.

Example:
```
BOUND  AX,Limits      ; dcl Limits DW Min,Max
```

CALL – Call a subprogram

Flags:	S	Z	A	P	C	Ov	TF	IF	DF
	i	i	i	i	i	i	i	i	i

Calls a subprogram directly or indirectly. CALL may also cause a task switch, in which the flags will be changed to the value read from the new TSS. Calls within segments are identical with the 8086 processor: where two words are used, these may be pointers to code segments (conformant or not), via a Call Gate, via a Task Gate (setting the NT flag), or via a TSS.

Example:
```
CALL    Help       ; IP := displacement of Help
CALL    Mem_W      ; near call indirect
CALL    Mem_DW     ; far call indirect
CALL    BX         ; indirect near call via register
CALL    TSS        ; call via TSS selector (2 words)
CALL    TSKGATE    ; call via Task Gate (2 words)
```

CBW – Convert byte to word

Flags: S Z A P C Ov TF IF DF
        i i i i i i   i   i

Converts a signed byte in AL to a sixteen-bit value in AX by extending the sign bit.

Example:
```
CBW                ; AL=87H -> AX=FF87H
```

CLC – Clear Carry bit

Flags: S Z A P C Ov TF IF DF
        i i i i 0 i   i   i

The carry bit is set to 0.

Example:
```
CLC
```

CLD – Clear Direction Bit

Flags: S Z A P C Ov TF IF DF
        i i i i i i   i   0

The direction flag is set to zero, causing the processor to increment SI and DI during string instructions.

Example:
```
CLD
```

CLI – Clear IF flag

Flags: S Z A P C Ov TF IF DF
        i i i i i i   0   i

Inhibits interrupts. In protected mode, this operation is only possible if the current privilege level is compatible with the IOPL field in the flags register.

Example:
```
CLI
```

CLTS – Clear TS flag

Flags: S Z A P C Ov TF IF DF
        i i i i i i   i   i   i

Resets the Task Switched (TS) flag bit. May only be executed at privilege level 0 in protected mode.

Example:

    CLTS

CMC – Complement carry flag

Flags: S Z A P C Ov TF IF DF
        i i i i m i   i   i   i

Inverts the state of the carry flag.

Example:

    CMC

CMP – Compare two values

Flags: S Z A P C Ov TF IF DF
        m m m m m m   i   i   i

Operates on operands of type RR, RM, RI or MM. The two operands must be of the same size. The flags are set to indicate the result of the comparison. If a word is compared to an eight-bit immediate value, the latter is sign-extended to 16 bits.

Example:

    CMP   AL,BL   ; AL ? BL
    CMP   AX,-3   ; AX ? -3

CMPS – Compare two strings

Flags: S Z A P C Ov TF IF DF
        m m m m m m   i   i   i

Comparing two strings (of words or bytes), the first is accessed by DS:SI, the second by ES:DI. If the direction flag is zero, the two index registers are then incremented (by two for a word compare), or decremented if the direction flag is set. This instruction may be the subject of a REPZ, REP or REPNZ prefix. The flags indicate the result.

Example:

         LEA   SI,Src
         LEA   DI,Dst
         MOV   CX,10
    REPZ CMPSB   ; compare 10 bytes

CWD – Convert from word to double word

Flags: S Z A P C Ov TF IF DF
        i i i i i i   i   i

Convert the signed value in AX to a 32-bit value in DX:AX.

Example:
```
CWD       ; AX=99F4H -> DX=FFFF, AX=99F4H
```

DAA – Decimal adjust after addition

Flags: S Z A P C Ov TF IF DF
        m m m m m u   i   i   i

Corrects (to BCD) the result of adding two BCD numbers.

Example:
```
ADD   AL,BL   ; AL=46H BL=27H
DAA           ; AL=73H (from 6DH)
```

DAS – Decimal adjust after subtraction

Flags: S Z A P C Ov TF IF DF
        m m m m m u   i   i   i

Corrects the result after subtracting two BCD numbers.

Example:
```
SUB   AL,BL   ; AL=61H BL=45H
DAS           ; AL=16H (from 1CH)
```

DEC – Subtract 1 from a register or memory operand

Flags: S Z A P C Ov TF IF DF
        m m m m i m   i   i   i

Decrements its operand. Warning: this instruction does not alter the Carry flag.

Example:
```
DEC   Count   ; (Count) := (Count) - 1
```

DIV – Unsigned Division

Flags: S Z A P C Ov TF IF DF
        u u u u u i   i   i

Divides AX by an 8-bit value (R or M). The quotient is left in AL, the remainder in AH. Alternatively, divides DX:AH by a 16-bit value (R or M), leaving the quotient in AL, the remainder in DX.

Example:
```
DIV     BL      ; AX/BL, AL:=Q, AH:=R
```

ENTER – Make entry into a procedure

Flags: S Z A P C Ov TF IF DF
        i i i i i i   i   i   i

Has two immediate operands, N and Level. N indicates the number of bytes of local variable space to allocate on the stack, and Level the lexical declaration level of the procedure. This is for languages such as Pascal, which permit access to non-local variables.

Example:
```
ENTER   6,0     ; Equivalent to:
                ; PUSH BP
                ; MOV  BP,SP
                ; SUB  SP,6
```

HLT – Halt processor

Flags: S Z A P C Ov TF IF DF
        i i i i i i   i   i   i

Enter into "halted" mode. Privileged: level 0.

Example:
```
HLT
```

IDIV – Signed divide

Flags: S Z A P C Ov TF IF DF
        u u u u u u   i   i   i

Divides AX by an eight bit value, leaving the quotient in AL and the remainder in AH, or divides DX:AX by a sixteen bit value, leaving the quotient in AX, the remainder in DX.

Example:
```
IDIV    BL      ; AX / BL, AL:=Q, AH:=R
```

IMUL – Signed multiplication

Flags: S Z A P C Ov TF IF DF
        u u u u m m   i   i   i

When IMUL is written with a single operand, AX (or AL) is multiplied by a 16-bit (or 8-bit) value to give DX:AX (or AX). With three operands, the first (R16) is given the result of multiplying the second (memory) by the third (immediate). The two operand case is a special case of the three operand case.

Example:

```
IMUL    BL       ; AX := AX * BL
IMUL    CX       ; DX:AX := AX * CX
IMUL    BX,CX,3  ; BX:= CX * 3
```

IN – Read input port

Flags: S Z A P C Ov TF IF DF
        i i i i i i   i   i   i

Reads an 8-bit or 16-bit peripheral port. AX or AL is overwritten with the value, which may come from an immediate address (less than 256) or be a variable port number in the DX register. In protected mode, the current privilege level must be compatible with IOPL.

Example:

```
IN   AL,56H   ; direct address
MOV  DX,678H
IN   AX,DX    ; port address indirectly specified
```

INC – Adds 1 to memory or register

Flags: S Z A P C Ov TF IF DF
        m m m m i m   i   i   i

Increments a register or memory location. Warning: does not modify the Carry flag.

Example:

```
INC   AX
```

INSB/INSW – Read string from a port

Flags: S Z A P C Ov TF IF DF
        i i i i i i   i   i   i

Transfers 8-bit (INSB) or 16-bit (INSW) data from the port specified in DX to the memory area indicated by DS:DI. The address in DI is incremented or decremented depending on the Direction flag. Using the REP prefix, the number of transfers is given by CX. The current privilege level must be compatible with IOPL in protected mode.

Example:

```
    MOV   CX,20
    MOV   DX,3456H
    MOV   DI,OFFSET Buf
REP INSB                    ; read string of bytes
```

INT/INTO – Call an Interrupt procedure

Flags: S Z A P C Ov TF IF DF
        i i i i i i   i   i   i

Provokes a program interrupt. INT specifies the vector number in the range 0 to 255, and always interrupts, while INTO interrupts only if the Overflow flag is set, and always uses interrupt number 4. The interrupt may cause a task switch if the interrupt table contains a task gate.

Example:
```
INT     56      ; Interrupt via IDT entry 56
```

IRET – Return from interrupt procedure

Flags: S Z A P C Ov TF IF DF
        m m m m m m   m   m   m

Used at the end of interrupt processing. The flags are restored from the interrupted state: if the Nested Task bit is set in the flags register, the return is via a task switch to the task indicated by the back link in the current TSS.

Example:
```
IRET
```

Jxx – Jump on condition

Flags: S Z A P C Ov TF IF DF
        i i i i i i   i   i   i

The instruction tests a combination of flag bits, which can be used to determine the results of signed or unsigned arithmetic. These instructions contain an 8-bit value which gives a destination of -128 to +127 bytes from the current PC.

Example:
```
; general
        JC              Label   ; j. if C=1
        JCXZ            Label   ; j. if CX=0
        JE              Label   ; j. if Z=1
        JNE/JNZ         Label   ; j. if <> (Z=0)
        JNO             Label   ; j. if not OVF (OV=0)
        JNP             Label   ; j. if P=0 (not Parity)
        JNS             Label   ; j. if S=0 (not Sign)
        JP/JPE          Label   ; j. if P=1 (Parity even)
        JPO             Label   ; j. if P=0 (Parity odd)
        JS              Label   ; j. if S=1 (Sign)
        JO              Label   ; j. if OV=1 (Overflow)
```

80286 instruction set

```
; unsigned:
        JA/JNBE         Label   ; j. if >   (C=0 and Z=0)
        JAE/JNB/JNC     Label   ; j. if >=  (C=0)
        JB/JNAE         Label   ; j. if <   (C=1)
        JBE/JNA         Label   ; j. if <=  (C=1 or Z=1)
; signed:
        JG/JNLE         Label   ; j. if >   (Z=0 and S=OV)
        JGE/JNL         Label   ; j. if >=  (S=OV)
        JL/JNGE         Label   ; j. if <   (S<>OV)
        JLE/JNG         Label   ; j. if <=  (Z=1 or S=OV)
```

JMP – Unconditional jump

Flags: S   Z   A   P   C   Ov TF IF DF
        i   i   i   i   i   i   i   i   i

The jump may be short (16 bits) or long (32 bits), direct or indirect via 16-bit register or 16-bit or 32-bit memory. Short direct jumps are relative to PC, while long jumps and indirect jumps are absolute. Inter-segment jumps may be effected using a TSS, a Call Gate or a Task Gate.

The following checks are carried out when a JMP instruction references a Call Gate:

- The gate must be present
- The privilege level of the gate must be (numerically) higher than the current level
- The privilege level in the gate descriptor must be higher than that in the selector used to access the gate
- the selector of the code segment in the gate must be non-null
- the selector must point within the limits of the GDT or LDT
- the access rights bits of the descriptor must indicate a code segment
- if the segment is non-conformant, the protection level must be (numerically) lower than the current level
- the code segment must be present
- IP must be within the limits of the segment.

With these checks validated, the processor can load CS and IP, loading the CS descriptor cache and changing the current protection level to the DPL of the new code segment.

Example:
```
        JMP     NearLabel       ; 16 bits relative to PC
        JMP     BX              ; IP := (BX)
        JMP     FAR There       ; via 32-bit pointer
```

```
JMP     TSS             ; task switch
JMP     DWORD PTR Tbl   ; via a table
```

LAHF – Load the flags into AH
Flags: S Z A P C Ov TF IF DF
        i i i i i i   i   i   i

The low-order 8 bits of the flags register are copied into AH.
Example:
```
LAHF
```

LAR – Load Access Rights
Flags: S Z A P C Ov TF IF DF
        i m i i i i   i   i   i

LAR's second operand is a register or memory location containing a selector. If the descriptor referenced by this selector is visible at the current privilege level and at the RPL of the selector, the destination is loaded with the top half of the descriptor, and the lower half set to zero. The Zero flag is set to 1 if the operation is correctly executed, or zero if it fails for any reason (index out of table limits, *CPL > DPL*, or *RPL > DPL*).

Example:
```
LAR     AX,Selector     ; AH := DA, AL := 0
```

LDS/LES – Load segment and index register
Flags: S Z A P C Ov TF IF DF
        i i i i i i   i   i   i

Loads a register pair DS:R or ES:R wih a 32-bit pointer. The first word is the displacement, the second the selector. In protected mode, the cached values are loaded. Loading a null selector is prohibited.

Example:
```
LES     SI,Ptr_32
```

LEA – Load effective address
Flags: S Z A P C Ov TF IF DF
        i i i i i i   i   i   i

Loads the displacement of the specified memory operand into a register.

Example:
```
LEA     SI,Mem
LEA     DI,[BX]         ; same as MOV DI,BX
```

LEAVE – Leave a procedure begun by ENTER

Flags: S Z A P C Ov TF IF DF
        i i i i i i   i   i   i

Effects the inverse of ENTER, copying BP into SP and unstacking BP, to free space allocated at the beginning of the procedure.

Example:
```
LEAVE
RET
```

LGDT/LIDT – Load the system descriptors to GDT or IDT

Flags: S Z A P C Ov TF IF DF
        i i i i i i   i   i   i

The operand of these instructions is a 6-byte area of memory, giving the limit (one word) and the base (next 3 bytes) of the table. The last byte is ignored. A protection exception occurs if the current privilege level is not zero.

Example:
```
LGDT    ADGDT
```

LLDT – Load LDT

Flags: S Z A P C Ov TF IF DF
        i i i i i i   i   i   i

The operand is a memory word or register containing a selector into the GDT. The internal LDT registers are loaded with the limit and base address from that descriptor; the LDT field in the current TSS is unchanged. Privileged: level 0.

Example:
```
LLDT
```

LMSW – Load MSW

Flags: S Z A P C Ov TF IF DF
        i i i i i i   i   i   i

Load the Machine Status Word from memory. Privileged: level 0.

Example:
```
LMSW    MachStat
```

LOCK – Lock Prefix

Flags: S Z A P C Ov TF IF DF
        i i i i i i   i   i   i

LOCK is a prefix used with any instruction to assert the LOCK signal throughout the execution of the instruction. LOCK is used to ensure non-interference in a multiprocessor system, and is most commonly used with INC, DEC, or XCHG instructions. Because of its effect on the overall operation of the system, it is privileged and may only be executed at level 0.

Example:

```
LOCK XCHG     AX,SemX
```

LODSB/LODSW – Loads from a string

Flags:	S	Z	A	P	C	Ov	TF	IF	DF
	i	i	i	i	i	i	i	i	i

Loads AL (LODSB) or AX (LODSW) from DS:SI. SI is incremented or decremented (depending on the Direction flag) by 1 or 2. Used with the REP prefix, CX contains the number of bytes to transfer.

Example:

```
REP LODSW         ;AX := DS:SI++ (CX times)
```

LOOP/LOOPE/LOOPNE – Looping instruction

Flags:	S	Z	A	P	C	Ov	TF	IF	DF
	i	i	i	i	i	i	i	i	i

LOOP decrements CX and jumps (relative to IP) if CX is non-zero. When CX reaches zero, the LOOP instruction drops through. LOOPE also drops through if Z is set, while LOOPNE drops through if Z is clear.

Example:

```
LOOP    Again    ; until (--CX) reaches 0
```

LSL – Load Segment Limit

Flags:	S	Z	A	P	C	Ov	TF	IF	DF
	i	m	i	i	i	i	i	i	i

If the descriptor given by the second operand's selector is visible at the CPL, the segment limit is loaded into the first operand. Z is set if the operand is successful, cleared otherwise. LSL can be used to find the sizes of segments, the TSS or the LDT.

Example:

```
LSL    AX,Selec      ; AX := limit and Z := 1
```

LTR – Load TR

Flags:	S	Z	A	P	C	Ov	TF	IF	DF
	i	i	i	i	i	i		i	i

The Task Register is loaded with the value of the second operand, a register or memory location. The new TSS is marked "busy". LTR does not cause a task switch.

Example:
```
LTR     AX
```

MOV – Transfer data

Flags:	S	Z	A	P	C	Ov	TF	IF	DF
	i	i	i	i	i	i		i	i

The value of the second operand (16 or 8 bits) is loaded into the first operand. Operand combinations permitted are RR, RM, RI and MI. If a segment register (ES, DS or SS) is loaded, the descriptor addressed by the new selector is validated in the usual way.

Example:
```
MOV     AL,3
MOV     AX,BX       ; RR
MOV     Count,4     ; MI
MOV     AX,Value    ;FROM Value TO AX
```

MOVSB/MOVSW – Memory to memory copy

Flags:	S	Z	A	P	C	Ov	TF	IF	DF
	i	i	i	i	i	i	i	i	i

Transfer a byte or word from DS:SI to ES:DI, incrementing or decrementing (according to the Direction flag) SI and DI by 1 or 2. With the REP prefix, copies CX bytes or words. The operation is interruptible, as with all string instructions.

Example:
```
    LEA     Si,Src
    LEA     Di,Dst
    MOV     CX,LENGTH Dst
    CLD
REP MOVSB
```

MUL – Unsigned multiplication

Flags:	S	Z	A	P	C	Ov	TF	IF	DF
	u	u	u	u	m	m		i	i

Carries out an 8-bit or 16-bit multiplication. One of the operands must be in AL or AX, and the 16-bit or 32-bit result is given in AX or DX:AX.

Example:
```
MUL     CL      ; AX := AL * CL
MUL     BX      ; DX:AX := AX * BX
```

NEG – Two's complement
Flags: S   Z   A   P   C   Ov   TF   IF   DF
        m   m   m   m   m   m   i   i   i

Negate the operand in register or memory.
Example:
```
NEG     AL
```

NOP – No Operation
Flags: S   Z   A   P   C   Ov   TF   IF   DF
        i   i   i   i   i   i   i   i   i

Wastes time and space by doing nothing.
Example:
```
NOP
```

NOT – One's complement
Flags: S   Z   A   P   C   Ov   TF   IF   DF
        i   i   i   i   i   i   i   i   i

Gives the one's complement of a register or memory operand.
Example:
```
NOT     AX
```

OR – Logical OR of two operands
Flags: S   Z   A   P   C   Ov   TF   IF   DF
        m   m   u   m   0   0   i   i   i

Performs a logical OR of two 8-bit or 16-bit operands, of type RR, RM or RI. The two operands must be the same length.
Example:
```
OR      AL,BL
```

OUT – Write to a peripheral port
Flags: S   Z   A   P   C   Ov   TF   IF   DF
        i   i   i   i   i   i   i   i   i

Write to an 8-bit or 16-bit output port from AL or AX. The address may be given directly or in DX. A privilege exception is caused if the current privilege level is incompatible with IOPL.

Example:

```
OUT    56H,AL
MOV    DX,678H
OUT    DX,AX
```

OUTSB/OUTSW – Write a string to a port

Flags: S Z A P C Ov TF IF DF
       i i i i i i   i   i   i

Writes bytes or words to an output port from memory at the address DS:SI, incrementing or decrementing SI. With the REP prefix, a string of bytes or words are written. The current privilege level must be compatible with IOPL.

Example:

```
    MOV    DX,678H
    LEA    SI,Print
    MOV    CX,LENGTH Print
REP OUTSW  DX,AX
```

POP – Unstack a word

Flags: S Z A P C Ov TF IF DF
       i i i i i i   i   i   i

Unstacks the word addressed by SS:SP, loading it into the operand specified (R or M). If the destination is a segment register, the selector is validated, and interrupts are inhibited until after the following instruction (to permit SS and SP to be changed without peril).

Example:

```
POP    AX
POP    DS
POP    Word1
```

POPA – Unstack all registers

Flags: S Z A P C Ov TF IF DF
       i i i i i i   i   i   i

The general registers DI, SI, BP, SP, BX, DX, CX and AX are unstacked. This is the inverse order from the stacking performed by PUSHA.

Example:

```
POPA              ; restore all registers
```

POPF – Unstack flags

Flags: S Z A P C Ov TF IF DF
        m m m m m m   m   m   m

The word at the top of stack is removed and loaded into the flags register.
Example:
```
POPF
```

PUSH – Stack a word

Flags: S Z A P C Ov TF IF DF
        i i i i i i   i   i

Decrement the stack pointer by two and write the operand (R or M) to the address SP:SS. PUSH SP stacks the *old* value of SP, which is different from the 8086 implementation of the same instruction.

Example:
```
PUSH    AX
PUSH    Var
```

PUSHA – Stack all registers

Flags: S Z A P C Ov TF IF DF
        i i i i i i   i   i

Stacks the general registers in the order AX CX DX BX SP BP SI DI.
Example:
```
PUSHA            ; Preserve all registers
```

PUSHF – Push flags

Flags: S Z A P C Ov TF IF DF
        i i i i i i   i   i

The 16-bit flags register is stacked.
Example:
```
PUSHF
```

RCR/RCL – Rotate through carry

Flags: S Z A P C Ov TF IF DF
        i i i i m m   i   i

Performs a 9-bit or 17-bit rotate of a memory location or register through the carry bit in the flags register. The Overflow flag is undefined for multiple rotates. The number of bits to rotate may be specified in the CL register, and is limited to 31.

Example:

```
RCR     AX,1
RCR     Mask,CX
```

REP/REPE/REPNE – Repetition Prefixes

Flags: S Z A P C Ov TF IF DF
       m m m m m m i i i

The repetition prefixes can be used with the string instructions to cause a single-instruction loop. The loop terminates when the count (in CX) is exhausted, or when Z is set (for REPE) or when Z is clear (for REPNE). The flags are unchanged unless the REPeated instruction is CMP or SCA; the REPeated instruction is interruptible.

Example:

```
REP MOVSB
```

RET – Return from subprogram

Flags: S Z A P C Ov TF IF DF
       i i i i i i i i

Return after a near or far CALL. An optional operand specifies the number of bytes to unstack after unstacking the return address.

Depending on the declaration of the procedure, the return address may be a 16-bit offset within the current code segment, or a 32-bit far pointer. In this latter case, the return may involve a change in privilege level, which causes the processor to check that return is being made to a less privileged (higher numbered) level.

Example:

```
RET
RET     2*3      ; unstack 3 x 1 word parameters
```

ROR/ROL – Rotate without carry

Flags: S Z A P C Ov TF IF DF
       i i i m m i i i

Performs an 8-bit or 16-bit rotation, with the C bit retaining the last bit shifted out of the byte or word. The Overflow flag is undefined for multiple rotates. The number of bits to rotate may be specified in the CL register, and is limited to 31.

Example:

```
ROR     AX,1
```

SAHF – Store AH into flags

Flags: S Z A P C Ov TF IF DF
        m m m m m m   i   i   i

Stores the AH register into the low byte of the flags register.

Example:

```
SAHF
```

SAL/SAR – Arithmetic shift

Flags: S Z A P C Ov TF IF DF
        m m u m m m   i   i   i

Shifts the register or memory operand left or right by the designated count. Operates on byte or word operand, and shifting right preserves the sign bit. Shifting left injects zeros at the right hand end. The shift count is specified in an immediate operand or in CL, and is limited to 31 bits.

Example:

```
SAR     AX,1
MOV     CL,1
SAR     AX,CL    ; C656 -> E32B
```

SBB – Subtract with borrow

Flags: S Z A P C Ov TF IF DF
        m m m m m m   i   i   i

Subtracts two 8-bit or 16-bit values, accounting for the Carry flag. The operand combinations implemented are RR, RM, RI and MI.

Example:

```
SBB     AX,Diff
```

SCASB/SCASW – Scan bytes or words

Flags: S Z A P C Ov TF IF DF
        m m m m m m   i   i   i

Compare AL or AX with the byte or word at ES:DI, incrementing DI as appropriate. The flags give the result of the comparison.

Example:

```
REPE    SCASW          ; find first equal words
```

SGDT/SIDT – Store table registers

Flags: S Z A P C Ov TF IF DF
        i i i i i i   i   i   i

The contents of the internal CPU table register is written to a 6-byte memory area: the first word contains the limit and the next three bytes the base address, with the last byte unused. Privileged: level 0.

Example:

```
SGDT    SavedGDT
```

SHL/SHR – Logical shift

Flags: S   Z   A   P   C   Ov TF IF DF
        m   m   u   m   m   m   i   i   i

Shifts the register or memory operand left or right, inserting zeros. The shift count is specified in an immediate operand or in CL, and is limited to 31 bits.

Example:

```
SHR     AX,1    ; C656 -> 632B
```

SLDT – Store LDT selector

Flags: S   Z   A   P   C   Ov TF IF DF
        i   i   i   i   i   i   i   i   i

Stores the value of the current LDT selector at the memory address given. Privileged: level 0.

Example:

```
SLDT    CurLDT
```

SMSW – Store MSW

Flags: S   Z   A   P   C   Ov TF IF DF
        i   i   i   i   i   i   i   i   i

Stores the current value of the Machine Status Word.

Example:

```
SMSW    SavMSW
```

STC – Set Carry flag

Flags: S   Z   A   P   C   Ov TF IF DF
        i   i   i   i   1   i   i   i   i

Carry flag is set to 1.

Example:

```
STC
```

STD – Set Direction flag

Flags: S   Z   A   P   C   Ov   TF   IF   DF
        i   i   i   i   i   i   i   i   1

Set Direction flag to 1: indicates that subsequent string instructions use descending-order memory addresses.

Example:
```
STD
```

STI – Set Interrupt Flag

Flags: S   Z   A   P   C   Ov   TF   IF   DF
        i   i   i   i   i   i   i   1   i

Enable interrupts. Current privilege level must be compatible with IOPL.

Example:
```
STI
```

STOSB/STOSW – Store into string

Flags: S   Z   A   P   C   Ov   TF   IF   DF
        i   i   i   i   i   i   i   i   i

Stores the value in AL (STOSB) or AX (STOSW) into ES:DI, incrementing DI as appropriate. REPeatable using a prefix.

Example:
```
        XOR     AX,AX
        LEA     DI,Buf
        MOV     CX,LENGTH Buf
        CLD
        REP STOSB                ; clear memory area
```

STR – Store TR

Flags: S   Z   A   P   C   Ov   TF   IF   DF
        i   i   i   i   i   i   i   i   i

Stores the TR selector into the specified operand. Privileged: level 0.

Example:
```
STR     OldTR
```

SUB – Subtract

Flags: S   Z   A   P   C   Ov   TF   IF   DF
        m   m   m   m   m   m   i   i   i

Subtract two 8-bit or 16-bit values without carry. Operands may be RR, RM, RI or MI.

Example:

```
SUB     AX,Decrement
```

TEST – Logical and, setting flags

Flags:	S	Z	A	P	C	Ov	TF	IF	DF
	m	m	u	m	0	0	i	i	i

ANDs two 8-bit or 16-bit operands together, without writing the result to an operand, but setting the S, Z and P flags according to the result. RR, RM, RI and MI operand combinations are provided.

Example:

```
TEST    AX,0FF8FH
```

VERR/VERW – Verify access for read or write

Flags:	S	Z	A	P	C	Ov	TF	IF	DF
	i	m	i	i	i	i	i	i	i

This instruction takes a selector operand in memory or in a register. The instruction verifies if the segment addressed is visible and available for reading (VERR) or writing (VERW). The Z flag is set if the segment is visible, and cleared if not. Privileged: level 0.

Example:

```
VERR AX
```

WAIT – Wait while BUSY

Flags:	S	Z	A	P	C	Ov	TF	IF	DF
	i	i	i	i	i	i	i	i	i

Intended for synchronising with the 80287, the WAIT instruction does not finish execution until the BUSY pin on the processor is low.

Example:

```
WAIT
```

XCHG – Exchange

Flags:	S	Z	A	P	C	Ov	TF	IF	DF
	i	i	i	i	i	i	i	i	i

Exchanges two operands, of types RR or RM. The operands may be 8-bit or 16-bits long.

Example:

```
XCHG    AH,AL
```

XLAT – Table Translate

Flags: S Z A P C Ov TF IF DF
        i i i i i i   i   i

Translates the byte in AL using a (256 byte) table at DS:BX. The assembler uses the operand to generate a segment override prefix if necessary.

Example:

```
LEA     BX,Table
XLAT    Table               ; AL := Table[AL]
```

XOR – Exclusive Or

Flags: S Z A P C Ov TF IF DF
        m m u m 0 0   i   i   i

Perform an exclusive OR between two 8 or 16-bit operands, in the combinations RR, RM, RI or MI.

Example:

```
XOR     AX,AX               ; Clear AX
XOR     AL,BL               ; AL := AL XOR BL
```

Appendix B *80386 Instruction Set*

The 80386 instruction set is a superset of that offered in the 80286, and allows access to the full 32-bit structure of the machine. The 32-bit facilities are provided by introducing a number of instructions (suffixed by a D) acting on 32-bit words. The chief departure of this machine is the processing of bit fields: all 8- and 16-bit operations of the 80286 are available on 32-bit quantities in the 80386.

One new type of data appears in the 80386: the address, or an 80386 pointer, is a 48-bit value containing a 16-bit selector and a 32-bit displacement.

The 80386 is a more orthogonal machine than the 80286, implying that the general registers can be used in all arithmetic and logical operations, as well as in addressing modes.

In the assembly language, the pseudo-instruction USE is provided to indicate whether 16-bit or 32-bit displacements are to be planted.

The summary below indicates the chief enhancements of the 80386: the reader is referred to Intel's detailed documentation for a complete description of the enhancements made in the 80386.

B.1 Double-word Instructions

A number of instructions are provided to operate on 32-bit quantities. In most cases, these are double-word variants of the 16-bit instructions present in the 80286. Some examples are:

CMPSD: Double word compare
INSD: Input from 32-bit I/O port
MOVSD: Copy an area of double words
OUTSD: Write to a 32-bit I/O port
POPAD: Restore all 32-bit registers from stack
PUSHAD: Stack all 32-bit registers
POPFD: Restore EFLAGS, the 32-bit flags register from stack
PUSHFD: Stack EFLAGS
SCASD: Search area of 32-bit words
STOSD: Initialisation of area of 32-bit words

B.2 Additional Instructions

BSF/BSR – Find lowest or highest bit set

BSF finds the first bit set to 1 in a word or double word, and BSR finds the last bit set. ZF is set to indicate the result: 0 if the word is all zero, 1 if non-zero. In the latter case, the index to the bit found is left in the register operand.

Example:
```
BSF     AX,Mem          ; AX set to first bit set in Mem
```

BT – Bit Test

Loads the bit in the first operand designated by the second operand into the carry flag.

Example:
```
BT      AX,BX           ; Cy = bit (BX) of AX
```

BTC – Bit test with complement

As for BT, but loads the complement of the designated bit into the C flag.

BTR/BTS – Bit test with reset or set

As for BT, but following the test, the selected bit is set or reset.

CDQ – Convert double to quad

Converts the 32-bit signed integer in EAX to 64 bits in EDX:EAX.

CWDE – Convert word to double (extended)

Converts the signed integer in AX to EAX.

IBTS – Insert bit string

Copies a string of bits from a register into memory or a register. The source is right-justified in the register; the destination offset (in bits) is specified in AX or EAX, and the length of the bit string is given in CL.

Example:

```
MOV     AX,000111110111111B
MOV     CL,8
IBTS    Mem32,EAX,CL,Reg;  8 bits from Reg copied to
                        ;  Mem32 at displacement EAX
```

IRETD – Return from interrupt

Return from interrupt in 32-bit mode, indicating that EIP is restored from the stack rather than IP.

LSS/LGS/LFS – Load SS, GS or FS register and a displacement

These instructions function as LDS and LES in the 80286, but can be used with DS, ES, FS, GS or SS, and can operate with a 32-bit displacement.

Example:

```
LGS     ESI,Ptr_386     ; GS:ESI := a 386 pointer
```

MOVSX – Move with sign extension

Operates as MOV, but sign extends the source before the transfer.

MOVZX – Move with zero extension

As for MOV, but extends the source with zeros before transfer.

SETxx – Write condition to byte

This instruction sets its operand byte to 1 if the designated condition is true, or to 0 if not. The same conditions are provided as for the Jxx instruction.

Example:

```
CMP     AX,BX
SETEQ   Flag            ; 1 if AX = BX, else 0
```

SHRD/SHLD – Shift double word right or left

Shifts the first operand right or left inserting bits specified in a second operand by the number of bits specified in an immediate operand or in CL.

Example:

```
MOV     AX,011B
MOV     CL,3
SHLD    Mem,AX,CL      ; shift Mem left 3 places,
                       ; inserting 011 from AX
```

XBTS – Extract bit string

Extracts a string of bits from memory and inserts it, right-justified, into a register. The bit string is addressed by a base and displacement in AX or EAX, and its size is given in CL.

Example:

```
XBTS    EBX,ESI,EAX,CL  ; extract string, length CL
                        ; from EAX[ESI]
```

Appendix C *ETR_286 Real-time Monitor*

The following pages contain the listings of selected parts of the ETR_286 real-time monitor.

The appendix contains the following listings:

etr.h: Standard definitions
etrstr.h: Data Structure definitions
etrprc.h: User entry point definitions
etrt0: Test: task 0
etrt1: task 1
etrtf: task 2
etrsched.s86: task dispatcher (assembly language)
etrto: clock handler
etrford: timeouts
etrevms: events and messages
etrfifo: fifo operations
etrmemx: internal memory space
etrmemu: user memory space
etrbud: user memory allocator
etrcnf: configuration of tasks and I/O
etrdrv: I/O manager
etrexp: exception handlers
etrut: utilities
etrmain: Main program
etrinit: initialisation and internal memory
etres: peripheral initialising
etr286.bld: Builder configuration file

C.1 etr.h

```
/*-------------------------
ETR286 Literal Declarations
-----------------------*/
/*
General
*/
    declare dcl         literally 'declare';
    dcl lit             literally 'literally';
    dcl true            lit '0FFH' ;
    dcl false           lit '00H'  ;
    dcl boolean         lit 'byte' ;
    dcl lx_ends         lit '00'    ;   /* End of String                    */
    dcl lx_nbitw        lit '16'    ;   /* No. of bits in word              */
    dcl lx_nilw         lit '0FFFFH';   /* 16 bits invalid value            */
/*
GDT-related
*/
    dcl lx_al_gdt       lit '   8'; /* Alias to gdt in GDT                  */
    dcl lx_al_idt       lit '  16'; /* Alias to idt in GDT                  */
    dcl lx_firstgdt     lit '80 ' ; /* First free GDT entry                 */
    dcl lx_egdt         lit '  10'; /* No. of aliases in GDT                */
    dcl lx_index_otd    lit '  02'; /* Index to task's OTD in GDT           */
    dcl lx_index_fifo   lit '  03'; /* Index to task's fifo in GDT          */
    dcl lx_index_ldt    lit '  01'; /* Index to task's LDT in GDT           */
    dcl lx_index_t0     lit '0050'; /* Index to task 0 in GDT               */
    dcl lx_index_tss    lit '  00'; /* Index to task's TSS in GDT           */
/*
Descriptor-related
*/
    dcl lx_bpres        lit '80H'     ; /* Present bit in Desc.             */
    dcl lx_dpl0         lit '   00'   ; /* Dpl 0                            */
    dcl lx_ti           lit '04'      ; /* TI bit in selector               */
    dcl lx_typseg       lit '00000'   ; /* Segment type for selector        */
    dcl lx_ar_rw        lit '  00H'   ; /* RW access rights                 */
    dcl lx_msk24B       lit '0FFFFFFH'; /* Mask for L.S. 24 bits in 32      */
    dcl lx_msk_idx      lit '0FFF8H'  ; /* Mask for index in selector       */
/*
Sizes
*/
    dcl lx_szotd        lit '  000';    /* Size of task's OTD               */
    dcl lx_szfifo       lit '  004';    /* Fifo size                        */
    dcl lx_nbint        lit '08'   ;    /* No. of INT's handled             */
    dcl lx_ndesc_tsk    lit '    4';    /* No. of GDT entries per task      */
    dcl lx_ti_isgdt     lit '00000';    /* GDT selector                     */
    dcl lx_ti_isldt     lit '04'   ;    /* LDT selector                     */
/*
Error codes
*/
    dcl lx_succes       lit '00000';    /* return code: Success             */
    dcl lx_check        lit '00001';    /* ``check'' return code            */
    dcl lxes_no_name    lit '100'  ;    /* IO name not found                */
    dcl lxe_except      lit '1000' ;    /* Exception error                  */
    dcl lxe_err_bud     lit '300'  ;    /* Memory allocator error           */
```

```
    dcl lxe_err_tol     lit '400'    ;    /* Timeout errors                        */
    dcl lxe_mff_full    lit '001'    ;    /* Message fifo full                     */
    dcl lxe_fifo        lit '500'    ;    /* Fifo errors                           */
    dcl lxe_unknown     lit '600'    ;    /* Cancel: task not found                */
    dcl lxe_memx        lit '700'    ;    /* Internal memory allocator error       */
    dcl lxe_nobloc      lit '001'    ;    /* External memory: none free            */
    dcl lxe_noevt       lit '101'    ;    /* No such event                         */
    dcl lxe_nofifo      lit '102'    ;    /* No message fifo for task              */
    dcl lxe_nomsg       lit '103'    ;    /* No message (receive)                  */
    dcl lxe_fifo_full   lit '002'    ;    /* Fifo full                             */
    dcl lxe_tacx        lit '105'    ;    /* Invalid task number                   */
    dcl lxe_size        lit '003'    ;    /* Mem. allocator: request too big       */
    dcl lxe_timout      lit '106'    ;    /* Invalid timeout request               */
    dcl lxe_empty_cn    lit '005'    ;    /* Timeout cancel: empty list!           */
    dcl lxe_empty_dq    lit '006'    ;    /* Fifo: empty on dequeue                */
/*
IO related
*/
    dcl lx_tick_max     lit '1000'   ;    /* How many ms in 1 s?                   */
    dcl lx_clk          lit '  50'   ;    /* Clock interval (ms)                   */
    dcl lx_attach       lit '00'     ;    /* I/O Attach procedure                  */
    dcl lx_detach       lit '01'     ;    /* I/O Detach procedure                  */
    dcl lx_open         lit '02'     ;    /* I/O Open procedure                    */
    dcl lx_close        lit '03'     ;    /* I/O Close procedure                   */
    dcl lx_read         lit '04'     ;    /* I/O Read procedure                    */
    dcl lx_write        lit '05'     ;    /* I/O Write procedure                   */
    dcl lx_iofree       lit '0FFH'   ;    /* I/O Free (idle)                       */
    dcl lx_iobusy       lit '000H'   ;    /* I/O Busy                              */
    dcl lxin_ckint      lit '00'     ;    /* INT number of clock                   */
    dcl lxin_ttyint     lit '06'     ;    /* INT number of TTY input               */
    dcl lxin_ttyoint    lit '07'     ;    /* INT number of TTY output              */
    dcl lxp_nilb        lit '0FFH'   ;    /* End of I/O initialisation data        */
    dcl lxp_usdata      lit '00'     ;    /* 8251 Data port                        */
    dcl lxp_usstat      lit '02'     ;    /* 8251 Status port                      */
    dcl lxp_ustrdy      lit '01'     ;    /* Usart TX RDY bit                      */
    dcl lxp_ad_pic      lit '0C0H'   ;    /* Address of PIC                        */
    dcl lxp_ad_pit      lit '0B6H'   ;    /* Address of PIT                        */
    dcl lxp_ad_tty      lit '0D8H'   ;    /* Address of TTY                        */
    dcl lx_ttyspd       lit '9600'   ;    /* TTY speed in baud                     */
/*
Task status bits
*/
    dcl lxs_timout      lit '0001H'  ;    /* Timeout ended                         */
    dcl lxs_wevt        lit '0004H'  ;    /* Waiting for event                     */
    dcl lxs_wevtto      lit '0008H'  ;    /* Waiting for event (with timeout)      */
    dcl lxs_wmsg        lit '0010H'  ;    /* Waiting for message                   */
    dcl lxs_wmsgto      lit '0020H'  ;    /* Waiting for mess. (with timeout)      */
    dcl lxs_wtimout     lit '0040H'  ;    /* Simple timeout                        */
    dcl lx_notimout     lit '0FFFFH' ;    /* No timeout                            */
    dcl lx_waitto       lit '00000'  ;    /* Wait with timeout                     */
/*
Memory allocator
*/
    dcl lx_block0       lit ' 5'     ;    /* First two memory                      */
    dcl lx_block1       lit ' 9'     ;    /*   block sizes.                        */
```

```
dcl lx_max_idx    lit '15'    ;   /* Size of block size table    */
dcl lx_max_memu   lit '2000'  ;   /* Max segment size in memu    */
dcl lx_max_memx   lit '2000'  ;   /* Max segment size in memx    */
```

C.2 etrstr.h

```
/*--------------------------------
ETR286 Data Structure Declarations      NB: COMMENTS INSIDE STRUCTURES
---------------------------------       MUST BE REMOVED BEFORE COMPILING
*/
/*
Operational Task Descriptor
*/
        dcl dx_otd literally 'structure (
                number  word,           /* task number                   */
                prior   word,           /* priority                      */
                status  word,
                event   word,           /* pending events                */
                ce      word,           /* N times task scheduled        */
                ctick   word,           /* timeout count (clock ticks)   */
                p_fifo  pointer,        /* pointer to tasks message fifo */
                p_otd   pointer,        /* pointer to task's own otd     */
                next    pointer,        /* next task                     */
                prev    pointer         /* prev task                     */
                )' ;

/*
Descriptors
*/
        dcl dx_desc literally 'structure(       /* hardware defined      */
                limit   word,
                base_l  word,
                base_h  byte,
                rights  byte,
                rsv     word                    /* reserved              */
        )';
        dcl dx_desc2 literally 'structure (     /* alternative view      */
                limit   word,
                base    dword,
                rsv     word
        )' ;

/*      dcl dx_ldt literally 'structure(
                lnum    word,
                unk     word,
                codet   selector,
                datat   selector
        )' ; */
                        /* unused */

        dcl wd lit 'word';

/*
Task State Segment
*/
        dcl dx_tss literally 'structure (
                bl      wd,
                sp0     wd,
                ss0     wd,
```

```
                    sp1     wd,
                    ss1     wd,
                    sp2     wd,
                    ss2     wd,
                    ip      wd,
                    fl      wd,
                    ax      wd,
                    cx      wd,
                    dx      wd,
                    bx      wd,
                    sp      wd,
                    bp      wd,
                    si      wd,
                    di      wd,
                    ds      wd,
                    cs      wd,
                    ss      wd,
                    es      wd,
                    ldt     wd
            )' ;
/*
Message fifo header
*/
            dcl dx_fifo lit 'structure (
                    first   word,           /* index of first          */
                    last    word,           /* index of last           */
                    max     word,           /* size of buffer          */
                    nbr     word,           /* current occupancy       */
                    ptr(1)  pointer
            )';
/*
block info for memory allocator
*/
            dcl dx_block lit 'structure(
                    prev    pointer,
                    next    pointer,
                    free    byte,
                    size    word,
                    code    word
            )';
/*
head of timeout list
*/
            dcl dx_timeout lit 'structure (
                    next    pointer,        /* first entry             */
                    prev    pointer,        /* (NIL)                   */
                    ctick   word,           /* time until first        */
                    nbr     word            /* number of entries       */
            )';
/*
IO - peripheral initialisation
*/
            dcl dx_peri lit 'structure(
                    base            word,   /* peripheral address      */
```

```
                dper(32)        byte
        )';
/*
Static Task Descriptor - for initialisation
*/
        dcl dx_std literally 'structure (
                number          word,
                prior           word,
                stack_0         word,           /* stack size            */
                msgfifosz       word,           /* message buffer size   */
                name(8)         byte
        )' ;
/*
Date and Time
*/
        dcl dx_time lit 'structure(
                sec     byte,
                min     byte,
                hour    byte,
                day     byte,
                month   byte,
                year    word
        )';
/*
IO driver descriptor
*/
        dcl dx_iodesc lit 'structure(
                p_proc(7)       pointer,
                intlev          word,   /* interrupt level               */
                p_ios           pointer, /* to current io state record   */
                task            word,
                lnum            word,   /* logical driver number         */
                iofifo(4)       word,
                busy            byte
        )';

/*
IO - table of IO driver descriptions
*/
        dcl dx_ioptr lit 'structure(
                sta             byte,   /* free/busy                     */
                p_iodesc        pointer /* to an iodesc structure        */
        )';
/*
IO - initial configuration of device driver
*/
        dcl dx_ioconf lit 'structure(
                name(12)        byte,
                maj_dn          word,   /* major device number           */
                intlev          word    /* interrupt level               */
        )';
/*
IO - status of transfer
*/
        dcl dx_iostate lit 'structure(
```

```
        err          word,
        status       word,
        task         word,    /* for which task?            */
        function     word,    /* which IO function?         */
        evt          word,    /* event to send on completion */
        lnum         word,    /* logical driver number      */
        intlev       word,
        index        word,    /* next byte to transfer      */
        nchar        word,    /* transfer count             */
        p_zone       pointer, /* transfer buffer            */
        finished     byte     /* true/false                 */
)';
```

C.3 etrprc.h

```
/***************************
 ETR286 - Public Procedures
***************************/

/*
This file may be included in separately compiled tasks
*/

rq_dem: procedure(intlev) external;
        dcl intlev word;
end     rq_dem;
rq_msq: procedure(intlev) external;
        dcl intlev word;
end     rq_msq;


rq_send_msg: procedure(task,p_msg,p_err) external;
        /* Wc = 5 */
        /* send a message to a task */
        dcl task       word;
        dcl p_err      pointer;
        dcl p_msg      pointer;
end rq_send_msg;

rq_read_msg: procedure(timout,p_err) pointer external;
        /* Wc = 3 */
        dcl timout     word;
        dcl p_err      pointer;
end rq_read_msg;

rq_send_event: procedure(task,event,p_err) external;
        /* Wc = 4 */
        /* send an event to a task */
        dcl task       word;
        dcl event      word;
        dcl p_err      pointer;
end rq_send_event;

rq_await_event: procedure(timout,p_err) word external;
        /* Wc = 3 */
        dcl timout     word;
        dcl p_err      pointer;
end rq_await_event;

rq_timout: procedure(timout,p_err) external;
        /* Wc = 3 */
        dcl timout     word;
        dcl p_err      pointer;
end rq_timout;

rq_get_memu: PROCEDURE(n,p_err) POINTER external;
        /* Wc = 3 */
        /* external memory allocator */
```

```
        dcl n           word;    /* no. of bytes */
        dcl p_err .     pointer;/* Error code */
end rq_get_memu;

rq_free_memu: PROCEDURE(p_block_u,size) external;
        /* Wc = 3 */
        /* release memory area */
        dcl size        word;
        dcl p_block_u   pointer; /* area to be freed */
end rq_free_memu;
```

C.4 etrt0.pl6

```
$TITLE('ETR_286 - task 0')
tsk0_mod: do;
$NOLIST
$INCLUDE(etr.h)
$INCLUDE(etrprc.h)
$list
    dcl p pointer;
    dcl err word;
    do while 1;                     /* loop forever, */
        p = rq_read_msg(100,@err);  /* get a message */

        call rq_free_memu(p,30);    /* release its memory */

        call rq_timout(40,@err);    /* then wait */
    end;

end tsk0_mod;
```

C.5 etrt1.pl6

```
$TITLE('ETR_286 - task 1')
tsk1_mod: do;
$NOLIST
$INCLUDE(etr.h)
$INCLUDE(etrprc.h)
$list
    dcl p pointer;
    dcl err word;
    do while 1;                             /* loop forever */
        p = rq_get_memu(30,@err);           /* allocate memory */

        call rq_send_msg(1,p,@err);         /* send it to task 1 */

        call rq_timout(40,@err);            /* and wait ... */
    end;

end tsk1_mod;
```

C.6 etrtf.pl6

```
$TITLE('ETR_286 - task f')
tstf_mod: do;
$NOLIST
$INCLUDE(etr.h)
$INCLUDE(etrprc.h)
$list
    dcl fnd dword;
    dcl err word;

    fnd = 0;
    do while 1;                         /* loop forever */
        fnd = fnd + 1;                  /* incrementing a counter */
        call rq_timout(10,@err);        /* and waiting */
    end;

end tstf_mod;
```

C.7 etrsched.s86

```
$TITLE('ETR286 : Assembly Language Procedures')
        NAME    etr_sched_V1P0A
;**********************************************************/
LX_TD_CE        EQU     08      ;Offset of ce in OTD
;
        extrn   sx_fnd_tready:far
        extrn   sx_get_tsk:far
        extrn   sx_wait:far
;
        extrn   vx_p_otd:dword
        extrn   vx_p_tss:dword
        public  vx_ctask
;
DATAX   SEGMENT RW      ; local variables for scheduler
vx_histo DB     512 DUP(?)      ;history: last 512 tasks scheduled
vx_ixh  DW      ?               ;history index
vx_ctask DW     ?               ;Current task
ad_vx_p_otd     DD      ?
ad_vx_p_tss     DD      ?
DATAX   ENDS

CODEX   SEGMENT EO
        ASSUME  DS:DATAX
        PUBLIC  sx_scheduler
sx_scheduler    PROC    FAR
        PUBLIC  sx_schedinit
                                ; suspend the current task
        push    vx_ctask
        call    sx_wait
                                ; Scheduler is initialised by entering HERE
sx_schedinit    label   far
                                ; find highest priority task
        call    sx_fnd_tready   ; Find ready task
        mov     vx_ctask,ax     ; task number
                                ; set up pointers for new task
        call    sx_get_tsk
                                ; increment execution counter
        les     bx,ad_vx_p_otd
        les     bx,dword ptr es:[bx]
        inc     WORD PTR [BX+LX_TD_CE]
                                ; note rescheduling in history buffer
schedul_20:
        mov     AX,vx_ctask
        mov     SI,vx_ixh
        mov     vx_histo[SI],AL
        inc     SI
        and     SI,size(vx_histo)-1
        mov     vx_ixh,si
schedul_99:
                                ;context switch
        les     bx,ad_vx_p_tss  ;Current TSS
        les     bx,dword ptr es:[bx]
        push    BX
```

```
              push      ES
              call      SX_SWITCH_TSS
              ret
sx_scheduler  ENDP

SX_SWITCH_TSS PROC      NEAR ;stack:= <VAL:RET:0:SEL>
              mov       BP,SP
              jmp       DWORD PTR [BP+2]
              ret       4
SX_SWITCH_TSS ENDP

CODEX   ENDS
        END
```

C.8 etrto.pl6

```
$TITLE('ETR286 - clock handling')
etrto_mod: do;
$NOLIST
$INCLUDE(etr.h)
$INCLUDE(etrstr.h)

sx_get_otd: procedure(task) pointer external;
    dcl task word;
end sx_get_otd;

sx_scheduler: procedure external;
end sx_scheduler;

sx_ready: procedure(task) external;
    dcl task word;
end sx_ready;

sx_init_to: procedure external;
end sx_init_to;

sx_timeout: procedure(p_new,ctick,p_err) external;
    dcl p_new pointer;
    dcl ctick word;
    dcl p_err pointer;
end sx_timeout;

sx_dequeue_to: procedure(p_err) word external;
    dcl p_err pointer;
end sx_dequeue_to;
$list
    dcl vx_p_otd pointer external;
    dcl ctask based vx_p_otd dx_otd;
    dcl vx_timeouts dx_timeout external;
    dcl vx_systime(2) dword;                /* 64-bit binary time */
    dcl vx_time dx_time;                    /* readable-time */
    dcl vx_maxdays(*) byte
        data(30,28,31,30,31,30,31,31,30,31,30,31);
    dcl vx_ticks word;                      /* count of clk ints */
    dcl vx_maxtick word;                    /* n. ints per sec */

    sx_maxday: procedure word;              /* check current day for wrap*/
        dcl crt word;

        crt = lx_succes;
        if(vx_time.day <= vx_maxdays(vx_time.month))
        then
            crt = lx_check;
        else do;
            if(vx_time.month = 2)           /* February */
                and ((vx_time.year mod 4) = 0) and (vx_time.day <= 29)
            then
                crt = lx_check;
            end;
```

```
        return crt;
end sx_maxday;

sx_timout: procedure(timout,p_err) public;   /* delay current task */
    dcl timout word;
    dcl p_err pointer;
    dcl err based p_err word;

    if(timout = 0) OR (timout = lx_notimout)
    then do;
        err = lxe_timout;               /* illegal request! */
    end;
    else do;
        err = lx_succes;
        call sx_timeout(vx_p_otd,timout,p_err); /* add to timeout list */
        if(err = lx_succes)
        then
            call sx_scheduler;          /* reschedule */
    end;
end;

sx_clkint: procedure public;            /* clock interrupt procedure */

    dcl p_task pointer;
    dcl dtask based p_task dx_otd;
    dcl task word;
    dcl err word;

    vx_systime(1) = vx_systime(1) + 1;  /* adjust binary time */
    if(carry)
    then do;
        vx_systime(0) = vx_systime(0) + 1;
        vx_systime(1) = 0;
    end;

    vx_ticks = vx_ticks - 1;            /* adjust seconds? */
    if(vx_ticks = 0)
    then do;
        vx_ticks = vx_maxtick;          /* set ticks to max */
        vx_time.sec = vx_time.sec + 1;
        if(vx_time.sec = 60)            /* adjust minutes? */
        then do;
            vx_time.sec = 0;
            vx_time.min = vx_time.min + 1;
            if(vx_time.min = 60)        /* adjust hours? */
            then do;
                vx_time.min = 0;
                vx_time.hour = vx_time.hour + 1;
                if(vx_time.hour = 24)   /* is it midnight? */
                then do;
                    vx_time.hour = 0;
                    vx_time.day = vx_time.day + 1;
                    if(sx_maxday = lx_succes)
                    then do;            /* increment month */
                        vx_time.day = 1;
```

```
                        vx_time.month = vx_time.month + 1;
                        if(vx_time.month = 13)
                        then do;                        /* Happy New Year! */
                            vx_time.year = vx_time.year +1;
                            vx_time.month = 1;
                        end;
                     end;
                  end;
               end;
            end;
         end;
         if(vx_timeouts.nbr <> 0)       /* attend to tasks in timeouts */
         then do;
            err = lx_succes;
            vx_timeouts.ctick = vx_timeouts.ctick - 1;  /* decrement first */
            do while (vx_timeouts.ctick = 0) and (err = lx_succes);

               task = sx_dequeue_to(@err); /* dequeue it */
               p_task = sx_get_otd(task);
               if(err = lx_succes)
               then do;
                   dtask.status = lxs_timout;
                   call sx_ready(dtask.number);    /* and mark it runnable */
               end;
            end;
         end;
      end sx_clkint;

      sx_init_clk: procedure(p_clk,freq) public;    /* initialise clock */
         dcl p_clk pointer;
         dcl freq word ;

         call movb(p_clk,@vx_time,size(vx_time));
         vx_maxtick = lx_tick_max / freq ;
         vx_ticks = vx_maxtick;
         vx_systime(0) = 0;                         /* binary time */
         vx_systime(1) = 0;
         call sx_init_to;                           /* timeout structure */
      end sx_init_clk;

   end etrto_mod;
```

C.9 etrford.pl6

```
$TITLE('ETR_286 - Timeouts')
etr_ford_V1P0A: DO;
$NOLIST
$INCLUDE(etr.h)
$INCLUDE(etrstr.h)
$list
/*
waiting tasks have their OTD chained onto the vx_timeout structure thus:

            vx_timeouts         OTD1          OTD2         Sentinel
           +-----------+    +---------+   +---------+    +---------+
  prev     ! NIL       !<-----!       !<---!       !<----!         !
           -------------    -----------   -----------    -----------
  next     !           !----->!       !--->!       !---->!  NIL    !
           -------------    -----------   -----------    -----------
  ctick    !    10     !    !   10    !   !   30    !    !   0     !
           -------------    -----------   -----------    -----------
           !           !    !         !   !         !    !         !
           -------------    -----------   -----------    -----------

                              new
                         -----------
                         !         !
                         -----------
                         !         !
                         -----------
                         !         !
                         -----------

*/

    dcl vx_sentinel dx_otd;
    dcl vx_timeouts dx_timeout public;   /* head of timeout list */
    dcl vx_p_head pointer;               /* pointer to list head */
    dcl vx_p_sent pointer;               /* pointer to last element */

    sx_init_to: procedure PUBLIC;        /* initialise the timeout list */

        vx_p_sent = @vx_sentinel;
        vx_p_head = @vx_timeouts;
        vx_sentinel.next = NIL;
        vx_sentinel.prev= vx_p_head;
        vx_sentinel.ctick = 0;
        vx_sentinel.number = 65535;
        vx_timeouts.next = vx_p_sent;
        vx_timeouts.prev = NIL;
        vx_timeouts.ctick = 0;
        vx_timeouts.nbr = 0;
    end sx_init_to;

    sx_timeout: procedure(p_new,ctick,p_err) PUBLIC;   /* add new timeout */
```

```
    dcl p_new pointer;        /* pointer to task to be entered */
    dcl ctick word;           /* waiting time */
    dcl p_err pointer;        /* return code */

    dcl err based p_err word;
    dcl p_next pointer;
    dcl p_prev pointer;
    dcl t_new based p_new dx_otd;
    dcl t_next based p_next dx_otd;
    dcl t_prev based p_prev dx_otd;
    dcl sum_ctick word;       /* total timeout time */
    dcl sum_ctickp word;      /* total time (without last one) */

    p_prev = vx_p_head;
    p_next = vx_timeouts.next;  /* point to first in list */
    sum_ctick = t_next.ctick;
    do while (ctick > sum_ctick) and (p_next <> vx_p_sent);
        p_prev = p_next;        /* follow list */
        p_next = t_next.next;
        sum_ctickp = sum_ctick;
        sum_ctick = sum_ctick+t_next.ctick; /* sum timeout times */
    end;
    if p_prev <> vx_p_head      /* found insertion point: 2 cases: */
    then do;
        t_new.next = p_next;    /* insert somewhere in list */
        t_new.prev = p_prev;
        t_prev.next = p_new;
        t_next.prev= p_new;
        t_new.ctick = ctick-sum_ctickp;
        if p_next <> vx_p_sent
        then                    /* adjust following time if not at end */
            t_next.ctick = t_next.ctick-t_new.ctick;
    end;
    else do;                    /* insert at head of list */
        t_new.next = p_next;
        t_new.prev = vx_p_head;
        vx_timeouts.next = p_new;
        t_next.prev= p_new;
        vx_timeouts.ctick = ctick;
        t_new.ctick = ctick;
        if p_next <> vx_p_sent
        then                    /* adjust following time */
            t_next.ctick = t_next.ctick-ctick;
    end;
    vx_timeouts.nbr = vx_timeouts.nbr + 1;  /* increment timeout count */
    err = lx_succes;
end sx_timeout;

sx_cancel_to: procedure(number,p_err) PUBLIC;  /* cancel a timeout */
    dcl number word;            /* task no. */
    dcl p_err pointer;

    dcl err based p_err word;
    dcl p_can pointer;
    dcl p_next pointer;
```

```
    dcl p_prev pointer;
    dcl t_can based p_can dx_otd;
    dcl t_next based p_next dx_otd;
    dcl t_prev based p_prev dx_otd;

    err = lx_succes;
    if vx_timeouts.nbr <> 0
    then do;                          /* non-empty list: find task number */
        p_prev = vx_p_head;
        p_can = vx_timeouts.next;     /* follow list */
        do while (p_can <> vx_p_sent) and (t_can.number <> number);
            p_prev = p_can;
            p_can = t_can.next;
        end;
        if t_can.number = number      /* found right one? */
        then do;
            vx_timeouts.nbr = vx_timeouts.nbr - 1; /* got it! */
            if p_prev = vx_p_head
            then do;                  /* it was first */
                vx_timeouts.next = t_can.next;
                p_next = t_can.next;
                t_next.prev = vx_p_head;
                if p_next <> vx_p_sent
                then do;
                    vx_timeouts.ctick = t_can.ctick+t_next.ctick ;
                    t_next.ctick = vx_timeouts.ctick ;
                end;
            end;
            else do;                  /* elsewhere on list */
                p_next = t_can.next;
                t_prev.next = p_next;
                t_next.prev = p_prev;
                t_prev.ctick = t_prev.ctick + t_can.ctick;
                if t_prev.prev = vx_p_head
                then
                    vx_timeouts.ctick = t_prev.ctick;
            end;
        end;
        else
            err = lxe_err_tol+lxe_unknown;
    end;
    else
        err = lxe_err_tol+lxe_empty_cn;
end sx_cancel_to;

sx_dequeue_to: procedure(p_err) word PUBLIC;
    dcl p_err pointer;                /* dequeue first task from list */

    dcl err based p_err word;
    dcl ct word;
    dcl number word;
    dcl p_cur pointer;
    dcl p_next pointer;
    dcl t_cur based p_cur dx_otd;
    dcl t_next based p_next dx_otd;
```

```
            err = lx_succes;
            if vx_timeouts.nbr <> 0
            then do;                           /* list not empty */
                p_next = vx_timeouts.next;
                number = t_next.number;
                ct = t_next.ctick;
                vx_timeouts.next = t_next.next;
                p_next = t_next.next;
                t_next.prev = vx_p_head;
                if p_next <> vx_p_sent
                then do;
                    vx_timeouts.ctick = t_next.ctick+ct; /* adjust head value */
                    t_next.ctick = vx_timeouts.ctick; /* And tick */
                end;
                else
                    vx_timeouts.ctick = 0;
                vx_timeouts.nbr = vx_timeouts.nbr - 1; /* Decrement nbr */
            end;
            else
                err = lxe_err_tol+lxe_empty_dq;
            return number; /* number of first Task */
        end sx_dequeue_to;

END etr_ford_V1P0A;
```

C.10 etrevms.pl6

```
$TITLE('ETR_286 - events and messages')
etrevms_mod: do;
$NOLIST
$INCLUDE(etr.h)
$INCLUDE(etrstr.h)

sx_enqueue_fifo: procedure(p_fifo,p_val,p_err) external;
    dcl p_fifo pointer;
    dcl p_val pointer;
    dcl p_err pointer;
end sx_enqueue_fifo;

sx_dequeue_fifo: procedure(p_fifo,p_err) pointer external;
    dcl p_fifo pointer;
    dcl p_err pointer;
end sx_dequeue_fifo;

sx_cancel_to: procedure(number,p_err) external;
    dcl number word;
    dcl p_err pointer;
end sx_cancel_to;

sx_timeout: procedure(p_new,ctick,p_err) external;
    dcl p_new pointer;
    dcl ctick word;
    dcl p_err pointer;
end sx_timeout;

sx_ready: procedure(task) external;
    dcl task word;
end sx_ready;

sx_scheduler: procedure external;
end sx_scheduler;

sx_get_otd: procedure(task) pointer external;
    dcl task word;
end sx_get_otd;

$list
    dcl vx_timeouts dx_timeout external;/* Suspension list */
    dcl vx_p_otd pointer external;      /* Current task */
    dcl ctask based vx_p_otd dx_otd;    /* OTD of curr. task */
    dcl vx_maxtsk word external;        /* Max no. of tasks */
    dcl vx_p_fifo pointer external;     /* Ptr to mess. fifo for cur. task */
    dcl cfifo based vx_p_fifo dx_fifo;  /* Curr. tasks message fifo */

    sx_send_msg: procedure(task,p_msg,p_err) public; /* send msg to task */
        dcl task word;
        dcl p_err pointer;
        dcl err based p_err word;
        dcl p_msg pointer;
        dcl p_otd pointer;              /* destination task */
```

```
        dcl d_task based p_otd dx_otd;

        if(task > vx_maxtsk)           /* is destination valid? */
        then do;
            err = lxe_tacx;
        end;
        else do;
            p_otd = sx_get_otd(task);  /* get ptr to dest. task */
            if(d_task.p_fifo <> NIL)
            then do;                   /* does it have a msg fifo? */
                /* Oui envoi */
                call sx_enqueue_fifo(d_task.p_fifo,p_msg,p_err);
                if(err <> lx_succes)
                then
                    err = lxe_mff_full;
                else do;
                    if(d_task.status = lxs_wmsg)
                    then do;           /* is it waiting for this msg? */
                        if(d_task.status = lxs_wmsgto)
                        then do;       /* cancel timeout if applicable */
                            call sx_cancel_to(task,p_err);
                            d_task.status = d_task.status AND NOT lxs_wmsgto;
                        end;
                        d_task.status = d_task.status AND NOT lxs_wmsg;
                        call sx_ready(task);   /* set task ready to run */
                    end;
                end;
            end;
            else
                err = lxe_nofifo;      /* send to task with no msg fifo */
        end;
end sx_send_msg;

sx_read_msg: procedure(timout,p_err) pointer public;
    dcl timout word;
    dcl p_err pointer;
    dcl err based p_err word;
    dcl p_msg pointer;

    if(cfifo.nbr <> 0)
    then do;                           /* there's one here: */
        p_msg = sx_dequeue_fifo(vx_p_fifo,p_err);
    end;
    else do;                           /* no message: timeout? */
        if(timout = lx_notimout)
        then
            err = lxe_nomsg;           /* return immediately */
        else do;
            ctask.status = ctask.status OR lxs_wmsg;   /* wait here */
            if(timout <> lx_waitto)
            then do;
                call sx_timeout(vx_p_otd,timout,p_err);
                ctask.status = ctask.status OR lxs_wmsgto;
            end;
        end;
```

```
            call sx_scheduler;
        end;
        return p_msg;
end sx_read_msg;

sx_send_event: procedure(task,event,p_err) public;
dcl task word;                          /* send event to task */
dcl event word;
dcl p_err pointer;
dcl err based p_err word;
dcl p_otd pointer;                      /* destination task */
dcl d_task based p_otd dx_otd;

if(task > vx_maxtsk)
then do;
    err = lxe_tacx;
end;
else do;
    p_otd = sx_get_otd(task);           /* point to destination */
    d_task.event = d_task.event OR event;  /* OR in event */
    if(d_task.status = lxs_wevt)
    then do;                            /* waiting for an event? */
        if(d_task.status = lxs_wevtto)
        then do;                        /* timeout? */
            call sx_cancel_to(task,p_err);
            d_task.status = d_task.status AND NOT lxs_wevtto;
        end;
        d_task.status = d_task.status AND NOT lxs_wevt;
        call sx_ready(task);            /* destination is ready */
    end;
end;
end sx_send_event;

sx_await_event: procedure(timout,p_err) word public;
    dcl timout word;                    /* wait for any event */
    dcl p_err pointer;
    dcl err based p_err word;
    dcl event word;

    if(ctask.event <> 0)
    then do;                            /* happened already */
        err = lx_succes;
        event = ctask.event;            /* return ALL pending events*/
        ctask.event = 0;                /* and reset */
    end;
    else do;
        if(timout = lx_notimout)
        then
            err = lxe_noevt;            /* return immediately */
        else do;
            ctask.status = ctask.status OR lxs_wevt;
            if(timout <> lx_waitto)
            then do;                    /* wait for event */
                call sx_timeout(vx_p_otd,timout,p_err);
                ctask.status = ctask.status OR lxs_wevtto;
```

```
                end;
            end;
            call sx_scheduler;
        end;
        return event;
    end sx_await_event;

end etrevms_mod;
```

C.11 etrfifo.pl6

```
$TITLE('ETR_286 - Fifos for messages and timeouts')
etrfifo_V1P0A: DO;
$NOLIST
$INCLUDE(etr.h)
$INCLUDE(etrstr.h)
$list
/*

           +------------+
   first !                !-----------!
           --------------              !
    last !                !------------------------------------+
           --------------              !                        !
     nbr !      10      !              !                        !
           --------------   -----v-----  -----------  -----v-----
     max !              !  !         ! !!           !!         !  !
           --------------   -----------  -----------  -----------

*/

    sx_init_fifo: procedure(p_fifo,max) PUBLIC;  /* initialise */
        dcl p_fifo pointer;
        dcl fifo based p_fifo dx_fifo;
        dcl max word;

        fifo.nbr = 0;
        fifo.first = 0;
        fifo.last = 0;
        fifo.max = max;
    end sx_init_fifo;

    sx_enqueue_fifo: procedure(p_fifo,p_val,p_err) PUBLIC;
        dcl p_fifo pointer;                     /* insert at end */
        dcl fifo based p_fifo dx_fifo;
        dcl p_val pointer;
        dcl p_err pointer;
        dcl err based p_err word;
        dcl n word;

        err = lx_succes;
        if fifo.nbr <> fifo.max
        then do;
            /* Not full */
            n =fifo.first;
            fifo.ptr(n) = p_val;
            n = n + 1;
            if n >= fifo.max
            then
                n = 0;
            fifo.first = n;
            fifo.nbr = fifo.nbr + 1;
        end;
        else
```

```
            err = lxe_fifo + lxe_fifo_full;
    end sx_enqueue_fifo;

    sx_dequeue_fifo: procedure(p_fifo,p_err) pointer PUBLIC;
        dcl p_fifo pointer;                 /* return first value */
        dcl fifo based p_fifo dx_fifo;
        dcl p_val pointer;
        dcl p_err pointer;
        dcl err based p_err word;
        dcl n word;

        err = lx_succes;
        if fifo.nbr <> 0
        then do;
        /* Not empty */
            n =fifo.last;
            p_val = fifo.ptr(n);
            n = n + 1;
            if n >= fifo.max
            then
                n = 0;
            fifo.last= n;
            fifo.nbr = fifo.nbr - 1;
        end;
        else
            err = lxe_fifo + lxe_empty_dq;
        return p_val;
    end sx_dequeue_fifo;
END etrfifo_V1P0A;
```

C.12 etrmemx.pl6

```
$TITLE('ETR_286 - system memory allocator definition')
etrmemx_mod: do;
$NOLIST
$INCLUDE(etr.h)
$INCLUDE(etrstr.h)
$list
    dcl vx_memx(lx_max_memx) byte public;    /* segment for allocations */
end etrmemx_mod;
```

C.13 etrmemu.pl6

```
$TITLE('ETR_286 - user memory allocator definition')
etrmemu_mod: do;
$NOLIST
$INCLUDE(etr.h)
$INCLUDE(etrstr.h)
$list
    dcl vx_memu(lx_max_memu) byte public;    /* segment for allocations */
end etrmemu_mod;
```

C.14 etrbud.pl6

```
$RAM
$TITLE('ETR_286: Memory allocator using Fibonacci Buddies')
etrbud_mod: DO;
$NOLIST
$INCLUDE(etr.h)
$INCLUDE(etrstr.h)
$list
dcl vx_pmemu              pointer external;

DCL overhead              WORD;           /* allocater overheads */
DCL block_sizes(lx_max_idx) WORD;         /* Sizes of blocks */
DCL block_list(lx_max_idx) dx_block;
DCL err                   WORD;
DCL max_idx               WORD;           /* max index into list_blocs */
DCL lx_bud                WORD INITIAL(5);


add_ptr: procedure(p,n) POINTER;
    dcl p pointer;
    dcl n word;
    p = BUILD$PTR(SELECTOR$OF(p),(OFFSET$OF(p)+n));
    RETURN p;
end add_ptr;


sub_ptr: procedure(p,n) POINTER;
    dcl p pointer;
    dcl n word;
    p = BUILD$PTR(SELECTOR$OF(p),(OFFSET$OF(p)-n));
    return p;
end sub_ptr;


insert_block: PROCEDURE(p_block);   /* insert block into doubly-linked list */
    DCL p_block               POINTER;
    DCL block   based p_block dx_block;
    DCL nextp                 POINTER;
    DCL nextb   based nextp   dx_block;

    block.free = true;
    block.next = block_list(block.size).next;
    block.prev = @block_list(block.size);
    nextp      = block_list(block.size).next;
    nextb.prev = p_block;
    block_list(block.size).next = p_block;
    block_list(block.size).code = block_list(block.size).code +1;
END insert_block;


unlink_block: PROCEDURE(p_block);   /* extract block from doubly-linked list */
    DCL p_block               POINTER;
    DCL block   based p_block dx_block;
    DCL nextp                 POINTER;
```

```
    DCL nextb      based nextp      dx_block;

    nextp       = block.next;
    nextb.prev  = block.prev;
    nextp       = block.prev;
    nextb.next  = block.next;
    block_list(block.size).code = block_list(block.size).code-1;
END unlink_block;


empty_list: PROCEDURE(index) boolean;
    /* an empty list has its prev pointer pointing to itself */
    DCL index WORD;
    DCL Empty  BOOLEAN;
    Empty = block_list(index).next = @block_list(index);
    RETURN Empty;
END empty_list;


sx_init_memu: PROCEDURE public;     /* initialise lists */
    DCL j                   WORD;
    DCL p_block             POINTER;
    DCL block  based p_block   dx_block;

    overhead = SIZE(block);
    overhead = overhead + (overhead MOD 2);
    block_sizes(0) = lx_block0;
    block_sizes(1) = lx_block1;
    max_idx = lx_max_idx - 2;
    DO j = 2 to max_idx;
        block_sizes(j) = block_sizes(j-1) + block_sizes(j-2);
    END;

                              /* initialise pointers to empty block lists */
    DO j = 0 to max_idx;
        block_list(j).prev  = @block_list(j);
        block_list(j).next  = @block_list(j);
        block_list(j).code  = 0;
    END;

                              /* Allocate initial block */
    p_block      = vx_pmemu;
    block.size = max_idx;
    block.code   = 0;
    call insert_block(p_block);
END sx_init_memu;
/*================================================================*/
sx_get_memu: PROCEDURE(n,p_err) POINTER public; /* Allocate n bytes */
    DCL n                  WORD;     /* number requested */
    DCL p_err              POINTER;  /* error code */
    DCL err based p_err    WORD;
    DCL p_buddy            POINTER;
    DCL buddy based p_buddy  dx_block;
    DCL p_block            POINTER;
```

```
DCL block   based p_block    dx_block;
DCL size                     WORD;
DCL t_req                    WORD;    /* size requested*/
DCL p_block_u                POINTER; /* Block returned*/

/* Test that request is valid */
IF (n + overhead) <= block_sizes(max_idx)
THEN DO;                         /* valid;  look for correct block size */
    t_req = 0;
    DO WHILE (block_sizes(t_req) < n + overhead) AND (t_req< max_idx);
        t_req = t_req + 1;
    END;

                    /* Find the smallest block to satisfy this request */
    size = t_req;
    DO WHILE (empty_list(size)) AND (size < max_idx);
        size = size +1;
    END;

    IF not empty_list(size)
    THEN DO;                         /* Big enough block: extract it */
        p_block = block_list(size).prev;/* head of list */
        call unlink_block(p_block);      /* we'll use this one*/
                            /* divide this block to satisfy request */
        DO WHILE (size > t_req) AND (size >= 2);
            p_buddy=add_ptr(p_block,block_sizes(size-1)+overhead);
            buddy.code = 0;
            block.size = block.size -1;
            block.code = block.code +1;
            IF t_req > size-2
            THEN DO;
                            /* Allocate from larger, free smaller */
                buddy.size=size-2;
                call insert_block(p_buddy);
                size = size - 1;
            END;
            ELSE DO;
                            /* Allocate from smaller, free larger */
                call insert_block(p_block);
                size = size-2;
                buddy.size = size;
                p_block = p_buddy;
            END;
        END; /* DO WHILE */
                            /* hand over block, hiding system header */
        block.free = false;
        p_block_u = add_ptr(p_block,overhead);
    END; /* if not empty_list() */
    ELSE
                            /* No block is free */
        err = lxe_err_bud+lxe_nobloc;
END;
ELSE
                            /* request too large */
    err = lxe_err_bud+lxe_size;
```

```
                                        /* return pointer to user */
        RETURN p_block_u;
END sx_get_memu;


sx_free_memu: PROCEDURE(p_block_u,size) public; /* free user memory block */
    DCL p_buddy              POINTER;
    DCL buddy based p_buddy  dx_block;
    DCL p_block              POINTER;
    DCL block  based p_block dx_block;
    DCL size                 WORD;
    DCL bfree                BYTE;
    DCL p_block_u            POINTER;        /* Freed block */

    p_block = sub_ptr(p_block_u,overhead);   /* step back over header */
    bfree = true;
    DO WHILE bfree AND (block.size < max_idx); /* Try to coalesce */
        IF block.code > 0
          THEN DO;                            /* This is lower half of pair */
             p_buddy=add_ptr(p_block,block_sizes(block.size)+overhead);
             bfree  = buddy.free AND (buddy.size = block.size-1);
             IF bfree
               THEN DO;                       /* combine */
                  block.code = block.code -1;
                  block.size = block.size+1;
                  call unlink_block(p_buddy);
               END;
             ELSE                             /* can't combine */
                  call insert_block(p_block);
          END;
          ELSE DO;                            /* This is upper half of pair */
             p_buddy=sub_ptr(p_block,block_sizes(block.size+1)+overhead);
             bfree= buddy.free AND (buddy.size = block.size +1);
             IF bfree
               THEN DO;                       /* combine */
                  call unlink_block(p_buddy);
                  p_block    = p_buddy;
                  block.code = block.code -1;
                  block.size = block.size+1;
               END;
             ELSE                             /* can't combine */
                  call insert_block(p_block);
          END;
    END;
    IF block.size = max_idx
      THEN                                    /* Largest possible block */
         call insert_block(p_block);
END sx_free_memu;

END etrbud_mod;
```

C.15 etrcnf.pl6

```
$TITLE('ETR_286:  Configuration')
etrcnf_mod: do;
$NOLIST
$INCLUDE(etr.h)
$INCLUDE(etrstr.h)
$list
    dcl vx_std_0 dx_std              /* initial task configuration: */
        data(0,0,40,20,'T0');        /* num,pri,stksz,fifosz,name   */

    dcl vx_std_1 dx_std
        data(1,1,40,20,'T1');

    dcl vx_ioconf_0 dx_ioconf        /* initial IO driver config. */
        data('sysclk      ',0,0);    /* name, dev num, int. level */

    dcl vx_ioconf(*) pointer public
        data(@vx_ioconf_0);

    dcl vx_std(*) pointer public
        data(
             @vx_std_0,
             @vx_std_1
        );

end etrcnf_mod;
```

C.16   etrdrv.pl6

```
$TITLE('ETR_286: Input Output Manager')
etrdrv_mod: do;
$nolist
$include(etr.h)
$include(etrstr.h)

/* external declarations */

sx_enqueue_fifo: procedure(p_fifo,p_val,p_err) external;
    dcl p_fifo              pointer;
    dcl p_val               pointer;
    dcl p_err               pointer;
end sx_enqueue_fifo;

sx_dequeue_fifo: procedure(p_fifo,p_err) pointer external;
    dcl p_fifo              pointer;
    dcl p_err               pointer;
end sx_dequeue_fifo;

sx_init_fifo: procedure(p_fifo,max) external;
    dcl p_fifo              pointer;
    dcl max                 word;
end sx_init_fifo;

sx_send_event: procedure(task,event,p_err) external;
    dcl task                word;
    dcl event               word;
    dcl p_err               pointer;
end sx_send_event;

sx_mask: procedure(intlev) external;
    dcl intlev word;
end sx_mask;

sx_unmsk: procedure(intlev) external;
    dcl intlev word;
end sx_unmsk;

$list

    dcl intlev word;
    dcl idx word;
/*  dcl p_driv pointer;
    dcl drivers based p_driv(1) pointer;   unused */
    dcl vx_driv_6(7) pointer data(
        @sx_wser,
        @sx_intser);

    dcl vx_driver(*) pointer data(
        @vx_driv_6,
        @vx_driv_6,
        @vx_driv_6,
        @vx_driv_6,
```

```
          @vx_driv_6,
          @vx_driv_6,
          @vx_driv_6);

    dcl vx_ioconf(8) dx_ioconf;
    dcl vx_iodesc(8) dx_iodesc;      /* IO descriptors */
    dcl vx_ioptr(8) dx_ioptr;        /* pointers to IO descriptors */

    dcl p_iodesc pointer;
    dcl iodesc based p_iodesc dx_iodesc;
    dcl vx_pctask pointer external;
    dcl vx_ctask word external;
    dcl ctask based vx_pctask dx_otd;
    dcl vx_lnum word;

    sx_find_nam: procedure(p_nam,p_idx) word;    /* find p_nam in driver list */
        dcl p_nam pointer;
        dcl p_idx pointer;
        dcl idx based p_idx word;
        dcl err word;

        idx = 0;
        err = lx_check;
        do while (idx <= 7) and (err = lx_check);
            if(cmpb(@vx_ioconf(idx).name,p_nam,12) = lx_nilw)
            then
                    err = lx_succes;
            else
                    idx = idx + 1;
        end;
        return err;
    end sx_find_nam;

    sx_iomanager: procedure(p_ios) public;       /* carry out IO request */
    /* IO manager for ETR_286*/
    dcl p_ios              pointer;
    dcl iostate based p_ios   dx_iostate;
    dcl p_proci            pointer;
    dcl err                word;

    if(iostate.function <= lx_detach)            /* valid function request? */
    then do;
       do case iostate.function ;                /* switch on function */
          do;
                                                 /* lx_attach      */
                                                 /* Attach to IO driver */
              if(sx_find_nam(iostate.p_zone,@idx) = lx_succes)
              then do;
                  intlev = vx_ioconf(idx).intlev;
                  if(vx_ioptr(intlev).sta = lx_iofree)
                  then do;
                     vx_ioptr(intlev).sta = lx_iobusy;
                                                 /* make descriptor to iodesc */
                     p_iodesc = buildptr(selector$of(@vx_iodesc),
                         (offset$of(@vx_iodesc)+vx_lnum*14));
```

```
                                        /* insert into table */
            vx_ioptr(intlev).p_iodesc = p_iodesc;
            iodesc.lnum = vx_lnum;
            iodesc.intlev = intlev;
            iostate.lnum  = vx_lnum;
            vx_lnum = vx_lnum+1;        /* logical number */
            call movw(@vx_driver(vx_ioconf(idx).maj_dn),
                  @iodesc.p_proc,14);   /* copy procedure pointers */
            call sx_init_fifo(@iodesc.iofifo,40); /* initialise fifo */
            err = lx_succes;
        end;
    end;
    else
        iostate.status = lxes_no_name;
end;
do;
                                        /* lx_open */
    p_iodesc = vx_ioptr(iostate.lnum).p_iodesc;
    p_proci =iodesc.p_proc(lx_open);    /* lookup driver's open proc */
    call p_proci(p_ios);
    call sx_unmsk(iodesc.intlev);       /* enable this driver's ints */
    iostate.err = lx_succes;
    call sx_send_event(vx_ctask,iostate.evt,@err);  /* warn IO task */
end;
do;
                                        /* lx_read not implemented */
end;
do;
                                        /* lx_write */
    p_iodesc = vx_ioptr(iostate.lnum).p_iodesc;
    if(iodesc.busy = true)
        then do;                        /* enqueue this request */
            call sx_enqueue_fifo(@iodesc.iofifo,p_ios,@err);
            iostate.err = lx_check;
        end;
        else do;                        /* driver free: do it now! */
            p_proci =iodesc.p_proc(lx_write);
            call p_proci(p_ios);        /* driver's write routine */
            iodesc.p_ios = p_ios;
            iodesc.task = vx_ctask;
        end;
end;
do;
                                        /* lx_close */
    p_iodesc = vx_ioptr(iostate.lnum).p_iodesc;
    p_proci =iodesc.p_proc(lx_close);
    call p_proci(p_ios);
    call sx_mask(iodesc.intlev);        /* disable interrupts */
    iostate.err = lx_succes;
    call sx_send_event(vx_ctask,iostate.evt,@err);  /* warn IO task */
end;
do;
                                        /* lx_detach not implemented */
end;
do;
```

```
                                    /* lx_attach */
        p_iodesc = vx_ioptr(iostate.lnum).p_iodesc;
        vx_ioptr(iodesc.intlev).sta = lx_iobusy;
     end;

   end;      /* Case */
 end;        /* If   */
 else
    iostate.err = lx_check;
end sx_iomanager;

sx_wser: procedure(p_ios) public;
dcl p_ios pointer;
dcl iostate based p_ios dx_iostate;

    iostate.index    = 0;                   /* enable serial interface */
    output(lxp_ad_tty+lxp_usstat) = 1;      /* TX EN on 8251A */
    iostate.finished = false;
end sx_wser;

sx_intser: procedure(p_ios) public;         /* write to serial interface */
    dcl p_ios pointer;
    dcl iostate based p_ios dx_iostate;
    dcl p_zone pointer;
    dcl zone based p_zone(1) byte;

    p_zone = iostate.p_zone;                /* find data buffer */
    output(lxp_ad_tty) = zone(iostate.index);  /* output next byte */
    iostate.index = iostate.index + 1;
    if (iostate.index = iostate.nchar)      /* finished? */
    then do;
        call sx_mask(iostate.intlev);       /* turn off interrupts */
        iostate.finished = true;
    end;
end sx_intser;

sx_task_6: procedure public;                /* IO task for serial output */
dcl p_iodesc pointer;
dcl iodesc based p_iodesc dx_iodesc;
dcl p_ios pointer;
dcl iostate based p_ios dx_iostate ;
dcl err word;
dcl lnum word;

do while 1;                                 /* loop servicing interrupt */
    p_iodesc = vx_ioptr(6).p_iodesc;
    lnum    = iodesc.lnum;                  /* get logical driver number */
    p_ios   = iodesc.p_ios;
                                            /* call int. proc indirectly */
    if(iostate.finished = true)
    then do;                                /* signal to task */
        call sx_send_event(iostate.task,iostate.evt,@err);
        p_ios = sx_dequeue_fifo(@iodesc.iofifo,@err);   /* any more? */
        if(err = lx_succes)
        then do;
```

```
            call sx_iomanager(p_ios);
        end;
        else
        iodesc.busy = false;
    end;
    call wait$for$interrupt;                    /* wait for next interrupt */
  end;
  end sx_task_6;
end etrdrv_mod;
```

C.17 etrexp.pl6

```
$TITLE('ETR286 - Exception Handling')
etrexp_mod: do;
$NOLIST
$INCLUDE(etr.h)
$INCLUDE(etrstr.h)
sx_err_init: procedure(n) external ;
    dcl n word;
end sx_err_init;
$list

    dcl vx_exp(32) word public;

    /*-------------- 0 -------------------------*/
    except_0: procedure public;
        /* Division by zero */
        do while 1;
            vx_exp(0) = vx_exp(0) + 1;
            call sx_err_init(lxe_except+0);
            call wait$for$interrupt;
            halt;
        end;
    end except_0;
    /*-------------- 1 -------------------------*/
    except_1: procedure public;
        /* single step */
        do while 1;
            vx_exp(1) = vx_exp(1) + 1;
            call sx_err_init(lxe_except+1);
            call wait$for$interrupt;
            halt;
        end;
    end except_1;
    /*-------------- 3 -------------------------*/
    except_3: procedure public;
        /* Breakpoint */
        do while 1;
            vx_exp(3) = vx_exp(3) + 1;
            call sx_err_init(lxe_except+3);
            call wait$for$interrupt;
            halt;
        end;
    end except_3;
    /*-------------- 4 -------------------------*/
    except_4: procedure public;
        /* Overflow */
        do while 1;
            vx_exp(4) = vx_exp(4) + 1;
            call sx_err_init(lxe_except+4);
            call wait$for$interrupt;
            halt;
        end;
    end except_4;
    /*-------------- 5 -------------------------*/
```

```
except_5: procedure public;
    /* Bound range exceeded */
    do while 1;
        vx_exp(5) = vx_exp(5) + 1;
        call sx_err_init(lxe_except+5);
        call wait$for$interrupt;
        halt;
    end;
end except_5;
/*-------------- 6 --------------------------*/
except_6: procedure public;
    /* Invalid Opcode */
    do while 1;
        vx_exp(6) = vx_exp(6) + 1;
        call sx_err_init(lxe_except+6);
        call wait$for$interrupt;
        halt;
    end;
end except_6;
/*-------------- 7 --------------------------*/
except_7: procedure public;
    /* Processor Extension not available */
    do while 1;
        vx_exp(7) = vx_exp(7) + 1;
        call sx_err_init(lxe_except+7);
        call wait$for$interrupt;
        halt;
    end;
end except_7;
/*-------------- 8 --------------------------*/
except_8: procedure public;
    /* Double Fault */
    do while 1;
        vx_exp(8) = vx_exp(8) + 1;
        call sx_err_init(lxe_except+8);
        call wait$for$interrupt;
        halt;
    end;
end except_8;
/*-------------- 9 --------------------------*/
except_9: procedure public;
    /* Processor Extension segment overrun */
    do while 1;
        vx_exp(9) = vx_exp(9) + 1;
        call sx_err_init(lxe_except+9);
        call wait$for$interrupt;
        halt;
    end;
end except_9;
/*-------------- 10 --------------------------*/
except_10: procedure public;
    /* TSS invalid */
    do while 1;
        vx_exp(10) = vx_exp(10) + 1;
        call sx_err_init(lxe_except+10);
```

```
            call wait$for$interrupt;
            halt;
        end;
    end except_10;
    /*-------------- 11 --------------------------*/
    except_11: procedure public;
        /* Segment Not Present */
        do while 1;
            vx_exp(11) = vx_exp(11) + 1;
            call sx_err_init(lxe_except+11);
            call wait$for$interrupt;
            halt;
        end;
    end except_11;
    /*-------------- 12 --------------------------*/
    except_12: procedure public;
        /* Stack Segment Error */
        do while 1;
            vx_exp(12) = vx_exp(12) + 1;
            call sx_err_init(lxe_except+12);
            call wait$for$interrupt;
            halt;
        end;
    end except_12;
    /*-------------- 13 --------------------------*/
    except_13: procedure public;
        /* Protection Error */
        do while 1;
            vx_exp(13) = vx_exp(13) + 1;
            call sx_err_init(lxe_except+13);
            call wait$for$interrupt;
            halt;
        end;
    end except_13;
    /*-------------- 14 --------------------------*/
    except_14: procedure public;
        /* Processor Extension Error */
        do while 1;
            vx_exp(14) = vx_exp(14) + 1;
            call sx_err_init(lxe_except+14);
            call wait$for$interrupt;
            halt;
        end;
    end except_14;

end etrexp_mod;
```

C.18   etrut.pl6

```
$TITLE('ETR_286 - utility procedures')
etrut_mod: do;
$NOLIST
$INCLUDE(etr.h)
$INCLUDE(etrstr.h)
$list
    dcl vx_p_tss pointer external;
    dcl vx_index_tsk word external;
    dcl vx_sel_tss selector external;
    dcl vx_maxtsk word external;

    dcl vx_nb_egdt word public ;
    dcl vx_p_otd pointer public;
    dcl ctask based vx_p_otd dx_otd;
    dcl vx_p_fifo pointer public;
    dcl vx_bits(*) byte public
    data(00,
        01,02,01,03,01,02,01,04,01,02,01,03,01,02,01,05,
        01,02,01,03,01,02,01,04,01,02,01,03,01,02,01,06,
        01,02,01,03,01,02,01,04,01,02,01,03,01,02,01,05,
        01,02,01,03,01,02,01,04,01,02,01,03,01,02,01,07,
        01,02,01,03,01,02,01,04,01,02,01,03,01,02,01,05,
        01,02,01,03,01,02,01,04,01,02,01,03,01,02,01,06,
        01,02,01,03,01,02,01,04,01,02,01,03,01,02,01,05,
        01,02,01,03,01,02,01,04,01,02,01,03,01,02,01,08,
        01,02,01,03,01,02,01,04,01,02,01,03,01,02,01,05,
        01,02,01,03,01,02,01,04,01,02,01,03,01,02,01,06,
        01,02,01,03,01,02,01,04,01,02,01,03,01,02,01,05,
        01,02,01,03,01,02,01,04,01,02,01,03,01,02,01,07,
        01,02,01,03,01,02,01,04,01,02,01,03,01,02,01,05,
        01,02,01,03,01,02,01,04,01,02,01,03,01,02,01,06,
        01,02,01,03,01,02,01,04,01,02,01,03,01,02,01,05,
        01,02,01,03,01,02,01,04,01,02,01,03,01,02,01,05,
        01,02,01,03,01,02,01,04,01,02,01,03,01,02,01,01);

    dcl vx_mask_bits(*) word public
    data(
        0001H,0002H,0004H,0008H,
        0010H,0020H,0040H,0080H,
        0100H,0200H,0400H,0800H,
        1000H,2000H,4000H,8000H);

    dcl vx_tready(2) word;              /* bitmap of ready tasks */
    dcl vx_egdt word ;
    dcl vx_sgdt word ;

    sx_fnd_tready: procedure word public;   /* find highest pri. rdy task */
        dcl i word;
        dcl j word;
        dcl index word;
        dcl n word;
        dcl r word;
        dcl rr byte;
```

```
    i = length(vx_tready)-1;
    do while (i <> 0);
        r = vx_tready(i-1);
        if(r <> 0)                    /* one in this word? */
        then do;
            if (r AND 000FFH) <> 0H
            then do;                  /* it's in low-order byte */
                j = 0;
                rr = low(r);
                if(rr AND 0FH) <>0
                then                  /* low-order quartet */
                    j = j + vx_bits(rr)-1;
                else                  /* high-order quartet */
                    j = j + vx_bits(rr)+3;
                j = low(r);
            end;
            else do;                  /* high-order byte */
                rr = high(r);
                j = 8;
                if(rr AND 0FH) <>0
                then                  /* low-order quartet */
                    j = j + vx_bits(rr)-1;
                else                  /* high-order quartet */
                    /* Fort octet */
                    j = j + vx_bits(rr)+3;
            end;
            vx_tready(i) = vx_tready(i) AND vx_mask_bits(j); /* unmark */
            index = 16*(3-i) + j;
            i = 0;
        end;
        else
            i = i - 1;
    end;
    if(i = 0)
    then
        index = vx_maxtsk; /* Background task */
    return index ;
end sx_fnd_tready;

sx_ready: procedure(task) public;
    dcl task word;              /* mark task ready */
    if(task >= lx_nbitw)
    then
        vx_tready(0) = vx_tready(0) OR vx_mask_bits(task-16);
    else
        vx_tready(1) = vx_tready(1) OR vx_mask_bits(task);
end sx_ready;

sx_wait: procedure(task) public;
    dcl task word;              /* mark task not ready */
    if(task >= lx_nbitw)
    then
        vx_tready(0) = vx_tready(0) AND NOT vx_mask_bits(task-16);
    else
```

```
            vx_tready(1) = vx_tready(1) AND NOT vx_mask_bits(task);
    end sx_wait;

    sx_get_tsk: procedure(nt) public;
        dcl nt word;           /* set globals for nominated task */
        dcl n word;

        n = vx_index_tsk + nt*lx_ndesc_tsk + lx_index_tss;
        vx_sel_tss = sx_cv_ixgdt(n);
        vx_p_tss = buildptr(vx_sel_tss,0);
        n = vx_index_tsk + nt*lx_ndesc_tsk + lx_index_otd;
        vx_p_otd = buildptr(sx_cv_ixgdt(n),0);
        n = vx_index_tsk + nt*lx_ndesc_tsk + lx_index_fifo ;
        vx_p_fifo = buildptr(sx_cv_ixgdt(n),0);

    end sx_get_tsk;

    sx_get_otd: procedure(task) pointer public;
        dcl task word;         /* return pointer to task's otd */
        dcl n word;
        dcl s selector;
        dcl p pointer;
        n = vx_index_tsk + task*lx_ndesc_tsk + lx_index_otd;
        s = sx_cv_ixgdt(n);
        p = buildptr(s,0);
        return p;
    end sx_get_otd;

    sx_get_egdt: procedure word public;
        dcl index_gdt word;    /* return index to free entry in GDT */
        dcl v word;

        v = (vx_egdt + 1) MOD lx_egdt;
        if( v = vx_sgdt)
        then
        index_gdt = lx_nilw;
        else do;
            index_gdt = lx_firstgdt + vx_egdt;
            vx_egdt = v;
            vx_nb_egdt = vx_nb_egdt + 1;
        end;
        return index_gdt;
    end sx_get_egdt;

    sx_put_egdt: procedure public;
        dcl index_gdt word;    /* free entry last allocated in GDT */

        if(vx_sgdt = vx_egdt)
        then
            index_gdt = lx_nilw;
        else do;
            vx_sgdt = (vx_sgdt + 1) MOD lx_egdt;
            vx_nb_egdt = vx_nb_egdt - 1;
        end;
    end sx_put_egdt;
```

```
    sx_ini_egdt: procedure public;
        vx_sgdt = 0;              /* initialise GDT entry allocator */
        vx_egdt = 0;
        vx_nb_egdt = 0;
    end sx_ini_egdt;

    sx_get_agdt: procedure(sel_org,idx,p_sel) pointer public;
        dcl sel_org selector;    /* make a RW alias in GDT for segment idx */
        dcl idx word;
        dcl p_sel pointer;

        dcl dorg based sel_org dx_desc;
        dcl sel_alias selector;
        dcl dalias based sel_alias dx_desc;

        sel_alias = sx_cv_ixgdt(idx);
        call movw(@dorg,@dalias,4);      /* copy original descriptor */
        dalias.rights = dalias.rights AND lx_ar_rw ;    /* modify rights */
        return (buildptr(sel_alias,0));
    end sx_get_agdt;

    sx_put_agdt: procedure public;
        call sx_put_egdt;        /* return an alias */
    end sx_put_agdt;

    sx_cv_ixgdt: procedure(index) selector public;
        dcl index word;          /* make a GDT selector from an index */

        dcl v word;
        dcl s selector at(@v);
        v = shl(index,3);
        return s;
    end sx_cv_ixgdt;

    sx_cvtyp_s2w: procedure(s) WORD public;
        dcl s selector;          /* convert selector into word */
        dcl w word at (@s);
        return w;
    end sx_cvtyp_s2w;

    sx_cvtyp_w2s: procedure(w) selector public;
        dcl w word;              /* convert word into selector */
        dcl s selector at (@w);
        return s;
    end sx_cvtyp_w2s;

end etrut_mod;
```

C.19 etrmain.pl6

```
$TITLE('ETR_286 - main program')
ETRMAIN_MOD:
DO;
/* $NOLIST */
$INCLUDE(etr.h)
$INCLUDE(etrstr.h)

sx_get_adr_sel: procedure(p,n) dword external ;
    dcl n word;
    dcl p pointer;
end sx_get_adr_sel;

sx_get_egdt: procedure word external ;
end sx_get_egdt;

sx_put_egdt: procedure external ;
end sx_put_egdt;

sx_get_agdt: procedure(s,n,p) pointer external ;
    dcl n word;
    dcl s selector;
    dcl p pointer;
end sx_get_agdt;

sx_cv_ixgdt: procedure(ix) selector external;
    dcl ix word;
end sx_cv_ixgdt;

sx_cvtyp_s2w: procedure(s) WORD external;
        dcl s selector;
end sx_cvtyp_s2w;

sx_gmemx: procedure (n,p) pointer external ;
    dcl n word;
    dcl p pointer;
end sx_gmemx;

sx_init: procedure external;
end sx_init;

sx_init_clk: procedure(p_clk,fr) external;
    dcl p_clk pointer;
    dcl fr word;
end sx_init_clk;

sx_init_per: procedure(p) external;
    dcl p pointer;
end sx_init_per;

sx_schedinit: procedure external;
end sx_schedinit;

sx_ready: procedure(task) external;
```

```
        dcl task word;
end sx_ready;

sx_unmsk: procedure(intlev) external;
    dcl intlev word;
end sx_unmsk;

sx_ini_egdt: procedure external;
end sx_ini_egdt;

sx_init_fifo: procedure(p_fifo,max) external;
    dcl p_fifo pointer;
    dcl max word;
end sx_init_fifo;

sx_mak_desc: procedure(adr,index,sz,ty,dp,ar) external ;
    dcl adr dword;
    dcl (index,sz,ty,dp,ar) word;
end sx_mak_desc;

sx_err_init: procedure(n) external ;
    dcl n word;
end sx_err_init;
$list

    dcl vx_freq word public;
    dcl vx_tty word public;
    dcl vx_pgdt pointer external;
    dcl vx_pldt pointer external;
    dcl vx_index_tsk word external;
    dcl vx_maxtsk word public;

    dcl vx_std(1) pointer external;

    dcl gdt based vx_pgdt(1) dx_desc;
    dcl ldt based vx_pldt(1) dx_desc;
    dcl gdt2 based vx_pgdt(1) dx_desc2;
    dcl ldt2 based vx_pldt(1) dx_desc2;

    dcl cx_pic dx_peri external;          /* IO initialisation data */
    dcl cx_sysck dx_peri external;
    dcl cx_tty dx_peri external;

    sx_create_tsk: procedure(p_dst) public;
        dcl p_dst pointer;
        dcl dst based p_dst dx_std;
        dcl task word;
        dcl index word;
        dcl p_otd pointer;
        dcl otd based p_otd dx_otd;
        dcl err word;
        dcl xn word;
        dcl sel_otd selector;
        dcl sel_fifo selector;
        dcl adr dword;
```

```
dcl sel_ldt selector;
dcl sel_tss selector;
dcl p_ldt pointer;
dcl p_fifo pointer;
dcl p_tss pointer;
dcl p_alias pointer;
dcl tss based p_tss dx_tss;
dcl atss based p_alias dx_tss;

task = dst.number;                      /* find GDT area for task */
index = vx_index_tsk + lx_ndesc_tsk*task;

xn = lx_szotd + dst.stack_0;            /* create global memory area */
if(dst.msgfifosz <> lx_nilw)
then
xn = xn + dst.msgfifosz + lx_szfifo;
p_otd = sx_gmemx(xn,@err);

call sx_err_init(err);                  /* stop process if error */

sel_otd = sx_cv_ixgdt(index+lx_index_otd);  /* make GDT entries for */
sel_fifo = sx_cv_ixgdt(index+lx_index_fifo );/* OTD and fifo */

adr = sx_get_adr_sel(p_otd,0);
call sx_mak_desc(adr,index+lx_index_otd,    /* RW entries in GDT */
    lx_szotd,lx_typseg,lx_dpl0,lx_ar_rw);

if(dst.msgfifosz <> lx_nilw)
then do;
    adr = sx_get_adr_sel(p_otd,lx_szotd);
    p_fifo = BUILDPTR(selector$of(p_otd),lx_szotd);
    call sx_mak_desc(adr,index+lx_index_fifo,
    lx_szotd,lx_typseg,lx_dpl0,lx_ar_rw);
    call sx_init_fifo(p_fifo,dst.msgfifosz);
end;

                                        /* initialise LDT and TSS */
sel_ldt = sx_cv_ixgdt(task*lx_ndesc_tsk+lx_index_ldt);
p_ldt = buildptr(sel_ldt,0);
sel_tss = sx_cv_ixgdt(task*lx_ndesc_tsk+lx_index_tss);

index = sx_get_egdt;                    /* make TSS alias for SS0 */
p_alias = sx_get_agdt(sel_tss,index,@err);
if (err <> lx_succes)
then
    call sx_err_init(err);
atss.ss0 = sx_cvtyp_s2w(sel_otd);
atss.sp0 = lx_szotd + dst.stack_0;
call sx_put_egdt;

otd.number = task;                      /* fill in task's OTD */
otd.prior = task;
otd.status = lx_succes;
otd.p_fifo = NIL;
if( dst.msgfifosz <> lx_nilw)
```

```
            then
            otd.p_fifo = p_fifo;
            else
            otd.p_fifo = NIL;
            otd.p_otd = p_otd;
            otd.ctick = 0;

            call sx_ready(task);                    /* set task runnable */
        end sx_create_tsk;

    /*====== ===============================*/
    sx_create_tasks: procedure public;
        dcl bper(20) byte;
        dcl n word;

        call sx_init_per(@cx_pic);                  /* initialise PIC */

        /*
        For clock of 1.23 Mhz,
        TTY baud rate = 76875/baud rate
        Clock Interrupt = (interval*1536/10) at 153.6 Khz
        */

        call movb(@cx_sysck,@bper,20);              /* initialise system clock */
        vx_freq = lx_clk*1536/10; /* En ms */
        bper(4) = high(vx_freq);
        bper(2) = low(vx_freq);
        call sx_init_clk(@(14,06,86,0,0,0),lx_clk); /* date and time */
        call sx_init_per(@bper);

        call movb(@cx_tty,@bper,20);                /* baud rate generator */
        vx_tty = 76875/lx_ttyspd;
        bper(4) = high(vx_tty);
        bper(2) = low(vx_tty);
        call sx_init_per(@bper);

        n = 0;                                      /* create all tasks */
        do while (sx_cvtyp_s2w(selector$of(vx_std(n))) <> lx_nilw);
            call sx_create_tsk(vx_std(n));
            n = n + 1;
        end;
        vx_maxtsk = n-1;                            /* background task */

        /* Enable All Interrupts */
        call sx_unmsk(lxin_ckint);
        call sx_unmsk(lxin_ttyint);
        call sx_unmsk(lxin_ttyoint);
    end sx_create_tasks;

/* main program */

    call sx_init;
    call sx_create_tasks;
    call sx_schedinit;
end etrmain_mod;
```

C.20   etrinit.pl6

```
$TITLE('ETR_286 - initialisation and general utilities')
etrinit_mod: do;
$NOLIST
$INCLUDE(etr.h)
$INCLUDE(etrstr.h)

sx_ini_egdt: procedure external;
end sx_ini_egdt;

sx_cv_ixgdt: procedure(n) selector external;
     dcl n word;
end sx_cv_ixgdt;

sx_cvtyp_s2w: procedure(s) word external;
     dcl s selector;
end sx_cvtyp_s2w;

sx_init_memu: procedure external;
end sx_init_memu;
$LIST

/*    dcl vx_bgdt(3)     word    public;       */
 /* unused */
/*    dcl ldt based vx_sel_ldt dx_ldt;*/
 /* unused */

   dcl vx_pgdt pointer public;
   dcl vx_pldt pointer public;
   dcl vx_index_tsk word public; /* 1er index tsk ds GDT */
   dcl vx_p_tss pointer public;
   dcl vx_sel_tss selector public;
   dcl vx_sel_ldt selector public;
   dcl tss based vx_sel_tss dx_tss;
   dcl gdt based vx_pgdt(1) dx_desc;
   dcl gdt2 based vx_pgdt(1) dx_desc2;
   dcl ldt2 based vx_pldt(1) dx_desc2;

/* memory allocator variables */
   dcl vx_memx(1) byte external; /* memoire interne */
   dcl vx_memu(1) byte external; /* memoire user */
   dcl vx_sel_memu selector public;
   dcl vx_sel_memx selector public;
   dcl vx_pmemu pointer public;
   dcl vx_pmemx pointer public;
   dcl vx_max_memu word public;
   dcl vx_max_memx word public;
   dcl vx_basx word; /* Base memoire interne */


       sx_init: procedure public;      /* initialise ETR_286 variables */
          vx_pgdt = build$ptr(sx_cv_ixgdt(lx_al_gdt),0);  /* GDT */
          vx_sel_tss = task$register;
```

```
        vx_p_tss = buildptr(vx_sel_tss,0);          /* TSS */
        vx_sel_ldt = sx_cv_ixgdt(tss.ldt);
        vx_pldt = buildptr(vx_sel_ldt,0);           /* LDT */

        vx_basx = 0;                /* internal memory allocator */
        vx_pmemx = @vx_memx;
        vx_sel_memx = selector$of(vx_pmemx);
        vx_max_memx = lx_max_memx;
        vx_pmemu = @vx_memu;        /* user memory allocator */
        vx_sel_memu = selector$of(vx_pmemu);
        vx_max_memu = lx_max_memu;
        call sx_init_memu;

        call sx_ini_egdt;           /* GDT entries allocator */

        vx_index_tsk = lx_index_t0; /* task indices into GDT */
    end sx_init;

sx_gmemx: procedure(val,p_err) pointer public;      /* intern. mem alloc */
    dcl val word;
    dcl p_err pointer;
    dcl err based p_err word;
    dcl p pointer;

    if (vx_basx + val ) < vx_max_memx               /* possible? */
    then do;
        p = buildptr(vx_sel_memx,vx_basx);
        vx_basx = vx_basx + val;
        err = lx_succes;
    end;
    else
        err = lxe_memx;
    return p;
end sx_gmemx;

sx_get_adr_sel: procedure(ptr,sz) DWORD public;
                                /* real (24-bit) address of sz(ptr) */
    dcl ptr POINTER;
    dcl sz WORD;
    dcl v_s WORD;
    dcl adr DWORD;

    v_s = sx_cvtyp_s2w(SELECTOR$OF(ptr));
    if (v_s AND lx_ti) = lx_ti_isgdt
    then do;                        /* from GDT? */
        adr = gdt2(SHR((v_s AND lx_msk_idx),3)).base;
    end;
    else do;                        /* or LDT */
        adr = ldt2(SHR((v_s AND lx_msk_idx),3)).base;
    end;
    adr = (adr AND lx_msk24B) + sz;
    return adr;
end sx_get_adr_sel;

sx_mak_desc: procedure(adr,index,sz,typ,dpl,rights) public;
```

```
        dcl adr dword;                  /* make GDT entry */
        dcl index word;
        dcl sz word;
        dcl typ byte;
        dcl dpl byte;
        dcl rights byte;
        dcl desc dx_desc;
        dcl desc2 dx_desc2 at(@desc);

        desc.limit = sz-1;              /* segment limit */
        desc2.base = adr ;              /* 24-bit base address */
        desc.rsv = 0 ;                  /* reserved */
        desc.rights = lx_bpres + 64*dpl + rights;
        call movw(@desc,@gdt(index),4);
    end sx_mak_desc;
end etrinit_mod;
```

C.21 etres.pl6

```
$TITLE('ETR286 - IO routines')
etres_mod: do;
$NOLIST
$INCLUDE(etr.h)
$INCLUDE(etrstr.h)
$list
    dcl vx_imask_bits(lx_nbint) byte data(1,2,4,8,16,32,64,128);
    dcl vx_ioptr(lx_nbint) dx_ioptr public;      /* pointers to iodescs */
    dcl vx_iodesc(lx_nbint) dx_iodesc public;    /* The iodescriptors */
    dcl vx_lnum         word public;             /* logical driver no */
    dcl vx_mask_pic     byte public;             /* current PIC mask */

/* initialisation data */
    dcl cx_pic dx_peri public                    /* interrupt controller */
        data(
            lxp_ad_pic,                          /* base address */
            0,17H,2,20H,2,0DH,                   /* interrupt 32 */
            2,lxp_nilb,lxp_nilb,                 /* start with all masked */
            lxp_nilb);                           /* end */

    dcl cx_sysck dx_peri public                  /* system clock */
        data(
            lxp_ad_pit,                          /* 8253 address */
            6,036H,0,00,0,00,                    /* chan 0/mode 2/binary */
            lxp_nilb);

    dcl cx_ttyb dx_peri public                   /* TTY baud rate */
        data(
            lxp_ad_pit,
            6,0B6H,4,8,4,00H,                    /* 9600 Baud */
            lxp_nilb);

    dcl cx_tty dx_peri public                    /* serial interface */
        data(
            lxp_ad_tty+lxp_usstat,
            2,0,2,0,20,20,
            2,40H,2,4EH,2,37H,                   /* asynchronous */
            lxp_nilb);

    sx_init_io: procedure public;                /* initialise IO structure */
        dcl i word;

        do i = 0 to lx_nbint-1;
            vx_ioptr(i).sta = lx_iofree;
            vx_ioptr(i).p_iodesc = NIL;
        end;
        vx_lnum = 0;
    end sx_init_io;

    sx_init_per: procedure(p_per) public;        /* initialise IO device */
        dcl p_per           pointer;
        dcl peri based p_per dx_peri;
        dcl base            word;
```

```
        dcl i               word;

        i = 0;
        base = peri.base;
        do while (peri.dper(i) <> lx_nilw);
            output(base+peri.dper(i)) = peri.dper(i+1);
            i = i + 2;
        end;
    end sx_init_per;

    sx_get_mask: procedure byte public;         /* return current PIC mask */
        dcl intlev word;

        return vx_mask_pic;
    end sx_get_mask;

    sx_mask: procedure(intlev) public;          /* inhibit a PIC line */
        dcl intlev word;

        vx_mask_pic = vx_mask_pic OR vx_imask_bits(intlev);
        output(cx_pic.base) =vx_mask_pic;
    end sx_mask;

    sx_unmsk: procedure(intlev) public;         /* enable a PIC line */
        dcl intlev word;

        vx_mask_pic = vx_mask_pic AND NOT vx_imask_bits(intlev);
        output(cx_pic.base) =vx_mask_pic;
    end sx_unmsk;

/*======    Routines for debugging and error messages     ===============*/

    sx_outser: procedure(p_per,c);              /* output to serial line */
        dcl c           byte;                   /* BY POLLING */
        dcl p_per       pointer;
        dcl peri based  p_per dx_peri;
        dcl base        word;

        base = peri.base;
        do while (input(base+lxp_usstat) AND lxp_ustrdy <> 0);
        end;                                    /* wait for ready */
        output(base) = c;                       /* and output */
    end;

    sx_print: procedure(p_zone,p_peri);         /* print a string */
        dcl p_zone              pointer;
        dcl zone based p_zone(1) byte;
        dcl p_peri              pointer;
        dcl i                   word;

        i = 0;
        do while (zone(i) <> lx_ends);
            call sx_outser(p_peri,zone(i));
            i = i + 1;
        end;
```

```
    end sx_print;

sx_err_init: procedure(err) public;         /* print error message & no. */
    dcl err     word;
    dcl i       word;
    dcl s(9)    byte;

    call sx_print(@('ETR_286 Error = ',0),@cx_tty);
    do i = 0 TO 4;                          /* convert err to decimal */
        s(4-i) = (err mod 10) + '0';
        err = err / 10;
    end;
    s(5) = 0;
    call sx_print(@s,@cx_tty);
    call sx_print(@(0DH,0AH,0),@cx_tty);
end sx_err_init;

end etres_mod;
```

C.22 etr286.bld

```
-- ************************
-- * ETR286 : Build file *
-- ************************
--
ETR286_SYS;
-- Stack Segments
CREATESEG
    STKINT6 ;
SEGMENT
    STKINT6 (LIMIT=200H,DPL=0);
SEGMENT
    ETR286 (DPL=0);
-- GATE ETR ==========================================
GATE
        RQ_GET_MEMU (
                ENTRY=sx_get_memu,
                DPL=3,
                WC=3,
                CALL
        );
GATE
        RQ_FREE_MEMU (
                ENTRY=sx_free_memu,
                DPL=3,
                WC=3,
                CALL
        );
GATE
        RQ_DEM (
                ENTRY=sx_unmsk,
                DPL=3,
                WC=1,
                CALL
        );
GATE
        RQ_MSQ (
                ENTRY=sx_mask,
                DPL=3,
                WC=1,
                CALL
        );
GATE
        RQ_SEND_MSG (
                ENTRY=sx_send_msg,
                DPL=3,
                WC=5,
                CALL
        );
GATE
        RQ_READ_MSG (
                ENTRY=sx_read_msg,
                DPL=3,
                WC=3,
```

```
                CALL
        );
GATE
        RQ_SEND_EVENT (
                ENTRY=sx_send_event,
                DPL=3,
                WC=4,
                CALL
        );
GATE
        RQ_AWAIT_EVENT (
                ENTRY=sx_await_event,
                DPL=3,
                WC=3,
                CALL
        );
GATE
        RQ_TIMOUT (
                ENTRY=sx_timout,
                DPL=3,
                WC=3,
                CALL
        );
-- LDT ==================================================
TABLE
        LDTI (DPL=0,ENTRY=(ETR286));
TABLE
        LDT0 (ENTRY=(t0),RESERVE=(1..2));
TABLE
        LDT1 (ENTRY=(t1),RESERVE=(1..2));
TABLE
        LDTF (ENTRY=(tf),RESERVE=(1..2));

-- TSS ==================================================
-- TSS for initial task
TASK
        TINIT           -- task name
        (
                OBJECT = ETR286,
                LDT    = LDTI,
                INITIAL );
-- TSS application
TASK
        TSK0            -- task name
        (
                OBJECT = T0,
                LDT    = LDT0
        );
TASK
        TSK1            -- task name
        (
                OBJECT = T1,
                LDT    = LDT1
        );
TASK
```

```
              TSKF        -- task name
                (
                    OBJECT = TF,
                    LDT    = LDTF
                );
-- TSS for exception handlers
TASK
    TSS_EXP0 (CODE=except_0,
              DATA=ETR286.ETREXP_MOD_DATA,LDT=LDTI);
TASK
    TSS_EXP1 (CODE=except_1 ,
              DATA=ETR286.ETREXP_MOD_DATA,LDT=LDTI);
-- TSS for interrupt handlers
TASK
    TSS_INT6 (CODE=sx_task_6,
              DATA=ETR286.ETRDRV_MOD_DATA,
              STACKS=(STKINT6),DPL=0,LDT=LDTI);
-- Gates for interrupts and exceptions
GATE
    GEXP0 (TASK,ENTRY=TSS_EXP0);
GATE
    GEXP1 (TASK,ENTRY=TSS_EXP1);
GATE
    GINT6 (TASK,ENTRY=TSS_INT6);
-- IDT ==================================================
TABLE
           IDT  (DPL=0,
           ENTRY=(0 :GEXP0,
                  1 :GEXP1,
                 32:GINT6));

-- GDT ==================================================
TABLE
           GDT  (DPL=0,RESERVE=(0..19,52..53,56..57,60..61),
           ENTRY=(
               20:RQ_GET_MEMU,      -- System call gate
               21:RQ_FREE_MEMU,     -- System call gate
               22:RQ_SEND_MSG,      -- System call gate
               23:RQ_READ_MSG,      -- System call gate
               24:RQ_SEND_EVENT,    -- System call gate
               25:RQ_AWAIT_EVENT,   -- System call gate
               26:RQ_DEM,           -- System call gate
               27:RQ_MSQ,           -- System call gate
               28:RQ_TIMOUT,        -- System call gate
               30:LDTI,             -- Ldt for init. task
               40:TSS_EXP0,         -- TSS exceptions 0
               41:TSS_EXP1,         -- TSS exceptions 1
               42:TSS_INT6,         -- TSS interrupt  6
               50:LDT0,51:TSK0,     -- Ldt for task 0
               54:LDT1,55:TSK1,     --              1
               58:LDTF,59:TSKF      --              f (background)
                  ));
-- Define memory ranges
MEMORY (
           RANGE = (
```

```
              RAMT=RAM(10000..12000),
         RAMC=RAM(13000..16000)
              ),
     ALLOCATE = (RAMT=(*TABLES,*TASKS))
);
END
```

Bibliography

[1] Jean-Michel Trio (1985), *8086–8088 Architecture and Programming,* Macmillan, London.
Describes the original Intel family, from which the 80286 and 80386 derive.

[2] M.J. Bach (1986), *The Design of the Unix Operating System,* Prentice-Hall International, Englewood Cliffs, N.J.

[3] L. Bic and A.G. Shaw (1988), *The Logical Design of Operating Systems,* Prentice-Hall International, Englewood Cliffs, N.J.

[4] J.L. Petersen and A. Silberschatz (1985), *Operating System Concepts,* Addison-Wesley, Reading, Mass.

[5] E.I. Organick (1972), *The Multics System,* M.I.T. Press, Cambridge, Mass.

[6] M. Ben-Ari (1982), *Principles of Concurrent Programming,* Prentice-Hall International, Englewood Cliffs, N.J.

[7] J.G.P. Barnes (1982), *Programming in Ada,* Addison-Wesley, Reading, Mass.

[8] B. Stroustrup (1986), *The C++ Programming Language,* Addison-Wesley, Reading, Mass.

[9] N. Wirth (1983), *Programming in Modula–2,* Springer-Verlag, Berlin.

[10] B.W. Kernighan and D.M. Ritchie (1988), *The C Programming Language,* Prentice-Hall, Englewood Cliffs, N.J.

Bibliography

[11] Intel, *iAPX286 Hardware Reference Manual*, No. 210760.

[12] Intel, *PLM286*, No. 122469.

[13] Intel, *iAPX286 Programmer's Reference Manual*, No. 210498.

[14] Intel, *Operating System Writer's Guide*, No. 121960.

[15] Intel, *ASM286/R&L Language Reference*, No. 122439.

[16] Intel, *ASM286/R&L Utilities*, No. 122449.

[17] Intel, *iAPX286 Architecture Extension Kernel*, No. 121961.

[18] Intel, *80386 Application Note*, No. 23160

[19] Intel, *ASM386 Assembly Language*, No. 122332.

Index

A bit, 48, 81
abort, 140
ABS, 109
access bit, 48
access rights, 149
accumulator, 36
Ada, 98, 102
address, 1–3
    bus, 22
    calculation, 144
    decoder, 14
    effective, 44
    linear, 158, 160
    logical, 22
    network, 137, 138
    physical, 38, 149
    space, 33, 148
    space (virtual), 45
    translation, 149, 158
    unit, 20
    virtual, 44
addressing
    direct, 39
    indexed, 40
    indirect, 37
    modes, 39, 150
ADJUST$RPL, 113
AH, 145
AL, 37, 145
alias, 51, 84, 116
alignment, 35
    in memory, 22
allocation, 134
Apple, 1, 5

application, 2–6
    scientific, 31
architecture
    multiprocessor, 14
    system, 13
arguments, 107
arithmetic, 28
    real, 13
ARPL, 59
ASCII, 89
assembler, 95
Assembly language, 153
assignments, 106
ASSUME, 90
AT&T, 4
Atari, 6
attach, 132
attribute, 162
AX, 36, 145

back link, 63, 79
BASE, 99
base, 3
base address, 149, 155
BASED, 109, 116
BCD, 35, 153
BH, 145
BHE, 22
binary files, 96
Binder, 100
BIOS, 23
BIT, 144
bit field, 153
bit string, 153
BL, 145

Index

block
    DO, 106
    structured, 102, 104, 108
boolean, 35
boot-loadable, 98, 134
bootstrap, 23
BOUND, 73
bound
    check, 73
    check (none on CASE), 107
BP, 36, 145
branch
    multiway, 107
breakpoint, 73
broadcast, 137, 141
buddy system, 131
buffering
    bus, 14
    cache, 166
bug, 43
Builder, 96, 134
BUILDPTR, 110
built-in functions, 108
bus
    cycle, 22, 24
    local, 13
    saturation, 18
    serial, 16
    system, 13
    write, 23
busy, 132
busy bit (in TSS), 65
BX, 36, 145
BY, 106
BYTE, 103
byte, 89
byte operations, 35

C, 4, 101, 102
cache
    address translation, 35, 52
    memory, 145, 162
    optimum size, 163
    segment register, 149

CALL, 53, 108
call gate, 116, 125, 162
carry flag, 147
cascaded mode, 28, 69
check, 149
    presence bit, 161
    protection, 55
classified, 55
CLI, 72, 136
clock, 11
clones, 135
close, 132, 140
CMPB, 109
CMPW, 109
Cobol, 102
CODE, 99
collision, 138
communication, 2, 7, 119, 135
COMPACT, 113
compatibility, 2, 13, 30, 53, 74, 86, 143, 146
compilation, 85, 113
compiler, 3
component, *see* device
concurrent, 3, 4
confederation, 6
configuration, 17
    file, 98
    operating system, 121
conformant segment, 59
console, 133
constants, 105
contention, 7
context, 63, 119, 156
    switch, 66
contiguous memory, 115
control blocks, 121
controller
    bus, 10
conversion, 134
coprocessor, 13, 28, 119, 145, 148, 153
    connection, 28
CPL, 58

260   *Index*

CR0–3, 156
CR3, 159
CRC, 138
critical regions, 129
crystal, 11
CS, 38, 149
CSMA/CD, 136
CX, 36, 145

DATA, 99
data
    bus, 22
    field, 138
database, 6, 135
datagram, 140
DB, 89
DD, 89
debugger, 73
debugging, 2, 54, 133, 148, 157
    registers, 157
decentralised, 7
DECLARE, 103
defaults, 98
departmental, 6
descriptor
    80386, 155
    cache, 155
    file for ETR_286, 125
    format, 47
    gate, 56, 60
    initialisation, 97
    interrupt table, 74
    management, 116
    segment, 49, 53
    table, 34, 45, 47
design
    hardware, 9
    of operating system, 123
detach, 132
device
    80186, 136
    80287, 13
    80387, 148
    8207, 13

82284, 11
82288, 10
82289, 11
8251A, 136
82586, 22
82588, 136
8259A, 13, 28, 69, 127, 131
8274, 136
8282, 13
8283, 13
8286, 13
8287, 13
DI, 36, 145
directory, 142
disk, 3, 81
displacement, 3, 44, 149
display, 5, 6
DMA, 16
    controller, 137
DO, 106
DOUBLE, 109
double
    fault, 79
    precision, 89
    word, 89
DPL, 48, 58
DQ, 89
draw, 6
driver
    I/O, 119, 131
DS, 38, 149
DT, 89
DUP, 89
DW, 89
DWORD, 103
DX, 36, 145
dynamic, 119, 122
    RAM, 163
    system, 96

EAX, 145
EBP, 145
EBX, 145
ECX, 145

Index 261

EDI, 145
editor, 97
EDX, 145
EIP, 145
emulation, 13
enable
    byte high, *see* BHE
    interrupts, 76
END, 91, 106
ENTER, 91
ENTRY, 98, 99
EPL, 58
EPROM, 23
error
    code, 132
    general protection, 136
    handling in ETR_286, 124, 133
    programming, 116
    reporting, 54
    transmission, 138
ES, 38, 149
ESC, 28
ESI, 145
ESP, 145
Ethernet, 7, 136, 139
event, 125, 130, 136
    number, 132
exceptions, 72, 116
    in ETR_286, 133
exclusion
    mutual, 16
executive, 123
expiry, 128
expressions, 103, 105
extended precision, 89
EXTERNAL, 107, 110
EXTRN, 94, 101

FAR call, 91
faulty behaviour, 54
fictitious variable, 110
FIFO, 138
fifo, 126
file transfer, 141

filestore, 141
FINDB, 109
FINDW, 109
FIX, 109
flag byte, 138
FLAGS, 100
FLOAT, 109
floating-point, 35
Fortran, 85, 101, 102
FS, 149
function, 107, 108
    number, 132

Gates, 60
    interrupt, 62
GDT, 45, 126, 134
GDTR, 49, 53, 156
GET$ACCESS$RIGHTS, 112
GET$SEGMENT$LIMIT, 112
global, 156
granularity bit, 155
grouping segments, 52
GS, 149

header, 141
hierarchical protection, 54
HIGH, 109
HLDA, 22
HOLD, 22
hypervisor, 3, 143

IABS, 109
IDT, 62
IDTR, 156, 162
IEEE 802.3, 136
IF, 68, 106
IN, 136
iNA960, 140
indenting, 106
index, 49, 103
indexing, 134
indirection, 158
INITIAL, 99, 103
initialisation, 103

input/output, 23, 119, 135
    driver, 131
    in ETR_286, 131
    in PL/M, 112
    procedures, 136
INS, 136
instruction
    coprocessor, 28
    string, 25
INT, 109
INT k, 26
INTEGER, 103
Intel, 102
interfaces
    standard I/O, 119
intermittent bugs, 157
INTERRUPT, 107, 111
interrupt, 26, 68, 119, 162
    acknowlege, 28
    clock, 124, 127
    gate, 74
    hardware, 28, 75
    latency, 26
    level, 131
    priority, 26
    privilege checking, 76
    protected mode, 73
    real mode, 68
    response time, 136
    task switch, 78
    vector, 27
INTR, 26, 68
IOPL, 38, 112, 136, 147
IP, 38
IRET, 66, 77, 78, 111
iRMX/286, 85, 115, 140
isolation, 54
iteration, 106

jamming, 138
JMP, 53

kernel, 55, 115, 117, 119, 136, 154
keyboard, 7

language
    assembly, 2
    high-level, 102
    systems programming, 102
LARGE, 113
large model, 92
LAST, 109
latch, 24
LDS, 53
LDT, 45, 99, 134
LDTR, 49, 53, 156
least-recently-used, 83
LEAVE, 91
LENGTH, 109
LES, 53
LGDT, 53
librarian, 101
library, 45, 96
LIMIT, 100
limit, 56
    checking, 50
link editor, 96, 100
LITERALLY, 105
LLDT, 53
loadable, 98, 100
LOCAL$TABLE, 112
LOCATION, 99
LOCK, 16, 28, 136
logarithms, 28
logical number (I/O), 131
logical operators, 104
loop, 163
    do, 106
    while, 107
LOW, 109

MACHINE$STATUS, 113
Macintosh, 5
macro, 92
mailbox, 125, 141
mainframe, 3, 160, 163
MAP, 135
Mapper, 101
MEDIUM, 113

Index

memory, 3
    access time, 163
    address space, 2, 9
    allocators in ETR_286, 130
    bandwidth, 166
    management, 81, 115, 144, 158
    physical, 22
    virtual, 3, 33, 80, 119
message, 125, 136
    fifo, 129
    passing, 17
    queue, 129
    read, 128
minicomputers, 160, 163
Modula-2, 102
modular programming, 92, 110
Motorola, 1
MOV, 53
MOVB, 109
MOVW, 109
MSI, 19
MSW, 39, 113, 156
multi-user, 2, 119
Multibus
    arbiter, 11
    Multibus 1, 16
    Multibus 2, 16
multiprocessor, 13, 18
multitasking, 2, 119
multiway branch, 107
mutual exclusion, 16

NEAR call, 91
NETBIOS, 142
network, 6, 7, 135
    driver, 140
    interface, 137
    local area, 136
    processor, 139
NMI, 26, 68
NT, 38, 66, 77, 148

OBJECT, 99
object, 116

object files, 96
offset, 32, 44, 149
OFFSET$OF, 110
open, 132, 140
operands
    immediate, 39
operator precedence, 105
orthogonality, 144
OS/2, 4, 167
OSI, 7, 139
OTD, 126
OUT, 136
OUTS, 136
overflow, 73
overlays, 101

P bit, 81
packet
    receive, 138
    transmission, 137
page table, 158
paged segment, 158
paging, 154, 158
parameter, 107, 108
    copying, 91
    formal, 111
    pointer, 109
partitioning, 57
Pascal, 85, 101, 102
PC, 2, 135
PC/NETWORK, 142
performance, 2, 143
peripherals, 16
    drivers, 125
pipelining, 20, 21, 24, 144, 163
PL/M, 101
PLM/286, 102, 113
POINTER, 103
pointers, 35, 36, 44, 103, 109, 149
    80386 format, 153
POP, 53
portable, 2
preamble, 138
preemption, 124

prefetching, 25
presence bit, 48, 161
primitive, 116
priority
    bus, 11
privilege
    applications, 125
    changing, 61
    effective, *see* EPL
    I/O, 38
    level, 54, 57, 115, 120, 121
procedures, 91, 107
    calling, 146
    heading, 107
    return, 108
process, 117
programming
    modular, 50
PROM, 98
protected mode, 21, 102
protection, 34, 54, 121, 143, 149, 161
    attributes, 56
    check, 48, 55, 57
    error, 80
    hierarchy, 57
    in 80386, 144
    in descriptor, 48
    inter task, 55
protocol, 137, 139
    transport, 140
PUBLIC, 89, 101, 107, 110

RAM, 163
read, 132
READY, 11
REAL, 103
real
    address mode, 21
    memory, 162
    number, 30, 89, 103, 148
receive, 140
RECORD, 92
REENTRANT, 107, 112
registers, 36

32-bit, 144
    address, 32
    base, 3
    control, 39
    coprocessor, 148
    debugging, 157
    file, 30
    flags, 38, 68, 146
    initialisation, 113
    segment, 3, 35, 38, 90, 149
    system, 154
rejection (of segments), 83
relational operators, 104
reliability, 50, 121
repertoire, 158
repetition, 106
RESERVE, 99
RESET, 11
RESTORE$GLOBAL$TABLE, 112
RESTORE$INTERRUPT, 112
Resume flag, 148
retransmission, 139
RETURN, 108
RF, 148
ring structure, 57
routine, 163
RPL, 58, 113

SAVE$GLOBAL$TABLE, 112
SAVE$INTERRUPT$TABLE, 112
scalar data, 103
scheduler, 119, 125
segment, 3, 148
    accessed bit, 81
    aggregation, 89
    conformant, 59
    name, 88
    not present error, 79
    present bit, 81
    privilege, 58
    registers, 149
    root, 102
    selector, 149
    sharing, 93

    size, 149
    stack, 113
    visibility, 50
SEGMENT$READABLE, 112
SEGMENT$WRITABLE, 112
segmentation, 31
select, 107
SELECTOR, 103
selector, 33, 44, 53, 103, 149
    back link, 63
    format, 45
    LDT, 63
SELECTOR$OF, 110
semaphores, 121, 125, 129
send, 140
session, 140
SETB, 109
SETW, 109
SGDT, 53
sharing, 51
SI, 36, 145
signals
    control, 10, 22, 25
SIGNED, 109
single step, 73
single-user, 119
size field, 155
SKIPB, 109
SKIPW, 109
SLDT, 53
SMALL, 113
small model, 92
software structure, 154
SP, 36, 145
SS, 38, 149
stack
    changing, 61
    error, 79
    segment, 149
STACKS, 99
STACKSEG, 90
statement, 106
static
    system, 96

    task structure, 119, 122
status, 132, 140
STD, 125
STI, 72, 136
STL, 101
string instructions, 37
STRUCT, 91
structure, 106
structured data, 103
subprograms, 107
subscript, 103
super root, 141
supervisor mode, 55, 57
suspension, 128
swapped, 159
synchronisation, 119
system calls, 92, 116

tag store, 164
TASK, 99
task, 44, 63, 119, 156
    applications, 122
    construction, 120
    delayed, 128
    gate, 74, 78, 162
    input/output, 125
    privilege, 58
    run time, 133
    scheduling, 125
    suspended, 126
    switching, 160
TASK$REGISTER, 112
testing, 54
TF, 73
thrashing, 81
TI bit, 45
time, 128
timeout, 125, 128, 130
    call, 125
    list, 128
timesharing, 4
TLB, 161
token ring, 142
TR, 65, 156

transient bugs, 157
translating, 46
trap gate, 74
trigonometric function, 28
trusted software, 56
TSAP, 140
TSS, 63, 120, 126, 134, 156
TYPE, 107

undefined instruction error, 73
unit
    address, 20
    bus, 20
    execution, 20
    instruction, 20
Unix, 3, 117
UNSIGN, 109
user mode, 57

VAN, 135
variables, 113
    based, 109
    declaration, 104
    redefining, 112
vector, 103
version numbers, 101

virtual
    8086, 160
    circuit, 140
    execution, 148
    memory, 21, 80
VM, 148
VTL, 101

WAIT$INTERRUPT, 111
WC, 60, 91, 98
Western Digital, 7
WHILE, 107
windows, 2
WORD, 103
word, 89
    count, 60
    operations, 35
write, 132
    cache, 166
    cycles, 165

X.25, 139
Xenix, 3, 117, 142
XLAT, 109

zero flag, 147
Zilog, 1